Carter F. Henderson is Manager of Public Affairs for one of the nation's ten largest corporations, and was the company's first manager of stockholder information. He holds an economics degree from the Wharton School of Finance and Commerce, was London Bureau Chief and European correspondent for *The Wall Street Journal,* and has been a management consultant to corporations and financial institutions.

Albert C. Lasher is Director of Corporate Relations for Lily-Tulip Cup Corp., placing him in the mainstream of the Company's relationships with stockholders and the professional investment community. Formerly a U.S. correspondent for *The Wall Street Journal* and financial editor at *Business Week,* he has been financial and public relations consultant for a number of banks and corporations. A graduate of Columbia University, Mr. Lasher lives in New York City.

20 Million
Careless
Capitalists

CARTER F. HENDERSON
AND ALBERT C. LASHER

20 Million Careless Capitalists

DOUBLEDAY & COMPANY, INC.
GARDEN CITY, NEW YORK

In memory of Oliver J. Gingold (1885–1966), who was the dean of financial journalists, edited *The Wall Street Journal*'s "Abreast of the Market" column for thirty-three years, coined the expression "blue chip stocks," and educated many young business reporters (he called them his "termites"), including the authors of this book.

ACKNOWLEDGMENTS

This book, like the products made by the corporations discussed in its pages, is the result of group effort. It is appropriate, therefore, that the authors of record publicly acknowledge the assistance of those who participated in bringing it into readers' hands.

By far the most significant contribution was made by Mrs. Jeanne Curtis Webber, a former *Fortune* magazine editorial researcher, on whose research talents depended a substantial portion of the manuscript, especially those chapters outlining the history of the relationship between stockholders and the corporations they owned.

Our editor at Doubleday & Company, Inc., Sam Vaughan, is to be commended not only for his early encouragement, gratefully received, but for his sound suggestions and good-humored patience as the manuscript inched its way to completion.

Many persons had a hand in the book's development, either through gracefully submitting to interviews or offering authoritative comment or criticism solicited by the authors. Some are directly quoted in the book; others are not, for a variety of reasons, not the least of which was that the authors' desire to recognize the deserving gave way to their concern that the reader might be overburdened by extensive references to sources. A few individuals in this category, however, cannot go unremarked.

Our special thanks, then, to Manuel F. Cohen, chairman of the Securities and Exchange Commission, for his willingness to discuss the thesis of this book early in its inception. Lewis D. Gilbert and Mrs. Wilma Soss, two of the more outstanding of that small, embattled group of "professional" stockholders which has taken on the cause of small stockholders, with not inconsiderable success, and to Sol A. Dann, Detroit lawyer and stockholder, whose battles with a number of auto companies provided object lessons in the ability of a determined minority stockholder to make his influence felt in the councils of management; John S. Tompkins, finance editor of *Business Week* magazine, and George Harlan, formerly financial writer for the late *New York Herald Tribune,* for their guidance in connection with the chapter on the press; Richard S. Nye, Sr., president of Georgeson & Company, John J. Blake III, partner of the Kissel-Blake Organization, and Kenneth Schwartz, associate editor of *Forbes* magazine, for their assistance and suggestions regarding the chapter on the power of the proxy; Ralph W. Michaud, senior analyst for Dean Witter & Company, and DeWitt C. Morrill, director of public relations for Indian Head, Inc., for their advice on the subject of the role of the security analyst; Richard A. Lewis, president of Corporate Annual Reports, Inc., for his thoughts on stockholder communications; John C. W. Schaie, a management consultant with the auditing firm of Touche, Ross, Bailey & Smart, for his observations concerning the function of the corporate director; Robert H. Savage, director of investor relations for International Telephone & Telegraph, former *Wall Street Journal* colleague of the authors, whose experience was helpful from start to finish; and to Donald A. Robinson Esq., partner in the law firm of Shanley & Fisher, for his advice and counsel regarding the subtleties of the complex securities law described in these pages.

We are also greatly indebted to a number of interested people who reviewed the manuscript in various stages of its development, enabling the authors to avoid errors of omission and commission. Our thanks go to Dr. Willis J. Winn, dean of the Wharton School of Commerce and Finance, of the University of Pennsylvania; Irwin Lainoff, vice-president, administration of Tsai Management & Research Corporation; Thomas W. Phelps, partner, Scudder, Stevens & Clark; O. Glenn Saxon, Jr., formerly consultant on investor relations with the General Electric and now chairman of the Executive Committee of Booke & Company, Inc.; Ruddick C. Lawrence, vice-president, New York Stock Exchange; and Dr. Wayne G. Broehl, Jr., professor of business administration, The Amos Tuck School of Business Administration, Dartmouth University.

Most importantly, our thanks to two friends of the authors, Miss Doris Nathan, who first suggested that this book be written, and Miss Susan Cutter, our expert and indefatigable manuscript typist; and to Hazel Mustard Henderson, wife of one of the authors, who, in addition to acting as a sounding board for many of the ideas expressed in this book, was also responsible for its title.

Finally, the authors wish to make it clear that this book is their brain child, and that the corporations for which they work had no hand whatsoever in its preparation.

CONTENTS

PREFACE

This book is about the excitement, the adventure, and the rewards that await you as a stockholder. It was written to tell you what's going on, to tell you how to get more pleasure—and just possibly more profit—out of being a stockholder.

But this book was written for another reason. A very serious reason. It is to remind you how monumentally unconcerned you are about the money you've so painfully saved in order to invest in common stocks.

Suppose every stockholder took his responsibilities as seriously as some of those mentioned in the pages of this book, who have actually influenced management decisions by invoking the powers readily available today to all stockholders. A new force would certainly come into being in our economy that could be every bit as powerful as management and labor are today. The conduct of many of our corporations would undoubtedly change, and it's possible that they might be a good deal more sensitive to the fundamental and fast-changing needs of our society.

Owning a share in American business can be a profitable experience, which is the reason approximately one million new investors enter the stock market every year.

But owning a share in American business can also be an experience that holds the potential—whether or not it is ever realized —of enabling every stockholder to make his small contribution to improving the society of which he is a part.

This could be unusually important today, when America seems to be evolving from a private enterprise to a public enterprise society, from a society where the corporations you own decide what kinds of goods and services America needs, to one in which the Government increasingly provides the guidance under which these decisions are made. A well-publicized example of this was the federal government's decision—not the automobile industry's decision—that the American consumer needs safer cars.

The Government, responding to pressure from the electorate, has also decided that the companies you own should help assure our society pollution-free air and streams, a more beautiful country-side, improved urban transportation, and so on. John Kenneth Galbraith foresaw this in his book *The Affluent Society* published in 1958. "The final problem of the productive society," said Professor Galbraith, "is what it produces. This manifests itself in an implacable tendency to provide an opulent supply of some things and a nig-gardly yield of others. This disparity carries to the point where it is a cause of social discomfort and social unhealth. The line which divides our area of wealth from our area of poverty is roughly that which divides privately produced and marketed goods and services from publicly rendered services."

The whole point is that a very serious dialogue about the future of American business and what it will produce is underway. One that makes it more imperative than ever for you to understand your power and responsibilities as a stockholder, power and re-sponsibilities that are yours if you care enough to exercise them.

The first step toward this goal is learning how to be a better stockholder. That's what this book is really all about.

In the pages that follow you'll discover that, as a stockholder, you have something in common with the English merchants and noblemen who provided the venture capital that colonized the New World, with George Washington, who invested heavily in com-panies to improve navigation along the Potomac River and drain the Great Dismal Swamp south of Norfolk, Virginia, with Vander-bilt, Gould, Harriman, and the other tycoons who financed the railroads, and with J. P. Morgan and Andrew Carnegie, whose brains and money helped create the American steel industry.

You'll get a new insight into how newspapers and magazines handle business news on which you may make investment de-cisions, how companies romance reporters with everything from stuffed dwarfs to all-expenses-paid trips to Tangier, and what Bernard Baruch had to say about people who offered unsuspecting investors "inside" information on hot stocks.

You'll go behind the scenes to see how the financial reports your companies send to you are actually put together, what manage-ment does to seduce you into reading vital information about your company's progress, and about the most embarrassing annual report ever mailed to share owners.

You'll get to meet top Wall Street security analyst Ralph Michaud, learn how stock market professionals figure out what a corporation's securities are really worth, and how companies do everything in their power to woo and win the affection of these analysts whose opinions can make or break the price of their stock.

You'll get the lowdown on what company presidents really think about the annual stockholders' meeting, get a glimpse of the annual meeting displays (monkeys under the influence of drugs), free gifts (coloring books), and sumptuous lunches (boneless squab and wild rice) that are used to regale stockholders, and learn how you can go about getting your ideas for improving your company's operations put up for a vote before every one of your fellow share owners.

You'll step inside the paneled walls of your company's board room and observe how the directors you elect, and frequently pay, go about representing your interests to your company's management.

You'll learn about the power of your proxy, how men ranging from John D. Rockefeller to banking king A. P. Giannini have used it to gain control over rich corporations, and how to recognize the telltale clues that spell big money to hardened proxy fighters such as the late Robert R. Young, whom the press labeled a "proxy-teer," "raider," "pirate," and "corporation destroyer."

You'll learn what you can do as an individual to help boost your company's sales and earnings.

You'll read about that bizarre band of flamboyant stockholders who have been called everything from "crackpots" to "crusaders."

And finally you'll be shown how careful stockholders manage their investments and grow quietly richer. You'll see how the Rockefellers look after their billions, how the profession of investment counseling has grown to cultivate fortunes of lesser millionaires, how the mutual fund business has exploded into a vast new industry serving millions of small investors who are willing to pay self-styled authorities to look after their money and hopefully make it grow, and how the smallest investor—using the kitchen table as his office—can often do as well and occasionally better than the highest-paid investment experts in the nation.

You'll see how, in an effort to make wiser investments, small stockholders in growing numbers are banding together to pool their investment knowledge, their cash, and the power of their proxies. These modern investment clubs promise to be a growing force in the investment community in the years to come.

That's our story of American stockholders. A story that began more than 250 years ago, when some English speculators purchased shares in a little company that thought it could make a killing in the vast unmapped wilderness of the New World.

Carter F. Henderson
Albert C. Lasher
February 10, 1967

Book One

1

THE CARELESS CAPITALISTS

If you are one of the more than twenty million Americans who own stock in U.S. corporations, chances are you only know one fact about your investment—how much your shares were worth at the close of yesterday's stock market.

You probably don't know the size or trend of your companies sales and profits, the amount of their dividends, the names of their presidents, the range of the products they make, or that you have the power to influence the way they are managed.

To put it quite bluntly, you are a careless capitalist.

Even if you earn a relatively high income of $10,000 after taxes it still takes you an entire year to save $500 or $600, according to the United States Department of Commerce. You are able to save this money because you have decided to deny yourself some of the good things of life today so you can build a portfolio of investments that will grow in value and help make tomorrow's dreams come true. A college education for your children, a new home, a small business of your own, security in your old age, these are the kinds of things you can look forward to if you have capital working for you in the form of common stocks.

There's a good chance that your investment in stocks represents one of your largest single assets, possibly the largest, ranking with your life insurance and the equity in your home.

Common sense suggests that you would devote at least as much time to these hard-earned investments as you do to cleaning the family car, mowing the lawn, or watching television. But the fact is that the average American stockholder seemingly couldn't care less about what's happening to the corporations whose shares he owns.

A famous survey, for example, has shown that a staggering

percentage of stockholders can't name a single one of their companies' products. To make matters worse, many stockholders who do name them guess wrongly, i.e., Swift & Company makes trucks, General Motors makes gasoline.

It's a newsworthy event when more than 1 per cent of a corporation's stockholders turn up at the annual meeting. Many of those who do attend come for the free lunch, sample products, or the lack of anything better to do. When American Telephone & Telegraph told its stockholders that luncheon would be served at their 1960 meeting, more than 11,000 people jammed the hall. Several years later, when lunch was eliminated, attendance collapsed to less than 3000.

Not long ago, there was a sudden flurry of buying activity in the stock of a little-known company called Data-Control Systems, of Danbury, Connecticut. Wall Street was dismayed until someone realized that many people were apparently grabbing the company's shares thinking they were investing in the Control Data Corporation, of Minneapolis, a big and successful computer manufacturer.

United States Attorney offices across the nation are flooded with an unending stream of complaints from casual capitalists who have bought stock in companies solely on the basis of high-pressure solicitation. The treasurer of a large Midwestern bank, for instance, purchased $8000 worth of Canadian mining stock after a ten-minute telephone call from Jersey City, New Jersey. Four months later, the banker sold his shares for 25 cents on the dollar.

Every time American Telephone & Telegraph gives its stockholders the right to buy additional shares below the going market price, thousands of A.T.&T. investors casually allow hundreds of thousands of dollars worth of their "rights" to expire despite repeated warnings from the telephone company's management.

And in New York, Delaware, Pennsylvania, and other states where large numbers of companies are incorporated, a king's ransom in dividends cascades into the states' coffers every year because the stockholders legally entitled to these payments have lost or abandoned their stock certificates and have disappeared from sight without bothering to leave forwarding addresses.

Some cynical brokers who have grown rich buying and selling stock for America's share-owning millions brand the average stockholder as far more than a careless capitalist. They call him a down-right boob. "What would we do without them," says the thirty-eight-year-old vice-president of one of the biggest brokerage firms on Wall Street. "They buy when we're ready to dump, and they sell when we figure the market has bottomed out and is ready to turn around."

One of the favorite stock market barometers, as a matter of fact, is the odd-lot index that measures the buying and selling of less than one-hundred-share lots of stock. This index, in effect, reflects the activities of the Wall Street equivalent of the two-dollar bettor. When the little man is buying, many Wall Street pros figure the market is about to go lower. But when he gets scared and starts to sell, these same pros figure that's the time to jump in and grab the bargains before the market heads for higher ground.

In the face of evidence such as this, it would appear that the careless attitude of American stockholders would rule them out as a force in shaping the destinies of the companies they own. This conclusion has indeed been espoused over the years by a number of well-known students of business and finance.

Adolf A. Berle, Jr., and Gardiner C. Means were among the first to outline these views in their book *The Modern Corporation and Private Property*, published in 1932. Messrs. Berle and Means concluded that the widely dispersed ownership of most large corporations has resulted in a shift of operating control from the people who own these companies to the hired hands who manage them. This, in turn, makes it extremely difficult for stockholders to throw an inept management out on its ear, and extremely easy for these highly paid executives to retain effective control of the company until they retire or die.

"The stockholder in the modern corporation is neither willing nor able to exercise his legal sovereignty," says economist and management consultant Peter F. Drucker in *The Future of Industrial Man*. "In the great majority of cases he never casts his vote but signs a proxy made out beforehand to and by the management. He exerts no influence upon the selection of new managers who are chosen through co-option by the management in power. The stockholder exercises no influence upon the decisions of management. As a rule he neither confirms nor repudiates them;

he does not even know about them and does not want to know about them."

In his provocative book *The Paper Economy* lawyer David T. Bazelon proclaimed "Large publicly-held corporations are not private property and they are not controlled by their stockholders. Where did anybody get the idea that they were?"

It would be outrageously naïve to suggest that stockholders control the corporations they legally own. But it would be equally naïve to say that they have no control over them at all.

Consider the following random examples of how stockholders have influenced decisions affecting corporations whose shares they own:

General Baking Company stockholders rejected a one-third increase in the number of shares available for purchase at a discount by company executives, while the share owners of the Sayre & Fisher Company vetoed a similar executive stock option plan altogether.

Owners of New York's Oakite Products, Inc., rejected a management proposal to merge their company with Calgon Corporation of Pittsburgh.

Stockholders' objections caused Grow Chemical Company and Chris-Craft Industries, Inc., to break off merger talks before even bringing the proposal to a vote. Adverse stockholder reaction was also responsible for the collapse of merger plans between Consolidated Foods Corporation and United Artists, Inc. Said Consolidated's Chairman, Nathan Cummings, "The figures were right, but some of our stockholders thought it would be too radical a move."

After stockholders of Boise Cascade Corporation voted overwhelmingly in favor of a merger with Rust Craft Greeting Cards, Inc., Rust Craft's share owners turned it down.

Stockholders of the well-known Paramount Pictures Corporation and the lesser-known Elgeet Optical Company of Rochester, New York, were each able to gain representation on their companies' boards of directors by threatening long and costly proxy fights.

And an increasing number of stockholders of firms such as Atlantic Research, Transcontinental Investing and McCrory Corporation have used legal action—or the threat of legal action—to get

members of management to reimburse their companies personally
for what the owners insisted were costly business blunders.

The significant test is what you or any other individual stockholder could do on your own to influence the fortunes of a giant
corporation in which you have an infinitesimal interest—say less
than .0006 per cent of its outstanding shares.

One stockholder who took this test and passed it with colors
flying is a pepper-pot Detroit lawyer in his sixties named Sol A.
Dann, who apparently thinks of himself as the Don Quixote of the
corporate world. He even has a Sancho Panza in the person of Karl
S. Horvath, a small stockholder and disenchanted former employee
of the Chrysler Corporation—the auto giant against which Dann
rode to battle. (Mr. Dann has a propensity for auto companies as
adversaries, having previously tilted with General Motors, American Motors Corporation, and the old Studebaker-Packard Company.)

Sol Dann owned 5100 shares of Chrysler's stock, or less than
.0006 per cent of the company's 9 million shares outstanding when
he stood up at Chrysler's 1960 annual meeting and held forth on
the big corporation's ills for one hour and twenty minutes.

In the course of his harangue, Dann noted that Chrysler had lost
more than $34 million in 1958, and $5 million in 1959, and had
run up $250 million in long-term debt from a standing start in
1953. As if that wasn't enough bad news, the company had slashed
its dividend from $4 in 1957 to $1 in 1959.

Mr. Dann accused Chrysler's top brass of a variety of generally
undocumented sins, not the least of which were cupidity and stu-
pidity. One of the few specific charges he made was that Chrysler's
management was in cahoots with some of its suppliers. He accused
the company's executives of paying "up to $300 a ton for steel
while its competitors are paying only $150."

This charge was one of several that Chrysler Chairman L. L.
"Tex" Colbert attempted to refute—the rest he ignored. Mr. Dann
was also largely ignored by Detroit's daily newspapers, which
failed to mention, not only his lengthy exchange with Mr. Colbert,
but the fact that he was present at the meeting in the first place.

Sol Dann's obscurity did not last long. As it turned out, at least
one member of Chrysler's top management group had been a stock-

holder in a supplier company. Chrysler's newly appointed president, William C. Newberg, had held important interests in two of the auto maker's suppliers and resigned two months after the meeting.

Some of Dann's charges, loose as they were, seemed to have hit home. Suits and countersuits were filed in the Delaware courts by Dann, Chrysler, and an assortment of Chrysler stockholders, officers, and former officers, including Mr. Newberg. (The main legal battle emanated from Delaware because Chrysler, like many other U.S. companies, is officially domiciled in that state.) Recriminations were exchanged in the press between the battlers. On July 27, 1961, about a year after Newberg's resignation, Tex Colbert himself resigned as chairman and president of Chrysler and became chairman of the company's Canadian subsidiary. A new top management team was installed with ex-accountant Lynn A. Townsend as president.

A good many observers thought there was little that Townsend and his men could do to turn the ailing Chrysler Corporation around. The company's 1961 sales fell to $2.1 billion, compared to 1957's record $3.6 billion. In February 1962, Chrysler's shares of the new car market sank to a postwar low of 8.3 per cent. Stringent cost-cutting produced some profit, but the $1.24 a share Chrysler earned in 1961—down from $3.61 the year before—did little to assuage stockholders' fears that their company might be riding down the road to ruin.

But the new management took hold and Chrysler started hitting the comeback trail. The year 1966 was the most successful sales year in the company's history with volume at a record $5.6 billion, and its share of the new car market at a solid 16.7 per cent.

Today, Sol Dann, who spent most of the five years between 1958 and 1963 engaged in a legal war against Chrysler, is satisfied with the ways things came out, even though his claims against the company were thrown out by the courts. "When St. Peter asks me what I've done with my life," he says, "I'll tell him I've raised a good family and saved Chrysler."

But the rewards have been far more than spiritual for Chrysler stockholders who refused to ditch the company during its years of adversity. Mr. Dann, for example, paid about $350,000 for his 5100 shares. The stock was split twice in 1963, a 4 per cent stock dividend was declared the following year, and if Sol Dann had sold his shares when Chrysler hit its high he would have received the $350,000 he originally paid for his shares plus a bonus in excess of $1 million—not counting dividends.

The Chrysler case illustrates, among other things, one of the most important levers that stockholders have to pry concessions from management: the ability to embarrass the officers and directors personally by uninhibited public criticism. A pointed question raised at an annual meeting by the owner of ten shares, for example, is no less pointed than one asked by the owner of ten thousand shares. And management's handling of the question—be it brilliant or ludicrously inept—may, within hours, be relayed to every corner of the nation by private wire, news ticker, and the press.

There is no all-embracing reason why American stockholders are so lackadaisical about their painfully acquired investments.

Some stockholders say they don't understand what business is all about even though the federal government, stock exchanges, brokerage houses, enlightened corporate management, and the press have made it possible for today's investor to follow the fortunes of his shares with consummate ease.

Other stockholders take the position that the managements of their companies know best and should be left alone to run the business as they see fit. These investors would do well to pay more attention to the financial sections of their daily newspapers, which carry a steady flow of stories about management mishaps, such as the $250 million the Ford Motor Company lost on its Edsel, and the $425 million the General Dynamics Corporation frittered away on its 880 and 990 jet transport planes.

Still other stockholders simply don't want to be bothered looking after their investments, an attitude well calculated to produce only one kind of payoff—a bundle of beautifully engraved stock certificates ideally suited for papering the family playroom

How did American stockholders get this way? That tale begins several centuries ago when a group of English speculators began looking longingly at the investment opportunities an ocean away in the New World.

2

PROMOTING THE NEW WORLD:

THE STOCK COMPANIES THAT

HELPED BUILD AMERICA

America was founded by 659 English capitalists who in the early 1600s subscribed for stock in an interesting speculation known as "The Treasurer and Company of Adventurers and Planters of the City of London for the First Colony of Virginia."

Their dreams of making a killing in the New World were simple and plausible. The Virginia Company would ship settlers to America who, in the words of one stockholder, might discover "mines and minerals of gold, silver, and other metals," or "treasure, pearls, and precious stones." They might even find a northwest passage to the Orient.

If all else failed, the colonists could at least trade with the Indians living in the Virginia Company's domain, which stretched from North Carolina to New Jersey. And when the colonists were not swapping trinkets for the savages' furs and other valuables, they could certainly produce goods which would find a ready market in England. Stockholders, of course, would turn an extra profit by supplying the settlers with the necessities of life in the wilderness.

These early investors were by no means babes in the woods. A number of them were noblemen and rich London merchants who had profited from the other great trading organizations of the day. There was the old Muscovy Company, for example, which had traded with Russia for fifty years; the Levant Company, with a prosperous monopoly of trade with Turkey, and the great East

India Company, which paid its owners from 100 per cent to 200 per cent on their investments in its early years.

The English "Adventurers" who purchased shares in the Virginia Company—at twelve pounds ten shillings apiece—were entitled to a proportionate part of the profits, whatever they might be. They were also guaranteed a vote in the "General Court" of shareholders, who met quarterly to approve or disapprove the actions of the directors and admit new stockholders as capital was needed. A stockholder received only one vote, no matter how many shares he held, which was the general practice in those days. One share of stock also entitled its holder to one hundred acres of land, and another one hundred acres in a second division to be made later on.

With the proceeds from the first sale of stock, the Virginia Company dispatched two ships full of colonists to the New World, who, after months of severe privation, finally established Jamestown. The colonists, as if they didn't have troubles enough, were continually plagued by top-level advice from the company's officers in England. These worthy men instructed them to cut down trees for timber and pitch, grow flax and hemp, dig for iron, fish, establish vineyards, and, while they were at it, to send a few expeditions up and down the coast looking for a northwest passage. Some stockholders, pondering the situation from clubs and counting-houses in London, never ceased to wonder why these simple instructions weren't carried out to the letter. They had been assured that the Virginia Company's territory was overflowing with the riches of nature that any enterprising settler could have for the taking.

Most of the stockholders were counting on the profits of the first voyages to return enough to cover the second payment due on their stock, and profits from later voyages to cover the third and subsequent installments. They were disappointed. As the struggling colonists battled disease, Indians, and starvation in those early years, they could barely pay for importing the goods needed to keep body and soul together, let alone produce a surplus for sale in England.

The absence of profits prompted the Virginia Company's owners to divide themselves into warring factions, one of which wanted to oust the management, headed by a prominent London merchant named Sir Thomas Smythe, who was the company's treasurer and

chief executive officer. The dissidents were under the leadership of
Sir Edwin Sandys and the Earl of Warwick. They raised such a
rumpus that Sir Thomas prudently decided not to run for re-election.
The stockholders, however, decided to vote him a bonus of twenty
shares of stock when he left office, "in consideration of the great
trouble mixed often with much sorrow" that had attended his in-
cumbency.

Sir Edwin Sandys was named treasurer, and he immediately
plunged into the job of wringing some money out of the Virginia
Company. He set up subsidiary companies in the hope that specific
projects might attract new investors. One subsidiary had a monopoly
of fishing off the coast, while another handled trade with the private
plantations that the company had sold to entice settlers with capital.
But Sir Edwin's only really successful subsidiary, it is said, was the
"Joint Stock for Transporting 100 Maids to be Made Wives."

To attract new colonists, Sandys had glowing promotion pieces
printed and distributed in England. He granted the colonists more
self-government to get their minds off politics and onto business. He
urged sugar cane planting and silk production, and actually in-
veigled a few tons of crude iron ore out of the settlement.

Then, in 1623, the Governor of Bermuda turned up in London.
This honorable gentleman was fresh from a trip to Jamestown, and
he had an eyewitness account of affairs in the colony that he
insisted on making public. It was a grim exposé and to a large
extent news to the company's stockholders. There had been a terrible massacre by Indians in 1622, acres of plantations had been
abandoned, the colonists were miserable and discouraged. Of the
10,000 persons sent over since 1609, the governor proclaimed, less
than 2000 had survived and they were in no condition to produce
much of value to investors.

Again the stockholders turned on the management. Sandys was
accused of suppressing unfavorable news and "causing misleading
reports to be sent . . . which were written with the intention of
making it appear that the colony was in a satisfactory condition."
He was also blamed for "many wild and vast projects set on foot at
one time." A committee was set up to investigate the company's
finances, it was pronounced bankrupt, and the king revoked its
charter.

Some of the approximately 1000 investors in the Virginia Company did manage to hold on to their American land rights. The great majority, however, were sadly disappointed. To these hapless Englishmen the first settlement of what would eventually become the United States of America was nothing more than another stock play gone wrong.

The dogged English, however, simply refused to be discouraged about investing in America. All through the seventeenth and eighteenth centuries wild schemes were successfully promoted in London for exploiting the New World. Some of these figured prominently in the speculative fever of 1720 that produced the South Sea Bubble. This was a disastrous venture, sponsored by the English Government, which saw myriads of capitalists part with their meager savings to buy stock in a company which had been given a monopoly of trade (mainly in slaves) with South America and the Pacific.

During this period companies were floated "for a wheel of perpetual motion," "for wrecks to be fished for," for a system of wool making "which will effectively employ all the poor of Great Britain," "for insuring marriage against divorce," and for Puckle's Machine Gun, which discharged "round and square cannon balls and bullets thus making a total revolution of the art of war"—round to be used on Christians, square on Turks. There was even "A Company for Carrying on an Undertaking of Great Advantage, but No One to Know What It is." For that one the subscription books remained open only one day, for the promoter, a printer, collected two thousand pounds in deposits on his rather high-priced shares and disappeared into the London fog.

Since America was conveniently far away, promoters in London were able to get away with many ingenious frauds based on the New World's purported resources. They often turned up with samples of ore they said had come from newly discovered mines that would yield fabulous profits to investors. Even in 1721, after the collapse of the South Sea Bubble, and after thousands of angry investors had stormed the House of Commons to protest being fleeced, a fast-talking mining promoter turned up with shares in a silver deposit he said he had found on the Maine coast. And there were takers.

The grist mills, forges, glassworks, cabinet shops, newspapers, and general stores of colonial America did not require more capital than one man, one family, or a simple partnership could provide. Occasionally an ironworks was built in which a dozen or more people had fractional shares, in a rather loose arrangement that foretold the corporation. In New England, ships were sometimes built and outfitted for fishing, whaling, or trading by public subscription. There were a handful of water companies and wharf companies in New England that were jointly owned by their users, and these public utilities were given certain privileges by grants of the colonial legislatures. Thus the legislatures came to supplant the king in the giving of special business rights to groups of people, and paved the way for the state granting of charters of incorporation.

A New Nation Learns How to Raise Capital

Banks were the first privately owned American companies in which issuing securities became the accepted way of starting business. Shares in these banks cost from $300 to $500 each, and the subscribers were wealthy merchants of Philadelphia, Boston, and New York as well as the federal and state governments. The United States Government, which had a pressing need for a place to borrow money, became a stockholder in a number of the new banks. It held 633 shares in the Bank of North America, for example, which was one of its chief suppliers of credit. Pennsylvania put a million dollars into the capital of the Bank of Pennsylvania.

The constitution of one of these early banks, the Bank of New York, bore the stamp of Alexander Hamilton's financial genius and his enlightened interest in the welfare of stockholders. In Hamilton's day, there was still a general reluctance to make votes directly proportionate to the number of shares an investor owned. The feeling was that one person, or even the Government, might become unduly dominant. This was particularly true with regard to banks. The original scheme for the Bank of New York provided for a top limit of seven votes no matter how large the investment.

Hamilton wanted to encourage large investors, and he persuaded the Bank of New York's sponsors to allow one vote for every five shares held over the number of ten. Shares were made readily transferable. Stockholders could vote for directors only if they had held their shares for three months. Proxy voting was allowed, but only if the stockholder had been a resident of the state for twelve months preceding the election (this was to discourage out-of-state financiers from seeking control of the bank). Directors were required to be stockholders and stockholder meetings had to be advertised well in advance. It was a model plan in many ways. When Hamilton a few years later proposed setting up a National Bank, he bowed to the prevailing customs and agreed to a top limit of thirty votes per stockholder.

Early bank stocks were quite profitable. Many returned 8 per cent to 14 per cent, and they soon attracted speculators. By 1812 a regular bank mania was sweeping the country. Since a charter from the state was necessary, some bank sponsors conceived the idea, later to be applied on a more grandiose scale by the railroads, that quietly passing out stock and cash might influence legislators in the right direction. The state legislators, it is true, were only following the example set by their counterparts in Congress. When the first Bank of the United States was launched, for example, various congressmen were allotted shares. In the boom that followed the public subscription, the congressmen and other insiders unloaded and the stock collapsed from 195 to 108 in one month.

As time went by, auctioneers began handling the selling of securities along with other wares. Next came a special group of auctioneers who only handled securities, and the prices they fetched were published in Philadelphia and Boston newspapers. Then the stockbroker emerged in the form of a local merchant who sent agents out to buy stocks for resale and who handled buying and selling for the local gentry.

That speculative period saw the start of the New York Stock Exchange.

In May 1792, some of the prominent brokers in New York drew up an agreement to give preference to each other in all business, and to charge a minimum commission of one-fourth of 1 per cent as commissions on all shares bought or sold. Their first meetings were held under a buttonwood tree on Wall Street. Soon these men, now calling themselves the Board of Brokers, moved into a room at the nearby Tontine Coffeehouse. As the years went by, and the country grew, these brokers found themselves trading shares in a steadily increasing number of insurance companies, manufacturing firms, transportation companies, canals, toll roads and bridges. It was a time of experimentation, both as to the best way to build a viable business and to keep stockholders happy with their investments.

One of the young nation's earliest corporate successes was the Insurance Company of North America. This Philadelphia company was formed in 1792, when 60,000 shares of stock at $10 a share were sold to bankers, government officials, shipowners, storekeepers, and others. The company gave stockholders one vote for every share held, paid a good return, and faithfully reported to owners on its financial progress.

There were few publicly owned manufacturing enterprises prior to 1800. Of the 300 state charters granted up to that time, only a handful were for manufacturing and most of these were relatively short-lived, and not one paid a dividend. A fairly typical example was the Beverly Cotton Manufactory, with the Cabots as chief stockholders. The state of Massachusetts encouraged this company with a grant of land, and later, when it ran into starting-up difficulties, even gave it a share in a state lottery—but it failed in 1807. The Society for the Establishment of Useful Manufactures, a scheme of Alexander Hamilton's to make cloth, shoes, and consumer goods in New Jersey, was launched with state and federal aid in the bull market of 1791. It floundered through a series of disasters and ended up with no assets except land.

Almost all these early companies were undercapitalized, in view of the problems they faced in securing raw materials, distributing finished goods, training unskilled labor. One exception was the Boston Manufacturing Company, which was established in 1813, had authorized capital of $400,000 and started out with $100,000 paid in by wealthy Bostonians. It actually kept going one way or another until 1929.

Transportation companies were the speculative darlings of the post-Revolutionary period. To facilitate commerce among the newly formed states, better means of moving goods were needed, and that meant canals, highways, and bridges. As neither states nor federal government had funds equal to the magnitude of the job, it fell to private capitalists. The states assisted, however, with loans and tax exemptions.

George Washington was always one of the leading enthusiasts for better waterways. With the Potomac near his front yard, he naturally had an interest in making it an important highway for commerce. As early as 1772 he invested five hundred pounds in a plan to improve Potomac navigation. The proposal required the co-operation of both Virginia and Maryland, and for a long time Maryland was reluctant, fearing that its great port of Baltimore would suffer. Finally in 1785 the states signed a compact and the Potomac Company was formed. Shares were subscribed by both states and by people in the towns bordering the river. Washington was elected president at the first stockholders' meeting.

The Potomac Company intended to deepen the waterway, build canals and towpaths, and bypass falls upriver with locks. The big problem turned out to be labor. The young company's free white workers appeared to have a "turbulent and insubordinate spirit," so the directors decided to hire slaves from nearby plantations, and also use free Negroes. All were to be paid wages plus "a reasonable quantity of spirits, when necessary." Perhaps they were paid more spirits than necessary, for soon the directors were reporting more "turbulent dispositions" and work was going ahead only fitfully. To make matters worse Potomac Company stockholders were slow in paying installments on their stock, and both persuasion and law had to be brought to bear. By 1798 Washington was obliged to put up his own stock as collateral for loans to keep the work going. New capital was raised. Tolls on the completed locks, which had been counted on as a source of new construction money, were all used up in maintenance. At length, in 1802, the last locks were finished and the company paid a lone dividend.

Washington also took considerable interest in the Great Dismal Swamp Company, which was formed before the Revolution to drain the swamp south of Norfolk, Virginia, by putting canals through it. Washington, as a large shareholder and managing director, personally supervised the company's affairs for several years before the Revolution. After his death, Washington's executors collected dividends of $18,000 from a period of profitable operations between 1810 and 1825.

Canal building became almost a mania in the early nineteenth century. Cities rivaled each other to bring water transportation to their doors. Promoters advertised extensively in the newspapers. "From the respectability of the characters who have already subscribed, we have reason to congratulate our fellow citizens in the prospect of the respective subscriptions being speedily and substantially filled," read one ad at a time when not one share of stock had been sold.

Turnpikes, or toll roads, also attracted local capital. The roads of those days were poor, and it frequently took many days to get from one major city to another. Toll rates were established by the states, and although 10 per cent to 15 per cent was not considered to be an unreasonable profit, toll roads were more successful in theory than in fact. From the beginning, these companies were plagued by a community relations problem. People who were used to going back and forth on free roads, however bad, simply did not take kindly to paying tolls. The turnpikes made some gestures toward their public, allowing soldiers going to military duty to pass free, and in Massachusetts churchgoers received the same generous consideration. Turnpikes naturally called for stagecoach companies, which specialized in the fast transportation of passengers, mail, and goods over the new roads. Most stage companies were small and privately owned, and even those which were investor owned had less than a hundred stockholders. There were a few spectacularly successful turnpike firms such as the Eastern Stage Company, which was capitalized with 500 shares at $200 each, made 8.3 per cent per year for twenty years, and distributed a bonus of $66 per share when it went out of business.

The Corporation Gets Off to a Slow Start

Of the 335 corporate charters issued by the colonies and states up to the end of 1800, transportation companies of all types made up two-thirds of the list, with banks, insurance companies, and water companies accounting for most of the remainder. There were a few manufacturing companies, including one called the Manhattan Company, that resisted classification.

The sponsors of the Bank of New York had successfully blocked the chartering of any competing banks in the city for several years when Alexander Hamilton and a group of associates including Aaron Burr managed to outwit them by setting up the Manhattan Company. New York City had just suffered a yellow fever epidemic, and the company applied for a charter to supply the city with pure drinking water produced by a horse-operated pump, so that such a thing could not happen again. The charter was granted. But inconspicuously set forth among its purposes was that of using its surplus for any other business, including banking. If any legislators were aware of the implications, they found it profitable to keep silent. At any rate, the Manhattan Company, with $1 million capital, operated as a bank, and when the city sued it on the grounds that it was not chartered for that purpose, the city lost. The Manhattan Company prospered, and its stockholders regularly visited the bank to collect their dividends which they signed for in a ledger book, now permanently on display at the head office of the Chase Manhattan Bank in Wall Street.

A few early banks and insurance companies had $500,000 to $1,000,000 in capital, but most of the corporations were relatively small with rarely more than a hundred stockholders. The big stockholders of the period were men with vast property and financial interests: Bostonians like the Lowells, Cabots, and Amorys; New Yorkers like John Jacob Astor, a stockholder in banks and canals as well as a real estate owner; Philadelphians like Robert Morris, or Stephen Girard, who was perhaps America's first millionaire, and John Ross, merchant and shipowner. The small stockholders were lesser merchants, shipowners living in port cities, and estate owners whose land produced an investable surplus. Their combined holdings were usually too small to give them much influence. They were not inclined to attend stockholder meetings, for a trip of only ten or twenty miles was a major undertaking.

Time after time corporate meetings in those days had to be adjourned for lack of a quorum. In order to get any business done at all the company often went right ahead with what representation it had on hand. In one bank election, for instance, only thirty shares out of two hundred voted for directors. Stockholders could not very well complain about the dividend rate, either, as they received whatever profits there were. They could and did complain if a company was not making any money at all, but they almost never ventured to get together to see that something was done about it.

In the early 1800s each corporation was granted a separate charter by a special act of the legislature. A few states were moving toward general incorporation laws—Massachusetts, for instance, had so many applications for charters for water companies that she provided a law under which they could all be handled. Most companies actually considered special charters to be a good thing. It made the charter a matter of negotiation, in which the sponsors asked for whatever they wanted, and the legislators trimmed it to something they considered reasonable. Individual charters also allowed a company to petition the legislature to have its enabling act amended whenever its influence with the state's lawmakers was running high.

So it was not the lack of legislative machinery that held back the birth of corporations before 1800 and in the years directly following. The truth is that people were a little suspicious of them. The old British joint-stock companies had always represented a monopoly of something, and part of the patriotic fervor preceding and following the Revolution was a distrust of anything smacking of the old system. The public simply did not like to see special privileges of the old English variety given to new combinations of wealth and power in America.

There were very few stockholders in early America, and the main reason was that most wealth was in the land. Although the great colonial estates had begun to melt away, there were still manorial holdings and ownership of land was a matter of prestige. When a shipowner accumulated some money, for example, he first bought land and built a fine house. After that, if there was anything left, he invested in banks, or canals, or government bonds, or set up a private company of his own. In the cities, land was rapidly appreciating in value and represented a good investment. In rural areas, when a man of moderate means acquired some surplus he bought more land. It was a tangible, familiar, and reassuring thing to possess. In a relatively few years, however, this feeling would change. The motive power behind the change was the steam locomotive.

3

RIDING THE RAILS TO CAPITALISM:

THE RAILROADS AS AMERICA'S FIRST

BIG STOCKHOLDER ATTRACTION

The railroads made stockholders out of people who had never intended to be and who knew nothing about investing. The launching of a railroad in the nineteenth century was a matter of intense civic pride. The new means of transportation, its promoters said, would bring a great influx of wealth to the area it served. No matter what the level of a town's commerce, it was not hard to demonstrate how it could be doubled or tripled by a link to a neighboring city. Trains would be faster than canal boats, and fixed tracks more reliable in bad weather than turnpikes. Ambitious cities and hamlets that had lost business to rivals on canal routes saw their salvation. Clearly it was every man's patriotic duty to see that his town got a railroad.

When it came to the rails, every man was a bull. Men who characterized themselves as "deserving citizens who have made and are willing to make sacrifices for the public good" undertook to raise capital among friends and relatives. Some were textile or iron manufacturing leaders with an eye to distant markets. Some were politicians who hoped to enlarge their sphere of influence. Others were retailers and wholesalers who wanted a bigger source of supplies and customers. Town fathers harangued from platforms, while newspaper editorial pages blazed with enthusiasm. Legislatures were deluged with petitions seeking railroad charters. Townsfolk offered special inducements to railroad companies to route the line their way. One Baltimore observer wrote: "Public excitement has gone far beyond fever heat."

Rival cities flung themselves into battle for the main routes. A Philadelphia lobby supporting the Pennsylvania Railroad fought for a charter in the legislature against a Pittsburgh lobby, which favored the Baltimore & Ohio. Counties around Pittsburgh threatened to secede unless they got their way. Harassed legislators compromised, by granting the B. & O. charter but promising to revoke it if the Pennsy could raise the necessary funds within one year. In a frenzied campaign, during which the religious-minded Philadelphians were told that the obligation to build the railroad had been imposed on them by God, the necessary capital was obtained. In almost every town railroad promoters could assure a generous subscription by painting a dismal picture of what would happen if the town were by-passed.

Railroad promoters did not promise great wealth to the individuals who bought stock. They found it difficult to calculate the benefits in dollars and cents when the project depended on a future volume of commerce and the exploiting of still undiscovered natural resources. Their dreams, though vague, had vast dimensions:

"Who then, even in imagination, can estimate the flourishing commerce, the swarming population, the boundless wealth, the cultivated and commodious life which this valley will present," rang a prospectus for Kentucky's Chattaroi Railway, "when its people are grown to perfection through a series of fortunate events and a train of successful industries? It will enable the producer to realize returns not too much diminished by transit charges, through a cheap method for the interchange of commodities, and all this, in time, will come about in the Valley of the Big Sandy."

To seduce capitalists into investing in a railroad serving Maine, its promoters predicted that the state would become a great industrial power because "the capacity of the human frame for labor is found to be greater in Maine, than in Massachusetts or any State, south or west of it."

So residents of small towns, prosperous farmers along the right-of-way, professional men and city merchants, and farsighted financiers bought railroad stock as a lien on the future. Local banks invested or made loans on railroad stock. Cities and towns themselves took blocks of stock, giving in return municipal bonds with interest secured by taxes. They endorsed loans to railroads during their construction. Local governments, in all, probably kicked in over $100,-000,000 in railway aid. Counties and states became heavily involved. Some states were partners from the beginning; when the B. & O. was chartered in Maryland in 1827, of a total of 30,000 capital shares, 10,000 were reserved for the state of Maryland and 5000 for the city of Baltimore. These governments were permitted to elect one director for each 2500 shares paid up, but were forbidden to vote for any other directors.

Every step in the planning, fund-raising, construction, and operation of the railroads was followed with intense interest. Early locomotives and their capabilities were discussed as avidly as baseball players and their records are today. When the states began to require reports from the railroads, they insisted that they include an accurate count of locomotives, their age, make and speed. The iron horses were believed extremely significant to the success of the railroad.

Thus the railroads, unlike most previous business ventures, began their corporate lives with a goodly number of stockholders. The price of the shares was set low by the legislatures—$25 to $50 each —and only a 10 per cent down payment was required, the rest to be paid in annual installments or as called for. There were usually some large investors, but, compared to earlier corporations, ownership was widely dispersed.

The charter stockholders were a militant bunch. They felt a peculiarly personal relationship to the railroad and its affairs. The plans, financing, and make-up of management frequently had been discussed at town "conventions" even before the company was formalized, so people generally were accustomed to public debate of railroad affairs. They carried this habit with them when they became stockholders. Stockholder meetings in the 1840s and 1850s were well attended. The Western Railroad, for example, which ran from Worcester, Massachusetts, to Albany, New York (west, that is, from Boston, where its principal backers lived), ended its first funding drive in 1835 with 1860 stockholders, and its meetings were frequently attended by 200 to 400 persons.

Stockholders could ride their railroad free to get to the annual meetings, usually held at a centrally located station or railway hotel; a stockholder had only to show his stock certificate to the conductor. If he had three or four shares, he could parcel them out among relatives and make a real holiday of it. The town fathers, ticket agents, reporters, legislators, and other "friends" of the railroad also sought free fares, and by 1881 some 50 per cent of the nation's rail passengers were riding gratis. The railroads finally clamped down on this largesse.

To be sure, these capitalists were not a sophisticated group; they did not probe deeply into financial matters. They discussed chiefly whether fares should be higher or lower, a matter that raised tempers and pushed other details to the background. Yet, before the Civil War, stockholders often had standing committees empowered to oversee various aspects of railway management. The Boston & Worcester Railroad, for example, had a stockholders' committee to examine the treasurer's report. The committee published its conclusions in the same pamphlet as the annual report of directors. Naturally such a committee had to depend on accounts kept by the management, and fraud-minded officers easily could juggle the figures. But the stockholders at least were interested; they still felt a sense of personal ownership and identification with their company.

No officer could afford to ignore his stockholders. For one thing, he had to get stockholders who were behind on their installment payments to ante up. Extending the road from town to town depended on how fast the money flowed in. Sometimes state aid depended on the railroad's completing a prescribed length of track before state funds could be used.

It was not easy to follow up each stockholder. When the Erie Railroad called for its first 2½ per cent after the initial 10 per cent, less than half the subscribers responded. The railroads in such cases had the choice of suing, which was hardly worth the trouble, or repossessing the stock and trying to resell it, or of waiting.

They tried waiting first, sending out plaintive pleas or firm demands. "Our road runs through the central wheat counties of the state, and the almost entire loss of the crop last harvest by rust has operated severely upon our subscribers and consequently upon the company," the president of the Indianapolis and Bellefontaine wrote in 1849. He urged stockholders to make payments in advance of the due dates. Other railway presidents used the annual report to deliver modest lectures on thrift and civic loyalty. They were usually a little more optimistic than was warranted. Dividends of 12 per cent to 15 per cent, "with a rapid increase from year to year," were predicted to encourage stockholders to hang onto their stock. As track laying proceeded, the officers assured stockholders that the terrain ahead lay flat and smooth, reminding them that new coal or mineral discoveries might mean a bulge in future profits.

The Little Man Loses Control

A shadow fell over the rails with the financial panic of 1837, in which many banks failed, the depression in New England in 1847, and the nationwide recession of the 1850s. Many small stockholders sold out when dividends ceased. Others could not keep up their installment payments. Control of the railroads became more concentrated. When the railroads repossessed their stock, they turned to wealthier men who were willing to take the stock outright and continue payments, or accept it as collateral for loans. Sometimes the rich rescuers took mortgages on the road, which, as senior obligations removed the underpinning from the common stock—that was the way the famous stock manipulators Daniel Drew and Cornelius Vanderbilt first got into the Erie Railroad. The consolidation of small lines into larger networks decreased stockholder influence, such as it was, for with ownership more widely dispersed it was harder for substantial numbers of stockholders to get to meetings and express any unified wishes.

The board of directors gained power. At the start, when directors were prominent citizens of the city where a large number of stockholders lived, the stockholders could feel reasonably sure of a measure of control over management. Their representative's local reputation depended on keeping them happy. But powerful and unfamiliar directors from distant financial centers, whose interests were dispersed among many corporations, seemed beyond the ordinary stockholders' reach. Without protest from the railroad's small stockholders, the directors assumed more and more authority, and in the scramble for routes and good rates the men who managed the roads had to be fast on their feet if they wanted to survive. The small stockholders would usually meet only when the railroad was on the verge of bankruptcy, and then it was usually too late. "At such times" wrote Henry Varnum Poor, editor of the *American Railroad Journal* and a campaigner for railway reforms, "stockholders are loud and often in their denunciations, but they are entirely unintelligent and would be no more successful were they placed in charge of their line."

Anything that aroused as intense public passion as did the railroads was bound to involve politics. The very obtaining of a charter required a knowledge of political infighting. Legislators who had thriving canals in their territories feared railroad competition, and every time they voted for a charter, groups of angry constituents arrived to protest. On the other hand, railroad promoters themselves came armed with citizens' petitions, as well as a liberal supply of cash or stock. One railroad had to issue stock to the governor before it got what it considered a suitable land grant. This was regarded as standard procedure by the promoters, and few stockholders objected. A certain amount of corruption was an accepted part of the democratic process. Some railroads, and even some early banks, were known to have allocated funds to spend in Washington, state capitals, county seats, and local city halls "to protect stockholders from injurious legislation."

The political character of charters did not end when several states adopted general incorporation acts under which the roads could be organized. But despite these laws, charters continued to be granted by special legislation. Politics necessarily continued to be a preoccupation of railroad managements who vied with each other in seeking favor. "Individuals and corporations . . . have of late not infrequently found the supply of legislators in the market even in excess of the demand," Charles Francis Adams, Jr., commented in 1869. Adams, a great-grandson of John Quincy Adams, was an expert on railway affairs and served on the Interstate Commerce Commission after it was set up in 1887.

The New England states took the lead in setting up state railway commissions. New Hampshire established one in 1844, but most came after the Civil War, when outraged farmers in the Grange movement were denouncing freight rates. The commissions were set up primarily to protect the railroad users, not the stockholders—

to protect what was loosely defined as the "public interest." It was the beginning of an effort, still going on, to reconcile equitably public and private interests in business. But rates were a far hotter issue than stockholder rights, and the commissions, although empowered to go into almost any aspect of railway operation, tended to concentrate on rate making. This did not always benefit stockholders. Western settlers regarded the railroads as the tools of bloated robber barons who were trying to squeeze profits out of poor farmers; naturally they wanted the commissions to lower fares. Easterners accused the commissions of setting such low rates that no dividends could be paid that provided a convenient excuse for directors who wanted higher rates so they could siphon off greater profits for their private gain.

About the time of the Civil War it became clear that financing a railroad through the sale of common stock did not provide enough funds fast enough, to meet the clamor for new railroads. A new pattern of financing evolved. If there was stock sold at all, it was only a token subscription to establish local backing, which was useful when petitioning for a charter. The railroad was financed mainly through the sale of bonds. Stock was thrown in as a sort of bonus; it represented hope that if the railroad prospered backers might receive a return on their investment exceeding bond interest alone. The Illinois Central, for example, began with $17 million in bonds and $1 million in stock.

Financing by means of bonds might have worked out fairly well except that the railroad always took longer to build and cost more than first estimated. Bonds were piled upon bonds. There were first, second, third, and fourth mortgages on portions of the track. There were income bonds, secured by a lien on future earnings—which did not even have to be allotted to the bonds unless the directors agreed. Equipment bonds went to purchase locomotives, cars, and ferryboats. Stations and stockyards were mortgaged. When the Atchison, Topeka and Santa Fe was up for reorganization in 1899 it had forty-one different classes of securities.

Railroads did not set up sinking funds to meet future bond redemptions until late in the nineteenth century. Poor's *Railroad Journal* was forever explaining that the roads could save money by setting up such funds, for the bonds, instead of being sold at enormous discounts, could be sold at par. But there appeared to be too many other uses for railroad income, particularly when control was frequently changing hands, with each set of new owners dipping freely into the company till.

Stocks and bonds were actually sold in such quantities that railway capital far outweighed the national debt all during the latter half of the nineteenth century. Early investors in railroad securities soon discovered that close to 50 per cent of all their capital was backed by nothing more than the insubstantial promises of the roads' promoters. The Arkansas Central Railway, for instance, was forty-eight miles long and built for less than $500,000, yet its promoters managed to unload $5 million of bonds and stock on the investing public. This amount of capital greatly exceeded any reasonable expectation of earnings plus the value of the physical assets. When the road went into receivership, only $40,000 was recovered, and that went to pay off, not the original bonds, but notes issued during the receivership.

Railroad common stock at the time represented little more than voting power alone. John Moody, publisher of *Moody's Manual of Corporation Securities,* speaking of the Wabash Railway stock, said, "The present value or cost, aside from temporary speculative manipulation, is measured almost entirely by the voting power, as there is no immediate prospect of dividend payments of any kind, and the equity back of it is so nebulous and uncertain that it cannot be sanely measured at all." Voting power was valued, of course, because it represented access to railroad earnings and to the public pocketbook via the issue of new stock and bonds.

Those who made the profits, however, were not those who took the risks. The real risk was assumed by the bondholders. Those stockholders who remained through bankruptcy and reorganization were often insiders. With their stock carrying only limited liability for debts, they made large fortunes manipulating both the company and the stock.

Railroad capital commonly was watered during mergers. The early pattern of the U.S. rail system was a network of small separate lines (at one time there were 6000 individual railroads). As commerce increased and the normal shipping routes became longer, the little lines were gradually linked to form fewer, larger properties. In a merger the new company always issued stocks and bonds far in excess of the value of the former lines. For example, the New York Central, formed by the merger of several smaller railroads, issued $9 million in securities over and above the par value of stock of the roads making up the consolidation.

On all this capitalization, interest had to be paid. It is no wonder that the railroads staggered under the burden, with defaults and reorganizations, while security holders watched their investments erode.

Bankruptcy proceedings occasionally wiped out entire classes of securities. Some of these bankruptcy actions, it should be noted in passing, served as devices to enable insiders to unload at a profit. Management would petition for bankruptcy before a friendly judge, and the president of the company, or one or two of the directors, would be appointed receivers. When the new receivers opened the books, they found that a few days before the bankruptcy petition was filed a large short-term loan had been made for unspecified purposes which naturally had to be taken care of before other bonds. And who had made the mysterious loan? Why the directors, of course, who were now the receivers. Stockholders sometimes sued when the double dealings became this obvious. But they seldom got anywhere, for in those days judges could be found who were only too glad to do favors for wealthy railroad magnates.

The Railroad Tycoons

A railroad stockholder of the nineteenth century had little protection against the dilution of his equity. While his road's charter generally fixed the amount of capital that could be authorized, and provided that a new capital issue had to be approved by stockholders, there was usually no prohibition against issuing mortgage bonds convertible into stock. This power was taken by the boards of directors and often used to the advantage of insiders.

The most famous instance of this took place in 1867 in a battle for control of the Erie Railroad between Daniel Drew, Jim Fisk, and Jay Gould on the one side, and Cornelius "Commodore" Vanderbilt on the other. These four men were among the most powerful and colorful railroad tycoons of the period. They were self-made men, shrewd and unscrupulous. Drew, tall, gaunt, pious, was often mistaken for a country deacon as he strode about Wall Street, shabbily dressed and carrying a battered old umbrella. He always spoke of the Erie as the "Airy."

Drew had established his fortune as a cattle drover and was credited with giving the world the term "watered stock" to describe company stocks backed by fictitious assets. He would feed his cattle salt on their drive down to the city and then allow them to drink their fill. This greatly increased their weight, and unsuspecting buyers would pay good money for water which they figured was solid beef.

Jim Fisk was as jolly as Drew was lugubrious—a plump, gaudy, ebullient little man who got his start with a circus and carried on a career in high finance with as much fun and show as if he were under the big tent. He loved luxury, excitement, and fast company.

Jay Gould was a loner. Quiet, frail, brilliant, he was given to secret maneuvering that made him feared and hated. He and Fisk made a good team—Fisk as the front man and Gould as the brains.

The trio's opponent in the contest for the Erie, Commodore Vanderbilt, had risen from a small-boat captain in New York Bay to a financier worth nearly $100 million. Big, bold, confident, opinionated, he was 73 and already in control of the New York Central when he decided to go after the Erie. The railroad was headed by Gould as president and Fisk as vice-president and comptroller. Drew was treasurer and a large stockholder.

When the Erie forces learned that Vanderbilt was to attempt to oust them, they armed for the attack. Under New York laws then, a railroad could issue its own stock in exchange for shares of any smaller road under lease to it that it wanted to consolidate. The Erie triumvirate bought a small railroad for some $250,000, leased it to their road, and upon consolidating it issued themselves convertible bonds worth $2 million. They also had the Erie directors authorize $10 million in convertible bonds for improvements to the road, which was in atrocious shape.

Through a series of court injunctions, Vanderbilt tried to tie up the bonds to prevent conversion. The Erie men brought forth a bondholder who demanded conversion and got a court order to compel it. Fisk and Gould printed up new stock certificates on a printing press, the story goes, which was conveniently located in the basement of Erie headquarters. Jim Fisk was said to have chortled, "If this press don't break down, we'll give the old hog all he wants of Erie."

After Vanderbilt had purchased $8 million worth of Erie stock, he gave up. His influence in the courts, however, was sufficient to force Drew, Gould, and Fisk to leave New York in the dead of night to avoid arrest, temporarily holing up in a hotel in Jersey City which they made into the railroad's headquarters. When a settlement was eventually worked out, the legislature was persuaded to legalize the phony issue. Vanderbilt was paid for some of it, which was recalled to the Erie treasury. Some Boston financiers who had been Vanderbilt allies were given a large amount of Erie bonds for a small railway they owned. Cash had to be spread around to soothe the wounded feelings of prominent market operators whom Erie did not want to offend and who had lost money by being caught in the crossfire between the warring factions. The fracas cost the Erie Railroad $9 or $10 million net of any value received. Not only was the stockholders' equity diluted, but there were more bonds to pay interest on before any dividends could be paid. Worse was yet to come. Under the stewardship of Gould and Fisk, Erie capitalization was watered by a total of about $54 million. Small wonder that after their regime the railroad did not pay a dividend for sixty-nine years.

This was by no means the only case of massive dilution of equity, although it may have been the most notorious. The president of the Vermont Central Railroad, for example, sold 10,000 illegal shares so widely that the legislature was forced to increase the capitalization because no one could disentangle the mess.

Stockholders protested such treatment, but history does not record that they altered or impeded in the least the flamboyant march of nineteenth-century railroad history. When a stockholder claimed that Jim Fisk damaged the Erie's good name by appearing in public with "women of bad repute," he was regarded as a crank. The public, as a matter of fact, liked to see Jim Fisk live it up; he was an appealing character. Nor did the stockholder get very far who complained that Fisk had put up around New York "showy and costly lampposts" at company expense, to advertise a theater he was interested in. Another dissident Erie stockholder sued Fisk and Gould for mismanagement; they had the case put before a friendly judge who threw it out and enjoined the stockholder from pursuing his efforts. When the stockholder persisted by bringing another suit, he was fined $5000 for contempt of court.

Some of the stockholder meetings of those free-wheeling days were as exciting as present-day TV Westerns. Fisk and Gould were trying to win control of the Albany and Susquehanna Railroad— a link of 140 miles between Albany and Binghamton, New York, they wanted to add to the Erie—but Fisk had been able to lay hands on only about a fifth of the stock when annual meeting time came. Undaunted, the irrepressible Fisk armed himself with an injunction against letting the rival group vote (which he obtained on some pretext or other), hired a group of hoods, and set out for Albany where the road's annual meeting was to take place. Once there, he took possession of the head office with the aid of a local sheriff who arrested the Albany and Susquehanna's president and other officials of the railroad. Fisk and his goon squad then held a "stockholders" meeting on the spot and elected their own slate of directors. The incumbent directors, however, persuaded the police to let them meet in another room in Erie's office suite before going to jail. This they did, and the resulting vote elected them to another term. It was left to the court to decide which team had really won. Eventually, Fisk lost his case and the presiding judge was moved to comment that "Mr. Fisk's attempt to carry the election by his contingent of 'toughs' was a gross perversion and abuse of the right to vote by proxy, tending to convert corporation meetings into places of disorder, lawlessness and riot."

Spotty reporting to stockholders was typical of all corporations in those days. United States Express, for instance, which was listed on the New York Stock Exchange, sent out no reports and held no meetings. American Sugar Refining issued no report although it was one of the largest companies in existence at the time. In the stockholder reports that did appear, financial details were scarce. While the pamphlet might go into fulsome details about the population and assessed valuation of the counties the railway served, and list the size of wheat and corn crops for ten years back, it often neglected to include such fundamental information as a balance sheet and statement of outstanding debt. Railroads frequently reported their income and expenses—out of character as this might seem—because most of them began to show operating profits soon after they were opened and they couldn't resist the temptation to toot their own horns. Without knowing the total debt and interest charges, however, a stockholder could not tell whether or not the operating profits were adequate.

Significant changes from year to year would be shown with no explanation of a big increase in the amount of stock outstanding, for instance. All sorts of accounting devices were used to make the reports look better. The Philadelphia & Reading Railway owned a profitable subsidiary producing coal; it once transferred a sizable amount of debt to the coal company's books to keep it off the railroad's annual report.

The *American Railroad Journal* published all the financial news it could find, and its editors crusaded for a more liberal corporate policy on information. They would make analyses of reports, with caustic comments such as "a studious attempt to conceal, if not suppress, facts material to be known." In 1868, Editor H. V. Poor began publication of his famous handbook of railroad securities, in which financial details were collected and compared, a milestone service to stockholders. The *Commercial and Financial Chronicle* also labored to mine full and accurate data. In 1875 it inaugurated an investors' supplement, attempting to cover most of the securities then actively traded. This paper also freely criticized railroad reporting. When one road was revealed to be in financial trouble, the *Chronicle* pointed out how hard it was to find out what was really going on: "The noteworthy fact is, that the several newspaper articles did not agree in their statement of those things which are mere matters of fact and not of opinion; for example, the amount of bonded debt; this is greatly to the confusion of the investor who cares little for speculation, but wants to know the real condition of his share property." On occasion the *Chronicle* would urge investors to join forces: "The stock and bondholders of this railroad should organize immediately for their own protection."

A number of states attempted to get a flow of financial information. Massachusetts, from 1833, required the filing of a yearly report with state officials. New York followed in 1843. These early reports did not have to contain much detail. Massachusetts gradually came to require more and more, and other states, especially after making loans and grants to the railroads, began to ask for a yearly accounting. Among the items desired was a statement of capital, income and expenses, cost of maintenance, cost of equipment and track mileage, including the radius of each curve.

The railroads were slow to comply with state requests for information. "They have a very great disinclination . . . to give information respecting their affairs," complained the Pennsylvania Auditor-General in 1859, even though states like Pennsylvania were large stockholders. The men on the board who represented state or city interests had a tough time of it. The other directors failed to invite them to meetings, would transact only minor business when they did attend, and ignored their requests for information. The penalties for failing to file yearly reports were nominal—$250 in New York State, for instance, and token compliance could be achieved by sending in a few figures; "reports required by law in several states are made in so perfunctory a manner that they are of very slight service," said the *Commercial and Financial Chronicle*. The trunk lines, which often sought help from the states, finally began to make yearly reports to them although they were not too informative.

Back in those days when Abraham Lincoln sat in the White House, there were no uniform accounting procedures. The Massachusetts Railroad Commission was empowered in 1876 to set up standard accounting procedures and compel state railroads to follow them; and nearby states shortly followed suit. Stockholders of the New England railroads benefited somewhat, but elsewhere it was not until the Interstate Commerce Commission was set up by Congress in 1887 that relatively complete reports were made available from all the railroads despite the fact that they were always a year or so behind the times.

The contrast between what the railroads told their stockholders and what was actually happening was so great that it was often downright amusing. One of the typically grandiose gestures of Jay Gould and Jim Fisk, when they were in command of the Erie, was to move company headquarters into a white marble edifice at

Twenty-third Street and Eighth Avenue, New York. On its lower floors the building housed a theater where a struggling impresario presented opera. Fisk, nicknamed "The Prince of Erie," had become a patron of the arts by taking as his mistress an actress who starred in the shows housed in the theater he built. While her shows were rehearsed and presented, and the halls of the building rang with music and the tinkling laughter of showgirls, the Erie Railroad carried on its business in lavishly decorated quarters upstairs. As a reporter described it:

> A huge admirably carved door swings open upon such a spectacle as was never before witnessed in any business place; in fact, there are but few palaces wherein so rich a coup d'oeil could be presented as that of the main offices of the Erie Railway Company. The carved woodwork, the stained and cut glass of the partitions, the gilded balustrades, the splendid gas fixtures, and above all the artistic frescoes upon the walls and ceilings create astonishment and admiration at such a blending of the splendid and practical.

How were the new headquarters described to stockholders? Gould, who was president, did not do anything so foolish as to call the building an opera house, though Fisk had renamed it the Grand Opera House and was advertising it far and wide. Gould modestly wrote in the annual report for 1869 that the Erie headquarters on the waterfront downtown had become hard to heat and was poorly ventilated. The company therefore decided to move to a more convenient location.

The first time stockholders were officially informed of the real character of the corporation's main office was in 1875, when one of Gould's successors announced that as part of his sweeping reform he was moving the Erie out of its opulent headquarters and back to its previous address. (The Grand Opera House, in later years, became a neighborhood movie theater and was torn down in 1961 to the accompaniment of sentimental newspaper reminiscences.)

If it was difficult for American stockholders to know what was going on, it was ten times more difficult for foreign stockholders to keep track of American investments. Foreign capital helped build

America. By the middle of the nineteenth century some $50 million of railway securities alone were held abroad, and the amount increased to $250 million during and after the Civil War. By the end of the century, total investments of foreign capital were close to $3 billion, mostly in rails. More than half of the shares of some railroads, and 25 per cent of all rail securities, were held overseas. The British in particular had continued, with a few lapses, to pour money into American railroads.

When they failed to get their dividends or interest, the British security holders held meetings in England to work out remedies. A common suggestion was that the railroad headquarters be moved to Britain—a vain hope considering the anti-foreign sentiment of American business.

Some English stockholders brought suit in American courts when their rights were violated. To supplement the meager supply of official information sent over from the U.S., they issued special reports for British consumption. Sometimes they sent over special emissaries to represent them on the board of directors or simply to look at the books. These gentlemen were given a difficult time by men like Gould and Vanderbilt, who posed as defenders of American investors against wily foreigners. At one of the meetings of English security holders of the Erie, a returning investigator reported: "It has been most demoralizing. Even one of our own Directors in New York, when asked to give us some information as to what had become of the English capital sent out—what do you think he said? He told us, 'Well, really, Sir, that is what I am always asking, but which I can never get to know.'"

An illuminating story of how annual reports could be doctored came up in connection with the difficulties English stockholders had after they finally succeeded in ousting Jay Gould in 1872. The man they had put in to succeed Gould promptly declared dividends, and kept on declaring them even during the desperate panic of 1873, when banks, brokerages, and commercial companies were failing one after the other. Erie's new comptroller, a man of high repute, resigned in a rage. He released a detailed statement showing that the official 1873 annual report had been falsified. Among other things, he charged that the floating debt was twice what was shown, and earnings had been manipulated to make it seem that the dividends were paid out of profits when they actually had been paid out of capital. In fact, at the time the dividends last had been paid, the railroad was a month behind on its payroll. The Erie board promptly declared the allegations "traitorous and false." But the loss of public confidence was enough to cause them to retire the Erie president, with thanks for his help.

4

SHEARING THE LAMBS FOR

FUN AND PROFIT:

THE UNREGULATED STOCK MARKET

OF THE 1800S

The nineteenth century was a glorious time for speculators. A stock could move fifty points a day from the time the market opened until it closed. Men were made rich in a few days, and they lost their bundle with equal speed. Wall Street buzzed with rumors. Anonymous pamphlets praising or disparaging certain stocks appeared out of the blue and were snapped up. Tip sheets in the guise of financial newspapers circulated sensation, false information, and biased advice to avid readers. "Men buy and sell through the columns of the press," said one contemporary. "The power of the press in financial matters is enormous."

Big speculators took advantage of the reliance placed on the written word. "The influence of a money article on a line of stocks is so great that if a favorable article can be secured for a handsome check, it is regarded as well laid out," a chronicler of Wall Street wrote. When Jay Gould found himself in possession of the New York *World,* he quickly devoted his attention to its financial columns. The *New York Times* charged, and pretty well documented, that Gould used his "Wall Street Gossip" column to print bearish tales about the Manhattan Elevated Railway in order to drive down the price of its shares while he was buying up control. Five months later, when the company was safely in Gould's hands, the *World* ran a series of favorable comments from "leading authorities" or "well known brokers" that enhanced the value of his investment.

While many newspapermen probably resisted the temptation to doctor the news, they understood that it did not do to write critically of Wall Street as an institution. One financial editor had to retire because, as a Wall Streeter wrote, "he indulged largely in opprobrious epithets when writing of the brokers and speculators of Wall Street, whereby he lost caste."

From the point of view of present business practices, there was plenty to be opprobrious about. Speculation had few effective restraints; it was limited only by the imagination of the speculator and the amount of money at his command. A few rich men, sitting around on a boring day, could cook up all sorts of exciting schemes for running up this stock, running down that one, outwitting rival cliques, or just "shearing the lambs" for fun and profit.

There was some gambling in stocks before the Civil War, but speculation didn't really hit its stride until after the war, when a new boom began. By that time, the telegraph enabled Wall Street's latest rumor to be flashed to other Eastern cities in seconds. Margin requirements were only a low 10 per cent for stocks listed on the New York Stock Exchange, still less for unlisted stocks or those traded on smaller exchanges, and this added more fuel to fires of speculation.

The passionate concern for quick wealth was enough to make James Bryce, an English historian who visited here in the 1880s, conclude that Americans "are naturally inclined to be speculative. . . . In the United States a much larger part of the population, including professional men as well as business men, seem conversant with the subject, and there are times when the whole community, not merely city people, but also storekeepers in country towns, even farmers, even domestic servants, interest themselves actively in share speculation."

Most of the more spectacular techniques for manipulating the stock market had already been invented, but they were ingeniously improved by the captains of Wall Street during the latter part of the century. A good example is the stock market "corner" which first occurred in the stock of the Morris Canal Company in the 1830s.

The stage is set for a corner when speculators are convinced that the price of a stock is too high and decide to sell it short. To sell short, a person sells shares of stock he does not own. He does this when the shares are in demand and he can get a high price. He agrees to deliver the shares by a definite date, gambling that in the meantime the price will go down and he can buy them back more cheaply, thus making a profit. If the market goes up instead of down, the speculator eventually has to buy anyway and loses money. There had been disapproval of short sales when they were first used. New York State outlawed them in 1812, Massachusetts in 1836, and Pennsylvania in 1841, but these laws were later repealed. Short selling during this period, incidentally, gave rise to the story of a company president who spotted a stranger at his firm's annual stockholders' meeting. The stranger persisted in asking detailed and searching questions of management, and when the president asked him to identify himself the interloper replied, "Oh, I represent the short interest in your company's stock."

A "corner" comes into being when a speculator decides to "squeeze" the short sellers by buying up all available shares of the stock so there are none available for the short sellers to buy when their contracts come due. Those who have to buy are at the mercy of the "cornerer," who can set his own price.

In the case of Morris Canal, it was the first time anyone had bought up all the floating shares. Those who had sold short were "cornered," not to mention astonished and displeased. They simply refused to settle their contracts, claiming unfair tactics had been used. The Board of Brokers, as the New York Stock Exchange was then called, agreed with them. It was the first and last time the exchange permitted short sellers to sneak out from under their obligations; after the storm of criticism that followed, the board decided it was better not to interfere with "the free play of the market."

Commodore Vanderbilt brought about some of the most famous stock corners in the annals of Wall Street. In 1863 he was interested in the New York & Harlem Railway, a short line running north from New York that was used to bring milk and construction materials to the city limits. Vanderbilt applied to the New York City Common Council for the right to extend the Harlem by a street railway down Broadway, right into the heart of Manhattan. As the Commodore generally got what he wanted, by one means or another, the Harlem's stock began to rise, and the council saw a wonderful chance to make money. They would pretend to go along, and when the stock hit a high point they would sell short. Then they would cancel the Harlem's valuable franchise, the price of the line's shares would immediately plummet, and they would buy back the shares they needed to cover their short sale for peanuts— making a killing. This the council did, and when Vanderbilt heard about this shocking bit of skulduggery he decided to corner all the Harlem's outstanding stock. When the time came for the councilmen to settle their contracts they discovered to their horror that Vanderbilt owned all the stock. The Commodore set a high price on his shares, and the councilmen lost a fortune.

One of the many mysteries of Wall Street is why Vanderbilt was able to repeat the same performance with the state legislature only a year later. He applied for permission to merge the Harlem with the Hudson River Railroad, which he also controlled. His application was accompanied by some monetary persuasion, and, being assured of favorable action, he began buying more Harlem stock, which had meanwhile been dispersed again. As the price rose the legislators made short sales, agreeing secretly that they would defeat the bill. They did defeat it, and the stock dropped sixty points. Not content with their paper profits, the legislators waited for it to go lower. In the interval, Vanderbilt raised money and bought heavily, forcing the price back up.

The Commodore did such a superlative job of cornering the stock that he actually paid for 27,000 more shares than were in existence. The old man was so angry he wanted to make the legislators settle at $1000 per share for stock they had sold at $150. Eventually he came down to $285, but a good many legislators were badly caught.

A corner that hurt little speculators badly, and in fact left a bad taste in the mouths of the financiers who took part, was the Northern Pacific corner of 1901. Edward H. Harriman, allied with John D. Rockefeller, was battling J. J. Hill, who was backed up by the House of Morgan, for control of the railway. In the last two days of the contest the price of the common stock was pushed up forty points. As neither side had revealed its hand, the general public was not aware of what was going on. The stock began to look far too high. Little speculators sold short in anticipation of a decline. The short selling went on so fast that 78,000 more shares were sold than actually existed. The rival factions, however, were immobilizing the stock as they snapped it up. Soon they had it all cornered between them. Speculators made frantic efforts to cover their short positions and bid the price up from $300 to $1000 in one day. They had to sell other securities, whose value fell 40 per cent in two days. People who held those other stocks on margin were wiped out. A panic set in that was felt in all financial centers of the world.

By this time maneuvers such as Vanderbilt and others were pulling off were considered the work of geniuses. "Gambling is a business now where formerly it was a disreputable excitement," wrote Charles Francis Adams, Jr., one of the few disapproving observers. "Cheating at cards was always disgraceful; transactions of a similar character under the euphemistic names of 'operating' and 'cornering' and the like are not so regarded." Wall Street did not tolerate thieves among its brokers and customers, but it admired a smart man who could make money, even though he used planted rumors, inside information, and conniving of all sorts as long as he got away with it. If a small stockholder lost everything during the gyrations of a big wheel, it was his misfortune. He should have been smarter. Henry Clews, head of a Wall Street firm for fifty years, called the panic of 1857 "a fine exemplification of the survival of the fittest. It proved that there was a law of natural selection in financial affairs," he said.

The Rules and Regulations—Such as They Were

The Stock Exchange, of course, attempted to set standards of conduct for its members. Prospective members, who were admitted by election and could be blackballed by three votes, had to appear before an examining committee and testify as to their financial resources. The charging of agreed-on commissions was strictly policed, as was the honesty of brokers in dealings with each other and their customers. There were even rules against the use of indecorous language, and during its early years the Exchange operated rather like an English gentlemen's club. Before the Civil War, the trading of stocks took place in deepest secrecy; the prices and volume were reported to the press only once a week. It was rumored that "outsiders" once dug a hole in the wall of the trading room to see what went on, and guards at the door were supposed to charge $100 a day for letting someone listen at the keyhole. Informal trading often went on in the street, and even at night. A rival Open Board of Brokers was formed to trade in more visible fashion and built up such a lively business that the older group agreed on a merger. It was consummated in 1869, and from then on the Exchange was open to the public. Stock tickers also appeared on the financial scene, bringing up-to-the-minute news of transactions on the Exchange to a still larger segment of the investing public.

In trying to regulate the companies whose stocks it dealt in, the Exchange usually moved in the most cautious manner. Up to 1869 the only requirements a company had to meet before its stock was listed consisted of satisfying the Exchange that the company was legally incorporated, had a transfer office, and had printed the stock certificates in such a way as to discourage forgery.

In 1869, the Exchange required listed companies to register their shares to prevent them from secretly issuing and selling large blocks before the public became aware such stock existed. When the Erie Railway refused to do this, it was temporarily delisted. The Exchange still made no examination of the corporation's financial condition, however, nor did it have any consistent rules to ban the listing of securities that had been obviously watered. It did refuse, in 1870, to admit the Atlantic and Great Western Railway, which had issued $120 million worth of securities on facilities that cost $20 million. But Henry Villard was able to get his Oregon Railway and Navigation Company listed although it had issued stock and bonds amounting to $12 million on visible assets of not more than $3.5 million. John Moody observed, "There never is, apparently, much difficulty in a big stock operator getting his issues upon the list . . . without the facilities of the Exchange, many of the stock watering frauds which have become historical never could have been successfully consum-

mated." For the benefit of companies that did not want to comply
with even the minimal rules, the Exchange maintained an Unlisted Department.

When there was a flagrant case of illegal stock manipulation,
such as an overissue, the Exchange stopped trading until things
were cleared up. Under a later ruling, thirty days had to elapse before a new issue could be traded. But brokers simply went short of it
for that period. Abuses such as "wash sales," where buying and
selling orders were entered at the same time by a manipulator who
wished to create the illusion of great activity in a stock, were deplored but not effectively stopped.

From time to time the Exchange suggested to its listed companies
that filing financial reports would be a good idea. In 1877, a committee reported to the Board of Governors the outcome of one
such campaign:

> The result of (our) effort was not cheering. After a delay
> of several months, about a score of companies consented to
> furnish the desired information, and have done so, but the lead-
> ing corporations declined, on various pretexts, to comply with
> our request. . . .
>
> Mr. Vanderbilt sent a courteous reply, so worded as to cause
> your committee to hope that he would give the desired returns.
> But we found to our regret, on seeking a more definite response,
> that his smooth words covered an inflexible purpose to give
> the public no more information than was required by law. . . .
>
> The Michigan Central Railroad furnished frequent returns
> while they were favorable, but ceased to do so when they showed
> a decrease in earnings. . . .

The committee thought it saw encouraging signs of a nascent
public demand for more information. It concluded its report with
an exhortation to stockholders to rise up and demand their rights.
It was not until 1900 that the Exchange felt it could insist that an
agreement to furnish regular financial reports be a prerequisite to
listing, although an independent audit of such reports was not required until 1933.

There was no prohibition against officers and directors secretly
trading in the stock of their own companies as there is today. They

did it all the time, and in huge amounts. Commodore Vanderbilt was one of the experts at this game. His manipulation of New York Central stock was described at the time as absolutely "hydraulic."

> Sending it up on one occasion at a bound, between Saturday and Monday, 20 per cent was a new move in manipulation which caused some of the boldest operators on the Stock Exchange to stand aghast. He kept working the stock up and down . . . until he "milked" the street sometimes very dry. He kept the tempting prize of a coming dividend glittering before the eyes of the dazzled imaginations of his friends who were dealing in the stock, but the "milking" process was so ably managed that, when the famous 80 per cent dividend was actually declared, they had become so poor that they were unable to carry any of the stock, so as to avail themselves of the profits.

Some faint stirrings of disapproval could be heard in the latter part of the century, to judge by a statement in the financial gossip columns of the *Times*. Two directors of a railroad had just returned from a tour of its route. They announced to all and sundry that the tour had shown them the railroad was in terrible shape. They were selling out their stock. "It shocked [Wall Street]," said the *Times*, "for when speculators 'bear' the stock of a road of which they happen to be Directors, etiquette requires that they at least shall not do it publicly."

Not having any sound information to go on, the small speculators followed as closely as they could in the wake of the big speculators, whose names and habits were familiar to all newspaper readers. So great a following did the financiers build up that Wall Street always expected a panic when one of them passed from the scene. When William H. Vanderbilt, the Commodore's son, died in 1885, his friends formed a $12 million pool to support the market the next day. But they did not have to use it. A temporary flutter of a few points was all that ensued—"scarcely adequate as a fitting tribute of respect to Mr. Vanderbilt's memory," remarked Henry Clews.

Up until the last decade of the nineteenth century, railroads were the principal securities listed on the New York Stock Exchange, other than banks and insurance companies. Only twenty industrials were traded. There was a special exchange for mining company shares, generally priced under $5 each, that handled trading in these corporations which were launched by the hundreds after the Civil War. Promoters would find a man with a valid claim and offer him stock in a company newly formed to exploit the claim. As there was a good deal of uncertainty as to what mining properties were worth, a mine that some geologists thought worth $50,000 might be capitalized at $1.5 million. "It is our belief, as well as the belief of experts, practical miners and mining authorities that we have properties that are certain to yield immense wealth," claimed a Colorado gold mining company, offering stock at five cents per share.

Back in those days, there was no Securities and Exchange Commission to protect unwary investors against exaggerations in a prospectus. By 1874, for instance, a man brought suit against a promoter who had induced him to buy a stock by saying it was worth 80 per cent of its par value. He found it worth only 40 per cent. The court decided the seller was not liable for damages because the value of stocks, in its view, was a matter of opinion and accordingly had no intrinsic value.

Land companies were also springboards for speculation. Promoters bought up tracts near railroads, or where railroads were likely to go, and sold acreage to settlers, especially immigrants. "The success of the Iowa Land Company is now apparent and firmly established," said its first report, when only 30 per cent of the stock had been paid in. "The only question in regard to it is, how large will be its profits." The Campbell Investment Company, which held some land near Chicago, also thought it had a sure thing. "Home buyers know nothing of real estate, either here or anywhere else," it told shareholders. "They 'use their own judgment'—they haven't any—which leads them to buy in flocks."

Outright fraud in land speculation was common. The promoters used the newspapers to promise 300 per cent to 500 per cent per year on investment. "Don't delay! Speculate conservatively!" they said, for land never seemed as risky as industry. A man would be induced to make a token investment. Soon a dividend would be forthcoming, along with a letter pointing out how much money he could make if he put in a lot more "before prices went up." He took out all he had in the bank and sent it along. The company was never heard from again. One firm alone swindled 10,000 people with this game.

There were more imaginative frauds. One was an egg company that put out an issue of 7 per cent "guaranteed" preferred. "The essence of the guarantee on the preferred stock appeared to be wholly based on the theory that the hens had somehow been forced into a promise to lay eggs night and day, if need be, in order not to allow the preferred stock dividends to lapse," wrote John Moody. Its promoters raised $80,000, mostly from city dwellers, and disappeared.

Another promotion was based on the fact that sea water contains minute amounts of various minerals, including gold. A man named Jergensen claimed to have invented a process for recovering the gold, in large amounts. He installed some machinery in a bay in Maine and invited prospective investors to visit the plant. Because of the necessity for deepest secrecy, lest someone steal the process and cheat the investors out of untold riches, he said, he could not actually show how he did it—besides, a good deal of the apparatus was under the water. Each morning, however, he exhibited a quantity of gold he said had been turned out during the night. He raised nearly $1 million. New Yorkers always liked to tell of the "sea water fraud," after it was exposed, because most of the money had come from Bostonians, who prided themselves on their hard-headed New England common sense.

In the midst of the speculative fever, the railroad battles, the engrossing financial scandals, there were of course companies that were run with scrupulous honesty and reported fully to their stockholders. These companies tended to be those with relatively few stockholders, perhaps two or three hundred, that had started as family affairs.

Andrew Carnegie, for example, fixed the value of his steel company's shares at $1000 to keep them from becoming easily marketed. They were not listed on the Exchange; in fact, Carnegie disapproved greatly of anyone parting with them. The Pepperell Company, which owned textile mills in Maine, was another conservative and solid investment. Its original $500 par stock was selling at $1000 by 1881, and it paid a 12 per cent dividend even in the panic year of 1873. The Dennison Company, a partnership until 1879, was two-thirds owned by the Dennisons even after incorporation. Dividends ran 10 per cent to 35 per cent from 1879 to 1893, plus some stock distributions. These were only a few.

While it appeared to some commentators that all American stockholders preferred to invest in companies whose shares were traded on stock exchanges, the actual percentage was probably about one-fifth of the just under one million Americans who owned stock at this time. Thus stockholder speculation, while it involved a good segment of the stockholding public, was not the whole story in the nineteenth century. But it was an exciting and well-publicized story nevertheless. After a good hard look at the country from coast to coast, James Bryce concluded:

> The habit of speculation is now a part of their character. . . . Some may think that when the country fills up and settles down, and finds itself altogether under conditions more nearly resembling those of the Old World, these peculiarities will fade away. I doubt it. They seem to have already passed into the national fiber.

5

THE RICH GET RICHER:

THE GROWTH OF TRUSTS AND

HOLDING COMPANIES

While corporations were growing in assets and importance in the last part of the nineteenth century, they were still personally managed by their owners. Vanderbilt, Gould, and others ran their railroads with the title of president, or treasurer and controlled them through direct or indirect stock ownership. Sometimes they had outright holdings of a majority of the stock; in other cases they were able to assemble a majority from among friends and associates. They would not have dreamed of letting their share interest drop to 10 per cent or 20 per cent; this would have been an invitation to some other financier to take over the enterprise. While these men certainly did not represent the majority of stockholders numerically, and had little regard for people with small holdings, they did, nevertheless, embody the combination of ownership and management that had been typical of companies built by American capital.

With the rise of the trust companies and holding companies, from 1890 on, ownership by stockholders was even further separated from the management of the companies they owned. By 1929 it was possible for one family with less than $20 million invested in a holding company to dictate the policies of companies having 55,000 stockholders who had invested $1 billion.

The combines of the "Trust Era" were so designated because some of the early ones were actually voting trusts. Railroaders had used that form of corporate control to give one man or group a free hand in running things when a railroad faced serious difficulties. Later, even without a financial crisis, stockholders in various industries were persuaded that, to end ruthless competition and effect economies in buying and selling, they ought to pool their resources and give sweeping powers to a few outstandingly shrewd men. They deposited their stock with trustees in exchange for trust certificates, and in doing so they gave up their votes and any voice in corporate affairs except the right to share in the profits.

John D. Rockefeller set the pattern with Standard Oil of Ohio in 1882 in an attempt to avoid coming under the Ohio corporation laws. Under his company, or trust, stockholders of forty or more oil producers and refiners exchanged their stock for stock of the Standard Oil companies in various states, and deposited the new stock with trustees, who issued trust certificates in return. Voting trusts were often employed during corporate reorganizations, on the theory that a crisis demanded a free hand for those in control. Some states declared voting trusts illegal. Gradually, however, they received legal sanction, though time limits were put on their duration. The later "trusts" were not trusts of this legal form, but simply large corporations created by the merger of many smaller ones. But because the earlier trusts had represented bigness, monopoly, and wealth in the public mind, the new combinations, similarly possessing those characteristics, also became known as trusts.

They seemed to stand for big, impersonal power beyond the grasp of most ordinary people. Because popular clamor tended to concentrate on the social and moral problems of big business, it failed to produce any effective controls from an economic point of view. The Sherman Anti-Trust Act, passed in 1890 to pacify the public, offered no real impediment to corporate consolidations.

The railroads were welded into larger networks run by fewer companies. The oil industry began to combine production, transportation, refining, and marketing. By 1899, when the Standard Oil Company (New Jersey) became the receptacle for holding all the Standard interests, Rockefeller and his associates were refining 85 per cent of all the oil in the country. American Can Company acquired 90 per cent of can production; American Tin Plate represented 265 tin mills; National Tube combined 90 per cent of iron pipe and tube capacity. These consolidations were dwarfed by the formation of the $1.4 billion United States Steel Corporation in 1901.

In the years 1898 through 1903, 300 industrial giants were born. There was a hiatus in the decade preceding World War I, and then the merger movement rose to full flood. Between 1919 and 1930 more than 8000 mining and manufacturing establishments disappeared as separate entities through merger or acquisition. Ten groups of holding companies came to control about three-fourths of all electric power production. Fourteen giant railway systems operated 87 per cent of the first-class railroad mileage. Just before the Depression, in 1928, of the 573 corporations whose securities were actively traded on the New York Stock Exchange, 92 were pure holding companies with no direct operations, while 395 were both holding and operating companies.

Some of the newly formed combinations ran into tough going. The important economies expected from their founding did not support the superstructure of bonds and stock. And they frequently needed capital, having outgrown the capacity of any one man or any small group of financiers to supply their needs. Since personal savings of the U.S. population had risen over the years, the big corporations had these resources to draw on—and they did. The number of owners grew rapidly as the public was encouraged to invest its cash in stock. Only a few of the largest corporations in the nineties had more than 5000 stockholders—Western Union had 9000; American Car and Foundry, 7700; and American Sugar Refining, 11,000. In 1901 and 1902 there was a boom in the stock market that attracted new investors in droves. "Sucker lists" made their appearance about this time. According to John Moody, who wrote *The Art of Wall Street Investing* in 1906, these lists carried the names of persons who, though relatively poor, nevertheless might take a $10 flyer in the market; the $25 investors who were country doctors, teachers and Methodist and Baptist ministers, $100 to $500 prospects including successful Big City doctors, merchants, and Episcopal and Presbyterian ministers; and large investors who could raise several thousand dollars when offered a good thing. A rash of tip sheets created visions of quick, fast profits in the stock market.

Still, when really big stock issues came up for sale, it took time to dispose of them. That's why underwriting became an important part of corporate finance—the investment bankers and brokers thus relieved the corporation of the extended job of disposing of a new issue of securities. When U. S. Steel was formed, it took two years to distribute the original public issue of stock.

World War I, with its sale of Liberty Bonds and frenzied market activity in 1916 and 1917, whetted the public appetite for securities. "Every Piker in Christendom has broken into Wall Street with his shoestring," one broker marveled.

Dispersal of ownership in the 1920s was partly the result of the increasing capital needs of corporations, and partly the result of a deliberate policy on their part to broaden the base of capital supply. In a period of rising stock prices, many companies split their stock to keep the price per share under $100. Employee ownership was encouraged through stock purchase plans. U. S. Steel had even begun such a plan in 1902, but the ups and downs of the market prevented any widespread adoption of the idea until the twenties, when the market seemed always headed upward. By mid-1927 there were 800,000 employee-stockholders in the U.S. owning perhaps $1 billion worth of stock.

Customer ownership was another method of dispersal. Utilities made particular use of customer campaigns as a major means of financing expansion. In the single year 1924, for example, the utilities claimed to have added a million new stockholders through offerings to customers. The Philadelphia Rapid Transit Company even marketed an issue of preferred stock to its car riders.

In the 1920s per capita income rose markedly, jumping 30 per cent between 1922 and 1928. Savings deposits and life insurance almost doubled in the decade. This prosperity was reflected in security purchases. More and more of this buying took place in cities outside of New York, Chicago, and other major financial centers.

Selling securities became so profitable that the commercial banks took it up. Forbidden by banking law to sell or underwrite securities, they organized special securities affiliates. This had been legal since before the war, but not many banks had availed themselves of the opportunity. In the bull market of the twenties almost every large commercial bank in New York had a securities arm. The National City Company, formed by the National City Bank, for example, launched a massive, nationwide campaign through its branches in 58 cities, using 350 special salesmen. In 1927 security affiliates of banks distributed about $19 billion worth of securities.

Some figures for specific companies illustrate the increase in numbers of stockholders from 1900 to the late twenties. General Electric had 2900 stockholders in 1900 and nearly 52,000 in 1928. Standard Oil of New Jersey had 3800 in 1900 and 62,000 in 1928. U. S. Rubber's ownership grew from 3000 to 26,000 during the same period. A.T.&T. had 7535 stockholders in 1900 and by 1928 could boast of 450,000 owners. U. S. Steel, which had about 50,000 stockholders when it was launched, had acquired 154,000 by 1928, while the Pennsylvania Railroad, already a big company in 1900, with about 50,000 share owners, had 158,000 in 1928.

The states charged fees for granting corporate charters, and competed to attract big corporations in an effort to increase state income. The attractions they offered seemed mainly to be means of reducing the accountability of management to stockholders. For instance, Arizona in 1908 advertised that "No public statement and no books need be kept for public inspection anywhere." This was great bait for mining promoters who had inflated the profit potential of their mines. Delaware asserted that under its laws "simple annual reports are necessary, but they do not require disclosure of the corporation's financial affairs." Delaware could also point out that permission of old shareholders was not necessary for the issuance of new securities unless the company particularly desired such a provision written into the charter. Delaware became the favorite home state for holding companies.

Although New Jersey had been the main nesting ground of the early trusts, it tightened up its laws and became less popular. Of the 92 holding companies with active stocks on the Exchange in 1928, 44 had been organized in Delaware. Only 13 were formed under the less liberal New York state law. Of the 573 corporations of all kinds whose securities were actively traded, 148 had Delaware charters. Some companies, in fact, changed over to Delaware from other states.

Since under all general state incorporation laws, business could be done out of the state, incorporators were able to pick and choose to meet individual requirements. The average stockholder did not grasp the significance of "A Maine Corporation" or "A New Jersey Corporation" below his company's name. He might have imagined that they maintained real head offices there, and would have been shocked to see the unprepossessing quarters, often little more than a pigeonhole for the receipt of certain items of official mail.

New York banking houses such as J. P. Morgan & Company, had become increasingly important as the capital needs of industry grew. A big corporation was dependent on the services of an investment banker not only for the issuance of new securities from time to time, but for continuous direction of its financial affairs as it acquired other companies, disposed of some, and borrowed from the commercial banks. The bankers played a tremendously important role then, as they do today. But the public of those days was not so much aware of the fact.

Who Protects the Rights of the Stockholder?

By 1930, a stockholder in a little operating company such as the Hocking Valley Railway, part of the Van Sweringen railroad empire, would have to find his way up through six companies before he caught sight of the Van Sweringen brothers who controlled it. First there was the Chesapeake & Ohio Railway, which owned 81 per cent of Hocking Valley. Then there was the Chesapeake Corporation, which held 54 per cent of the C. & O. Then came Allegheny Corporation with a 71 per cent interest in Chesapeake Corporation. General Securities Corporation dominated Allegheny with a 41 per cent interest. Vaness Company, 80 per cent owned by the Van Sweringens, owned 50 per cent of General Securities, which, coupled with the Van Sweringens' direct holdings, made up overwhelming control of that corporation.

A minority stockholder in an operating company at the bottom of such a pyramid was virtually helpless in a disagreement with those in control. Far off in the top holding company sat a group of men who actually controlled his company's affairs—control of the information he received, the valuation of assets behind his stock, the dividends he might get—even his right to participate in earnings at all, for these men had been upheld in the courts after they changed the participation rights of the various classes of securities. Unless the stockholder was prepared to prove that there was an intent on the part of these distant gentlemen to defraud him, that they were not acting in good faith, or had some private motivation for their actions, there was no use in appealing to the courts. The burden of proof was on the stockholder, who usually knew little, and could find out less, about the corporate affairs of the top holding company.

On most points of stockholders' rights there were so many diverse court opinions that legal action, at best, was a gamble. Moreover, no sooner had a series of opinions based on common law defined a stockholder's right that served to check the power granted to controlling groups than corporation lawyers drawing up charters began to insert waivers of that right. At first the courts had insisted, on the basis of a Massachusetts Supreme Court decision in 1807, that when new shares were to be offered by the corporation its shareholders had first right to subscribe to them pro rata—the doctrine of pre-emptive rights. Thus, the stockholder could prevent the dilution of his equity if he took his shares.

This was a good idea, but it did not last. First, exceptions were made in the case of shares issued in exchange for property. That was one way that water got into railroad stocks. Then some courts held that it did not apply if the total number of shares, including the newly issued ones, was still within the limits of the number of capital shares authorized in the original charter. Most effective of all, corporations began to put into their charters a specific waiver of pre-emptive rights. Some companies which had developed a group of loyal stockholders found it easier to market new issues by granting to each share owner the right to be first in line to purchase the new securities, but the decision whether to do so was up to management if the right was waived in the charter.

Did stockholders have a right to stop their company's directors from making deals with other companies in which the directors held an interest? After a few stockholders raised objections to this practice, charters were written with provisions specifically permitting directors to cause the corporation to deal with other companies in which they were interested. In this way, the stockholder found himself almost shorn of protection.

In *The Modern Corporation and Private Property,* Berle and

Means summed up the situation as it was at the end of the twenties:

> . . . the shareholder in the modern corporate situation has surrendered a set of definite rights for a set of indefinite expectations. The whole effect of the growth of powers of directors and "control" has been steadily to diminish the number of things on which a shareholder can count; the number of demands which he can make with any assurance that they must be satisfied.
>
> The stockholder is therefore left as a matter of law with little more than the loose expectation that a group of men under a nominal duty to run the enterprise for his benefit and that of others like him, will actually observe this obligation. In almost no particular is he in a position to demand that they do or refrain from doing any given thing. Only in extreme cases will their judgment as to what is or is not to his interest be interfered with. And they have acquired under the corporate charter power to do many things which by no possibility can be considered in his interest—whether or not they can be considered in the interest of the enterprise as a whole.

In some states, the stockholder might be able to gain real representation, or at least a source of information, through the requirement for cumulative voting for directors. Under cumulative voting a stockholder can take the votes he would normally cast for the company's entire slate of directors and give them all to a single director. The owner of one share, for example, could cast one vote for each member of his company's fifteen-man board or, if he prefers, cast all fifteen votes for just one director. A relatively small number of shareholders, by agreeing to vote all their shares for one person, can thus outvote a rival group that divides its votes among a number of candidates.

Cumulative voting was proposed so that minority shareholders would have a "watchdog" on the board of directors. This concept arose at the same time as the idea of proportional representation in political elections. When the Illinois legislature was writing a new constitution in 1870, its committee on corporations recommended a bill requiring cumulative voting. "We put our money into a stock company, and the first thing we know it is confiscated by the ring," said the committee chairman in a plea to the convention. "The men who get control of stock by proxies, which they coax or purchase on misrepresentation, elect the entire board and then do as they please. The remainder of the stockholders are in the dark. They have nobody on the board to watch their interests, or to protest against waste, extravagance or mismanagement, or to take any steps to protect them until it is too late."

Illinois passed the law, and Michigan passed a similar one. When other states came to consider the same piece of legislation, most of them decided merely to permit cumulative voting where the corporation included it in the charter or bylaws, rather than to require it in the state incorporation law. New York today has such a permissive law, along with twenty-two other states. Relatively few corporations in these states have adopted cumulative voting.

The stockholder, relatively powerless to protect his investment in the pre-1930 days, was rather passive. When management sought his proxy vote, he gave it. He may not have known what was going on in his company, but if dividends kept coming, and the value of the stock didn't decline, he was usually satisfied.

It was only when he felt short-changed in comparison to stockholders of other companies that he became vocal and critical. William C. Durant devoted some comments to this unreasonable habit in a report sent Durant Motors stockholders in 1928. He blamed stockholder "unfriendliness" for the poor financial state of the company.

> During the past five years many of our stockholders have manifested a noticeable spirit of criticism because of the failure of your corporation to progress to the point of giving them a return on their investment . . . This feeling of unfriendliness on the part of stockholders [has] exerted a hampering influence in obtaining new and better distribution of our products. It has slowed up the sale of our cars; it has furnished the basis for the disparaging statements of outsiders.

Generally, however, stockholders wanted to believe the best about their companies.

When the Teapot Dome scandal came to light, the men who uncovered it were called scandalmongers and character assassins. Stockholders of Sinclair Consolidated Oil Company would have disbelieved Harry F. Sinclair had he told them that he had siphoned part of its revenues into the coffers of a secret company and that about $760,000 of these funds found its way into his pockets. Stockholders were complacent and did not want to be disturbed from their dreams of big money to come. They did not go to stockholder meetings except in those few corporations which were conspicuous by their lack of success in a prosperous era. The annual stockholders' meeting became a mere formality which the officers would dispense with as quickly as possible. A typical report from the *Times* in 1927: "All directors were reelected today at the annual meeting of the Baldwin Locomotive Works. The annual report was approved and the meeting lasted but a few minutes."

Even when corporate officers did not control the company through ownership of a big block of stock, they did not worry about being ousted because the ownership of the company was so widely dispersed. In some companies no one group or individual held more than a fraction of 1 per cent of the stock, yet the directors were able to perpetuate themselves in office because they controlled the proxy machinery.

The states had made some mild attempts to strengthen stockholders' rights and powers in the use of proxies. Some early proxies were of unlimited duration, and, once handed over to management, they continued in effect until revoked. Then laws were passed that limited the duration of the proxy, and made it necessary to resolicit them. Some states also provided that stockholders had the right of access to the list of stock owners so they could solicit proxies themselves.

Two Proxy Fights

In spite of this there were few successful revolts by small stockholders. A J. P. Morgan & Company partner told the Pujo investigating committee in 1913 that he could not think of any case where little stockholders had successfully united to oust the management of a railroad. The same thing could have been said in 1929. There were only a handful of cases in corporations of any kind where small stockholders got together to battle entrenched management and directors, and only one or two in which they won.

John D. Rockefeller organized a successful proxy fight from a minority position in 1929. Though he held only about 15 per cent of the voting stock of Standard Oil of Indiana, the company had always been known as a "Rockefeller company." After its chairman, Colonel Robert Stewart, became publicly involved in the Teapot Dome scandals, Rockefeller asked him to resign. He refused. Rockefeller was forced to circularize stockholders at his own expense, asking their support; he engaged a battery of lawyers and publicity men for the job. On his part, Colonel Stewart counted on the existing directors and the stockholder-employees.

It was a hotly fought battle. Colonel Stewart's mightiest salvo was the declaration of a 50 per cent stock dividend shortly before the election. Stockholders also received, in Colonel Stewart's support, a telegram signed "Employees Committee." It read: "For years we, 25,171 employees of Standard Oil Company of Indiana, many grown grey in service, have been loyal to you. We now ask you to be loyal to us and to the management which has been loyal to both you and us."

The annual meeting on March 7, 1929, made front pages across the land. About 500 stockholders showed up for the big gathering in Whiting, Indiana, where an enterprising pickpocket stole three wallets. After Colonel Stewart's forces had presented the management slate of directors, Winthrop Aldrich, Rockefeller's brother-in-law, presented the insurgent slate. Then, to the surprise of both factions, a small stockholder named Joseph P. Hayes of Chicago rose to demand that two directors be nominated on behalf of stockholders at large, one to represent those with under 500 shares and one to represent those with larger holdings. He maintained that the ordinary stockholder was denied representation when the battles between titans took place. Mr. Aldrich, leader of the Rockefeller forces, protested that Hayes was out of order. Colonel Stewart, however, who was presiding, ruled that Hayes could "get it off his chest."

Rockefeller had the support of the company's Chicago bankers and at least one of the insurance companies holding blocks of stock. Stewart was the candidate of almost all the employee shareholders, whose combined stock ownership, however, amounted to only about 4 per cent. When the votes for directors were counted, the Rockefeller forces had 5.5 million out of a total of around 9.3 million shares. Stewart took his defeat stoutly. His farewell speech plugged what he said had been a project dear to his heart: paid annual vacations for all employees.

By coincidence, another battle for control reached its climax on the same day. That involved the Childs Company, owner of some hundred restaurants. The year 1928 was one in which the company was making a poor financial showing. A group of stockholders charged the chief trouble was that the Childs' menus contained few meat dishes and vigorously promoted vegetables. They hinted that William Childs, the president, was trying to turn the public into vegetarians. Childs abruptly adjourned the 1928 meeting and never reconvened it. In November, Childs sold a large part of his stock to Du Pont interests, announcing that he was moving up to the chairmanship, while his vice-president, S. Willard Smith, would be president. At the same time two new directors came on the board to serve until the next annual election. With these moves, he relinquished effective control of the chain.

But Childs did not like the way things went under the new president. In January 1929 he suddenly called the directors together and mustered enough support to oust Smith and the new directors, replacing them with various members of his family. He announced he was going to fight to regain control. In circulars to stockholders, many of whom were employees, he described the forty years of effort his family had devoted to the company. He placed posters in Childs restaurants, bought newspaper ads entitled, "The Truth about The Childs Co."

The opposition, now headed by the ousted officials, countered by saying that after the sale of stock to the Du Pont interests, Childs had agreed to resign. Any profits shown on the records, they said, came from the sale of various real estate properties, because the restaurants were losing money. Childs rejoined that what really reduced the net income was $250,000 in legal fees paid to the company's former legal counsel, one of the ousted directors.

About 200 stockholders attended the meeting in New York. Soon after it was opened, Childs, suspecting that he did not have enough votes to ensure victory, refused to produce his proxies and claimed no quorum was present. He suggested adjourning to the next day. Since it required unanimous consent to proceed, and unanimous consent to adjourn, some shouting ensued. Finally the votes were counted. Childs had lost by a relatively small margin. The Du Pont block and several brokerage houses holding stock voted against him. But like Colonel Stewart, he claimed to have a majority of the number of stockholders, though not of the number of shares voted. Childs's valedictory was rather poignant. "The company has been a child of my efforts," he said, probably unaware of the pun. "It is the strangest thing that anybody else should want it. . . . It is not easy to manage because it extends from the Atlantic to the Pacific and it has to have constant attention."

Keeping the Stockholder on the Outside

Few stockholders, in those days, were prepared to carry on such expensive challenges for corporate control. Rockefeller's campaign cost around $300,000; Childs's opposition did not have to spend as much only because they already had purchased virtual control. Almost without exception, stockholders acted like rubber stamps, acquiescing year after year in whatever the management proposed. The *Times* found something novel in the Standard Oil (Indiana) and the Childs fights, commenting, "The rank and file of stockholders of large corporations usually take little interest in the elections of directors, who are ordinarily chosen by a small group."

Sometimes the stockholder was pushed completely out of any possible influence in his company through the use of non-voting stock. Non-voting preferred had come into fashion in the nineteenth century in the course of rescue operations for companies in distress. When their debts were consolidated, the total was divided up into prior liens, which were represented by new bonds, and junior liens, whose claim on the company had to be assigned a priority slot between the bonds and the common stock. Not having originated as common stock, these securities, though "preferred" as to dividends, were not given a vote. Later, original capitalizations came to contain a class of preferred in order to attract investors who wanted stable income. In return for security the preferred stockholders sacrificed the vote.

When corporations became huge, it was no longer possible to maintain a majority ownership by purchasing a large amount of each issue of common as it appeared. So the new issues were divided into Class A and Class B common. Class A, though it had no vote, had first rights as to dividends, while the Class B, with the vote, was a numerically smaller issue placed into the hands of those in control. Later, these dual issues, whose differences attracted somewhat more attention than some managements would wish, were supplanted by complete issues of non-voting stock. The textbook example was a big issue of Dodge Bros. stock put out by Dillon, Read & Company in 1925. After the issue was sold, only one-fifth of the total common stock—the fifth controlled by Dillon, Read— could vote in elections of directors.

One suggested use for non-voting stock was to sell only this class to women. Obviously, the thinking went, they knew nothing about business, so why should they be given a vote? As might be expected, this reasoning got nowhere. A similar proposal was made in connection with stock to be issued to an employee, where it was felt that he would be hopelessly confused by being put in the triple role of owner, manager, and employee.

There was something about the idea of non-voting stock that offended the American sense of fair play, though it was admittedly legal. Reformers seized on non-voting stock as an example of the autocracy of big business. It was so overt an attempt to keep stockholders from exercising their rights that it suggested some legislative restraints were needed to keep the managers in line. That was the last thought that business wanted to raise. Even in financial circles the wisdom of non-voting stock was questioned. The New York Stock Exchange on several occasions refused to list such issues. Although tobacco companies and a few utilities put out non-voting stock, it never became very important or widespread.

A little less obvious was the idea of cutting down common stockholder power through giving a special class of stock enough votes to offset the common. Henry L. Doherty & Company, in 1929, obtained a million shares of Cities Service Company $1 preferred that had equal vote with $50 par common.

The first prerequisite for effective stockholder participation in the affairs of a corporation is, of course, information. From 1900 on there was a growing demand for facts. It was not always made directly by stockholders, but was frequently and loudly made in their behalf by a group of reformers that ranged from muckraking journalists to crusading college professors. Even conservative financial newspapers that found their reporting hindered by a scarcity of facts sounded a critical note. *The Wall Street Journal,* speaking of annual reports containing meager details, once said, "Whether by accident or design, such reports are drawn so as to withhold from the stockholder what he most desires to know. . . . He refrains from calling the report a mess of tripe only for fear of insulting an industrious and self-respecting animal."

The secrecy with which many big companies clothed their activities was one of the reasons bills to require federal incorporation were introduced into Congress again and again and appeared regularly as planks in party platforms. President Taft once recommended federal incorporation in a special message to Congress.

A number of scandals brought to public attention early in the century the need for accurate statements and reports. In an annual report of American Steel & Wire Company, a newly formed trust, John W. Gates, the president, boasted of the company's solid financial condition: "The common stock in the opinion of the directors occupies a position like that of the preferred stock of most other corporations," he wrote. Two months later he abruptly ordered twelve plants closed down. He told a reporter, "The steel and wire business is in bad shape. It has been getting worse steadily. . . ." The stock price broke fifteen points in one day. Many years later, it came out that Gates had made $1 million by selling his shares at the high prices partially inspired by his own optimistic annual report, and buying them back after the decline.

The United States Ship-Building Company, another trust, issued two prospectuses about a year and a half apart, one more optimistic than the other, though both were based on the same material. A receiver later charged that the debts of various companies that were to be merged were not correctly disclosed, and profits from work in hand exaggerated. The company, once launched, had circulated such reassuring statements as "The outlook for our company is absolutely satisfactory," and "We show enough [earnings] in half a year to pay our fixed charges for a whole year," even when insiders were preparing a reorganization plan because they could not meet the next interest payment due.

Two General Asphalt Company directors had made glowing statements about its condition two months before it went into receivership. There was talk of criminal proceedings against the directors, but they were never brought. The stock of Amalgamated Copper Company, the "copper trust," was actively traded in the Unlisted Department of the Stock Exchange. Amalgamated disclosed neither the reserves of its constituent companies nor their past operating records. It turned out the officers spent much of their time manipulating the stock, and they and other insiders were buying up copper companies and selling them to the trust at inflated prices. When the insiders tried to unload some companies at ten times their value, details leaked out and the deals were enjoined.

It was no wonder that public indignation flamed and prosecution of the trusts was called for, or that new antitrust legislation was passed. State and federal commissions made strong recommendations as to how the industrial giants could be kept within bounds.

The Beginnings of Reform

A number of businessmen, while recognizing that certain practices needed changing, opposed government regulation and believed the answers lay in publicity. If corporations had to function in full view of the public, they felt, most of the evils would disappear.

Henry Clews, broker on Wall Street for fifty years, called for reform through publicity in 1906. He thought corporations should issue at least semiannual statements, with complete financial details, verified by independent auditors. Then "large corporations would cease to be blind pools," he said.

Elijah W. Sells, the senior partner of Haskins and Sells, well known auditors, spoke to the Associated Advertising Clubs of America in 1911 about the need to advertise financial affairs of corporations. "However meritorious may be the advertising of the character we are accustomed to, advertising the financial affairs of the corporation is of far greater importance," he said. "Full publicity for the affairs of corporations would be beneficial not only to the public but to the corporations themselves. . . . The cost to the corporation of this publicity would be more than offset by the reduction in the expense of lobbying, defense against unjust legislation and blackmailing legislatures." Annual reports should be printed in paid ads, Sells thought, and not only in the financial press but in popular newspapers and magazines. Perhaps with tongue in cheek, he suggested that some of the advertising expense might be charged off as an investment, while lobbying could only be charged to current expenses.

Louis D. Brandeis, who later became a Supreme Court justice, saw publicity as a remedy for many of the evils he criticized in his influential little book, *Other People's Money,* written in 1914. "Publicity is justly commended as a remedy for social and industrial diseases," he said. "Sunlight is said to be the best of disinfectants, electric light the most efficient policeman." Brandeis particularly wanted the disclosure of underwriting commissions on new issues, for he thought the 7 per cent to 10 per cent rates, then not unusual, were excessive. "Let every circular, letter, prospectus or advertisement of a bond or stock show clearly what the banker received for his middleman services, and what the stock and bonds net the issuing corporation. That is knowledge to which both the existing security holder and the prospective purchaser are entitled." Not that the rate should be fixed by law—there should simply be disclosure, to the public as well as to the state or Exchange, and public opinion, he thought, would do the rest.

Many of the businessmen who opposed publicity were not trying to cheat the public. They believed it would put them at a competitive disadvantage, and those were highly competitive days. A Standard Oil spokesman at the time probably voiced a typical opinion when he said, "Private corporations should not be required to make public items of receipts and expenditures, profits and losses. A statement of assets and liabilities is all that can benefit the public. Items of receipts and expenditures, profits and losses can only benefit competitors." The fear of giving away valuable information that might injure the company was perhaps responsible for some abbreviated reports. But there were a good many instances where reports were meant to conceal information from stockholders, or were intended to assist insiders in racking up profits. It was particularly serious when the stockholder could not be sure dividends were being paid out of earnings, for if they were not it meant the stockholder's investment was being paid back to him little by little while he held onto a virtually worthless piece of paper. Some companies insisted they had to pay dividends to keep their credit rating high. All sorts of accounting devices could be employed to get the desired result. One company transferred inventory to its subsidiaries at a price yielding a paper profit, reported the profit, and paid dividends on it.

Under the pressure of public opinion, a change gradually began to come about. The change owed something to the "muckrakers" and reformers who dealt harshly with big business. The muckrakers were not interested in the rights of stockholders per se, though they protested against speculative maneuvers that wiped out people who could ill afford the loss. Their attack on the trusts was in terms of the dangers of monopoly to consumer prices, to labor, to the social structure. The pervasive influence of business in politics was deplored. Yet, indirectly, corporation democracy gained strength from the outcry. Business leaders learned that a public display of arrogance on their part, a flouting of law and public opinion, was no longer acceptable, nor was it tolerated. It fed the fire of a public anger that might, they thought, even lead to anarchy. Certainly it would lead to government reprisals. By the twenties the day of the Jim Fisks and Jay Goulds was past. Instead, business leaders took pains to insist that they had the interests of the little man at heart, be he consumer or stockholder.

"Investment by the public in the securities of a great corporation is an act of faith as well as an act of judgment," Alfred P. Sloan of General Motors wrote. "That faith must be justified not only by the good faith of management but also by management making accessible to the public all the facts that are necessary for the formation of that judgment." He called attention to the news letters he sent stockholders from time to time, describing new plants and products. He answered all stockholder letters personally.

John J. Raskob unveiled, in *Ladies' Home Journal,* a plan for a new type of investment company that would finance the purchase of stocks for a man who could not otherwise afford them, who could then pay off the debt in small monthly installments. It was an idea not unlike today's installment buying of securities—the New York Stock Exchange's Monthly Investment Plan—only somewhat more generous. The plan evoked enthusiastic comment, although it never gained the widespread acceptance its sponsors sought.

It was natural, perhaps, that the public utilities should cultivate customer and stockholder favor because their regulation, and, particularly, their rates, depended upon state agencies whose membership and activities reflected public sentiment. The utilities put vast effort and substantial sums of money into building up an image pleasing to the public. They got together to set up a speakers' bureau that would supply men to discuss the utilities and their role in the economy. All this public relations activity helped make them popular in the twenties, especially with stockholders.

Over the years the American Telephone & Telegraph Company developed what was perhaps the outstanding stockholder relations program in the country. The company was one of the first to send out letters welcoming new stockholders, and letters of regret when stockholders left the fold. It sent out frequent reports and news letters. It surveyed its stockholders to establish their age, sex, and economic characteristics. When the company found that about half the stockholders were women, it addressed communications to female interests, taking care to make its reports easy to understand. In dividend policy the company aimed at maintaining a stable dividend rate despite earnings fluctuations so that stockholders could count on the income—a big inducement to investment on the part of "widows and orphans" and ordinary wage earners.

While in the nineteenth century the circulars offering new securities usually contained most exaggerated promises of wealth, there were enough sadder but wiser people by the turn of the century to hold promoters to some kind of accountability. At first underwriters tried to evade responsibility by using quotations from the corporation president, usually drafted for him. The courts refused to countenance any such dodging. They maintained that the underwriter could be reasonably assumed to have gone into the company's business with some care, at least enough to catch any misleading statements its officers made. The omission of facts, as well as false statements, began to be interpreted as a lack of full disclosure, and grounds for damage suits. The misled stock purchaser, however, still had to prove that the banker or the company officer knew a particular statement to be false or its omission misleading.

The prospectuses of the twenties were a great advance over those

of fifty years before, but there was still plenty of room for improve-
ment. A committee of the Investment Bankers Association reported
in 1926 that "a considerable number of circulars offering the
securities of holding companies do not come up to the proper
standards." And Andrew Mellon, Secretary of the Treasury in
1928, estimated that stock and bond swindlers were milking the
public of $1 billion a year.

Tightening up requirements for companies listed on the New
York Stock Exchange was a favorite reform recommended in the
early part of the century. John Moody was always harping on it.
"The Stock Exchange does not even furnish trustworthy news. Nowhere is it so difficult to get reliable intelligence concerning any
stock dealt in there, as in Wall Street." The New York Commission in 1909 and the Pujo Committee in 1913 made strong
cases for the necessity of more detailed information at the time
stock was listed. In line with the change in public opinion the
Stock Exchange began to insist on more complete disclosure. Its
hand was strengthened by the fact that in the bull market of the
twenties companies needing money found it easy to get if they were
among the actively traded stocks.

After 1916 the Exchange required quarterly statements of earnings, assets, and liabilities from companies applying for listing, and
after 1926 a concerted effort was made to get the older companies
to file such reports. At that time only about 250 out of 950 listed
companies were furnishing them. The Exchange always maintained
an attitude of reserve toward the investment trusts which sprang up
so rapidly near the end of the speculative boom. These were first
admitted to trading in 1929, and then only if they agreed to
disclose both book value and market value of their portfolio item
by item. Not many trusts were willing to do so at the time, so they
were traded on the smaller, less regulated exchanges.

The Stock Exchange did not pretend to be the defender of the
stockholder. Its aim was to maintain a fair market for securities,
where investors were fairly treated in buying and selling. In the
hectic days after the 1929 market crash, few stockholders re-
membered that the New York Stock Exchange had ever taken any
measures in their behalf. Since it was extremely reticent about

publicizing its activities, this reaction was to be expected. But a good many stockholders saw the Exchange as the instrument of their destruction. Its ways were going to have to be changed—and they were.

6

TAMING THE WOLVES OF WALL STREET:

THE REGULATIONS THAT PROTECT

THE STOCKHOLDER

The stock market plunge of 1929–32 was not the most important event to occur in those years, but it was the one that attracted the most attention. In the popular mind the great crash had caused the national disaster that the Depression turned out to be.

There is some doubt about exactly how many individual stockholders took part in the frenzied market activity that preceded the break. Dozens of studies of security ownership have failed to come up with any reliable figures for the period prior to 1930. A United States Senate committee that queried member firms of all the exchanges found they had a total of just over 1.5 million customers on their books in 1929. Not all of those had margin accounts, so they could not be considered real speculators. John Kenneth Galbraith, in *The Great Crash,* comes to the conclusion that at the peak of speculative activity in 1929 the number of active traders was less—"and probably much less"—than a million. It just *seemed* enormous. In addition, there were thousands of small investors with five or ten shares of stock who were not interested in trading, and still other thousands of middle-class citizens who had shares they were accumulating like savings. Berle and Means, after studying tax and available stockholder records, decided there were anywhere from 4 to 7 million stockholders in 1929.

Everyone was incredulous and stunned by the sudden death of the great bull market. By 1932, when the Dow-Jones industrial average had fallen from 381 to 41, utilities from 144 to 17, and railroads from 189 to 13, it was pretty clear to those who still had any stocks that they could not expect to recover much of the lost value in the near future. Many investors had been wiped out in the first slide in the fall of 1929; others had to liquidate after the banks closed; or they lost their jobs. These people wanted to know what had happened. Congress, seeking legislative cures to prevent a repetition of the disaster, mounted a series of investigations which turned up front-page revelations that hit the public with stunning impact.

One of the particularly galling facts to emerge was that investors had purchased stock on the basis of false, incomplete, or misleading information. A notorious example involved the stock and debentures of Kreuger & Toll, a foreign company that had been listed on the Stock Exchange without even the minimum requirements asked of domestic enterprises. Kreuger & Toll, along with International Match Corporation, was controlled by the Swedish magnate Ivar Kreuger, who enjoyed at the time a formidable international reputation. The two companies had issued about $250 million worth of bonds through top U.S. underwriters. Even after the prices tumbled along with everything else in 1929, the underwriters expressed faith in those bonds. When Kreuger committed suicide early in 1932, his companies turned out to be chock full of fraud, false accounting, and inflated values. The securities he had deposited to back the bonds issued here were worth a fraction of what they were supposed to represent. They were not even the securities he had deposited originally. Through a clause in the contract, not known to the public, he had been allowed to substitute different securities of even less value.

As other revelations of inflated stocks and dubious assets followed, public indignation grew more vocal. The first step in protecting the stockholder, it seemed, was to make sure he received all the information necessary to evaluate intelligently a security when first issued.

The states had been trying since about 1900 to curb deceit in the issuance and sale of securities. State laws on the subject came to be known as "blue-sky" laws because they were intended to restrain the issuing of stocks "worth no more than a piece of blue sky," as the saying went in Kansas. Connecticut, in 1903, at the time of some wild speculation in mineral stocks, had provided that out-of-state mining and oil companies had to file statements of financial condition, property, work done, and other details before selling shares— but the law was more bark than bite. Nevada, in 1909, in an attempt to clamp down on mining frauds, decided that mining companies would have to file complete information (including officers' salaries) every six months with state officials and in each county where their operations took place. Mining men protested strongly that Nevada's booming business would be hurt by such disclosure. They succeeded in getting the law watered down in 1911, and repealed altogether in 1915, and Nevada has never had a blue-sky law since. Another pioneering effort was that of Rhode Island, which as an amendment to its general incorporation law in 1910 decreed that no out-of-state corporation could offer securities until it filed a report of financial condition and properties with the secretary of state.

Kansas must be given credit for passage of the first blue-sky law with teeth, following the 1910 elections that catapulted the Populist Party into power. The state's new bank commissioner was a Mr. J. N. Dolley, a retired bank director who was well aware of the frauds that had been perpetrated in the issuance of securities in Kansas. He enthusiastically embarked on a publicity campaign to warn the gullible investing public and his office encouraged people to make complaints. In 1911, the legislature passed a law which Mr. Dolley had been pressing for that strengthened his hand against fraudulent stock promoters.

The law required a company to get a permit from the state before issuing stock, and the commissioner was given broad powers to squelch a stock issue if he decided that the firm's charter or bylaws were unfair to any class of security, if its finances or assets were not as set forth, or even if he felt that the stock did not promise a fair return. Semiannual reports were required thereafter, with the commissioner empowered to inspect the books whenever he wanted to. The firm could be put into receivership for fraud, for impairment of assets, or failure to register its securities. Brokers, underwriters, and dealers had to get licenses, and the maximum rate of commission could be fixed by the state. Moreover, and probably most important of all, criminal penalties were provided for violations.

Mr. Dolley circulated copies of the law to his counterparts in other states along with periodic glowing reports of progress. In one report, Dolley wrote: "This law, as you know, was something entirely new in the business world, but I am pleased to inform you that we have worked the same out in a very nice shape and accomplished some wonderful results."

Of 1500 companies applying for permission to issue securities in the first eighteen months after the law took effect, only 100 were cleared by Dolley's department. Possibly he was too zealous; later investigators cast doubt on some of his claims. However, within two years, twenty-three states had followed Kansas' lead. All but six laws were identical or very similar to that of Kansas. Though in office only two years, Dolley managed to leave a lasting monument in the corporate world.

The blue-sky laws generally contain one or all of the following:

1. Antifraud provisions. The designated state official, such as bank examiner, secretary of state, or attorney general, can investigate suspected frauds and get an injunction against the sale of suspect securities. If fraud is found and the sale has taken place, it can be rescinded.

2. Securities to be sold to the public have to be registered and relevant information on the issuing company disclosed. Usually some affirmative action from the state official has to be given before the sale can commence. Old established companies with a record of operation often can just make notification instead of "qualifying," as new companies must. New companies often have to submit information on holdings of more than 10 per cent of the stock. In the case of mortgage bonds, appraisals of the property mortgaged are often required.

3. Underwriters, brokers, and other persons engaged in the business of marketing securities have to register with the state and sometimes post bond.

New York State's equivalent of a blue-sky law was the Martin Act, passed in 1921. But the New York Penal Law, apart from that act, prohibits untrue, deceptive, or misleading assertions in the offering of securities for sale, and broadly defines fraud, so as to include statements which were made without actual intent to defraud. As early as 1901, a man was prosecuted for inserting ads containing false information in the newspapers which predicted a fall in the price of a security.

Under the blue-sky laws, and the various state laws and court decisions preceding them, there had been a gradual development and strengthening of stockholders' rights. In New York, as far back as 1826, a court held that in an election contest management could not vote the authorized but unissued stock it held in the company treasury. Later, the courts defined more carefully the duties of the proxy committee. It was to accept proxies as valid unless there was some good reason to believe that they were not. In addition, the proxy committee was not to set itself up as a court, but to provide the machinery for corporate elections and let the challengers go to court.

Concealment or nondisclosure of an important fact in a prospectus had been established as equivalent to false representation if the stock buyer had reasonable grounds for relying on the statement. The case, tried in New York in 1909, involved a man living abroad who had been given a prospectus saying that a cold storage company in Manhattan had purchased land and was about to put up a building. The fact was that the promoter only had an option on the land, and it wasn't until he got the stockholders' money that he was able to purchase it. The court held that the stockholder could get his money back even though by the time the case came to court some of the statements in the prospectus were true.

When the blue-sky laws came along, it became necessary to define the scope of their application in each state. In Florida, for instance, it was determined that the state's law on disclosure applied to corporations selling their own securities without benefit of underwriters. In Michigan, an exchange of stock by the corporation was ruled to be a sale and hence within the scope of the law. In 1916, courts in Iowa and Nebraska ruled that the duty of disclosure of any pertinent inside information affecting stock value applied when officers or directors were buying or selling stock, even to one stockholder.

The constitutionality of the blue-sky laws was naturally challenged soon after they were passed. Three cases came to the Supreme Court of the United States in 1917 and are known as the Blue Sky Cases. Upholding the blue-sky laws of Michigan, Ohio, and South Dakota, the Supreme Court established the principle that while the laws do limit freedom of contract, such limitation is a valid exercise of the police power of the state. The court pointed out that the states are conceded to have the power to prevent fraud in the sale of food, so why not in securities.

Since then, parts of the laws have occasionally been invalidated, and since the early ones were rather hastily drafted, they have been extensively revised. But there has been no basic challenge to the idea that the states can exercise great regulatory powers over the issuing of securities, in the interests of protecting their citizens from fraud. The blue-sky laws of the United States (and the provincial laws of Canada, which are similar and were often modeled on those of the United States) are unique.

As they existed in 1933, the state laws differed a great deal in what information should be disclosed. They also had different machinery provided for their enforcement; some states had never provided enough money or personnel to do an adequate job. They differed also in the extent of their exemptions. Federal, state, county, and city issues were usually exempt; as were banks and trust companies, building and loan associations, insurance companies, issues for stock dividends, and sometimes real property mortgage bonds. Sales to fewer than fifteen persons were exempt in some states, while others put the maximum at fifty persons. Nearly half the states exempted companies doing business wholly within their borders which meant that many small mining or oil companies—where fraud often occurred—were exempt.

The most serious drawback to the blue-sky laws was that they applied only within each state's boundaries, and by 1930 most corporations of any size were doing business interstate. The laws of a strict state could be circumvented by establishing an office in another state and contacting sales prospects across the border by mail or telephone. Though the state where the sale took place might brand the company's stock issue as fraudulent, it could not get at the offender because in those days it was nearly impossible to extradite him. He was perfectly secure as long as he never entered the state where he was breaking the law. Securities salesmen knew this very well.

In a report for the year 1927, Pennsylvania complained bitterly that in spite of its own vigorous administration of its law, tipster sheets were flooding in from New York and New Jersey and unsound securities were being sold by mail and phone in great quantities. The state said it was "nearly helpless to protect the citizens of Pennsylvania who are foolish enough to deal over the telephone, by mail and telegraph with concerns located outside the state."

The United States Congress finally held a series of hearings which revealed that such evasion of state blue-sky laws was widespread. Federal legislation was needed, and it came in the form of the Securities Act of 1933, which was written to leave the state laws as the primary deterrents but to supplement them and plug loopholes by regulating the issuance of securities sold in interstate commerce—which included most of the actively traded ones. The act required a detailed registration statement to be drawn up and filed with a federal agency before any interstate offer of securities could take place. The statement had to contain copies of the charter and bylaws under which the company proposed to operate, details about capital structure, a balance sheet, a three-year record, where possible, of the company's profits and losses, and the rights attaching to each class of security. The names of the promoters and of all who owned or would own 10 per cent or more of the stock were to be included in the statement. This disclosure was specifically meant to reveal where control lay, heretofore usually extremely difficult to determine. The details of the underwriting agreement also had to be set forth. National banks and insurance policies were exempt, as were companies issuing less than $300,000 worth of stock if deemed appropriate by the commission. Moreover, if the securities were not being sold to the public, no registration was required. What exactly constituted a "public issue" was not defined and had to be developed case by case.

The Coming of the SEC

The stories of pools, pegged prices, faked publicity, and the intricate manipulation of stocks on the exchanges had also roused public ire. Pools were formed by a small group of insiders who paid newspaper columnists to print bullish news about a particular company's stock. As the stock started to move up, the pool would begin to buy, forcing the price still higher. Then the pool (which often included several of the company's directors) would raise the dividend and as the stock soared even higher the pool would quietly sell out at a handsome profit. Men went down in Wall Street legend if they directed a pool that was unusually successful in duping the investing public. One pool that achieved historic fame was organized in 1928 and manipulated the stock of the Radio Corporation of America so beautifully that the public was milked of $5 million in seven days flat. Another notorious pool was created in the stock of Kolster Radio Corporation. Kolster stock was run up twenty points, and the pool manager made over $1 million for himself plus $20 million more for the pool.

It was obvious that if the investing public was to be protected, a way had to be found to prohibit the manipulation of security prices by insiders or anyone else. The Securities Exchange Act of 1934, which also established the Securities and Exchange Commission, was designed to do this.

The average investor of the twenties had not the remotest idea of the tremendous amount of trading that insiders did in the stocks of their own companies. It was all legal and had been going on for centuries. Insiders with South Sea Company stock, for example, got out before the bubble burst in 1720. In the 1920s the majority of the states, New York included, took the view that an officer or director could trade in his own company's securities exactly as he might in the securities of any other company. All through the history of corporations officers with inside information had used it to make profits for themselves in the market. They were under no obligation to disclose the facts that only they were privy to as insiders. Their legal position was upheld on the ground that directors had a quasi-trustee relationship only to the corporation as an entity—not to individual stockholders. When a director, knowing something unfavorable was about to happen, unloaded his stock before the price declined, courts in a few Southern states had allowed damages. But the Supreme Court, in the few instances that came before it, held that except in unusual situations, where there was a material decline in the value of the stock, the director could not be held accountable for any harm suffered by other stockholders.

Certain few corporations themselves had imposed rules on insiders and directors. When Judge Elbert Henry Gary headed U. S. Steel, he insisted that dividend actions be announced to the press before the directors left the board room. In contrast to this, and more consistent with prevailing practice, Union Pacific concealed for two days the news that it had raised its dividend, while insiders bought up all the stock they could.

But advance knowledge of dividends was only the most obvious kind of insider information; the actions of a big company were so numerous and far reaching that it was very difficult for it to police insider trading even when it was contrary to policy.

Financial men themselves in the twenties were divided on the question of insider trading. Some thought profits from such trading were simply extra compensation for the job of being an officer or director, provided the company itself was not harmed. Others thought insider trading normally was all right, but drew the line somewhere in terms of the amount of profit. Investors, in the meantime, had only the vaguest notion that it must be going on, and the implications largely were unsuspected.

One of the astonishing discoveries of the congressional investigations that preceded the Securities Exchange Act concerned the speculations of Albert Wiggin, head of the Chase National Bank. In the big market slide in the fall of 1929, Wiggin had been continuously selling his bank's stock short. That is to say, he borrowed Chase stock and sold it at its present price level, expecting to return the borrowed stock later on when he'd be able to buy it at a lower price. He was, therefore, betting on a decline.

Wiggin had a number of dummy corporations, including one in Canada, where he took his profits to avoid U.S. taxes. Such companies were not unusual. What was unusual was that Wiggin was selling short at the very time the Chase directors had authorized a pool to try to stem the decline of the stock; he had sold some shares short to this pool and borrowed money from his own bank to carry the sales. Stockholders who had watched the price of their shares plunge from $500 to $200 a share, while Wiggin had garnered a $4 million profit, were not favorably impressed by his fast footwork.

Such practices led directly to a clause in the Securities Exchange Act providing that, for listed companies, any profit made by an insider through a sale within six months of the time he acquired his stock was to go to the corporation. The profit in question could be recovered by suit, either by the corporation or by a stockholder on behalf of the corporation. The law also required that new officers and directors file with the SEC their holdings of company stock within ten days of election. Thereafter, holdings were to be listed at the end of each month, by officers, directors, and anyone else who owned 10 per cent or more of the capital stock. Short selling by insiders was prohibited. Congress did not go so far as to outlaw short sales, but did give the SEC comprehensive powers over short selling in listed securities.

One of the most noteworthy effects of the new measures was to give the fledgling Securities and Exchange Commission the power to oversee proxy solicitation in listed companies. Rather than set definite rules, the law left it to the SEC to work out appropriate procedures. Over the years the commission, with its jurisdiction enlarged by later laws, developed rules through which it could regulate closely proxy solicitation in most large corporations.

The rules provide that proxy solicitations for annual meetings where directors are to be elected must be accompanied or preceded by a financial report. The form of the proxy itself is carefully set forth, even to the size of type that may be used. Proxy statements explaining what is to be presented at the meeting have to be filed with the SEC at least ten days before they are mailed out.

By meeting certain requirements, any security holder entitled to vote can insist that his own proposals for stockholder action be included in the official proxy solicitation or, he can ask management for a list of stockholders and solicit proxies on his own. If the management intends to oppose the stockholder's proposal, it has to include in the proxy material a hundred-word statement by the stockholder in support of what he wants done. To protect management from being pestered by a host of crackpot proposals, the SEC reserves the right to determine whether the proposals are of the proper type to come before the stockholders, and sets a limit on how frequently they may appear. On management's part, it has to disclose any officer's or director's special interest in any proposals it advances. In the case of the directors put up for election, stock ownership must be listed.

The framers of the Securities Acts of 1933 and 1934 had as guideposts the English Companies Act, as well as laws with similar intent in other countries. English securities law can be traced all the way back to 1697, when an attempt was made to curb the "ill practice" of London brokers who manipulated share prices. After the South Sea Bubble, a law called the Bubble Act sought to restrain the sale of shares in companies having irregular charters. It was whittled down and finally repealed. The English Companies Act itself dates to 1844 and was the first to contain a requirement about filing a prospectus before issuing securities to the public. This was strengthened in 1890 by making the directors liable for certain mis-statements of fact. The law was amended several times in succeeding years and was given a good going over in 1928. The result proved extremely useful to the men writing the U. S. Securities Acts. Belgium and the Netherlands also had revised their laws in 1928, and Germany had strengthened hers in 1931. So between those national laws and the U.S. and Canadian state and provincial laws, there was no lack of models.

The U.S. laws tend to go further than any others. The English Companies Act, for example, applies only to corporations, whereas the U. S. Securities Acts applies to partnerships and even special associations if they issue securities.

Under the Securities Acts a buyer was empowered to sue for damages if the registration statement contained untruths or omitted important facts, without having to show that he actually was misled by what was or wasn't said. This is a much broader range of liability than that contained in English law, where the issuing corporation is never liable to the original subscribers as they are not the public. The question of liability comes up only at the second step, when securities are put before the public. Then either issuer or underwriter may be liable for false information. The penalties, moreover, are more severe in the United States. In England fines alone are involved even in rare cases of criminal liability, whereas jail sentences may also be imposed in the United States. There is no equivalent in any other nation of America's Securities and Exchange Commission.

Strangely enough, the Securities Acts of 1933 and 1934 were belittled by most ardent New Dealers as not going far enough, despite the opposition they aroused in financial circles. William O. Douglas, before he was made chairman of the SEC (and later a justice of the Supreme Court) called the Securities Acts a "nineteenth century piece of legislation." Yet while some of the more spectacular examples of New Deal legislation are no longer with us in their original form, the Securities Acts endure. Joseph P. Kennedy, the first chairman of SEC (and a Wall Street wheeler dealer from way back), was considered a most unfitting appointment by some New Dealers. In moving cautiously, however, he partially succeeded in getting Wall Street to accept the new rules of the game especially as economic conditions improved and the market revived. Over the years the commission has slowly developed a set of rules covering prospectuses and the use of proxy machinery that are now cornerstones of stockholder democracy.

Slaying a Corporate Monstrosity

Congress next turned its attention to public utilities that over the years had been quietly creating corporate monstrosities known as holding companies.

The utility holding company device permitted a few men at the apex of the pyramid to control a host of operating utility companies that produced and sold gas and electricity. Some of the companies between the operating utilities and the top control were only one-room offices where, presumably, great minds were at work. The securities issued by these intermediate firms were greatly in excess of the asset value of the operating companies they controlled. The men at the top paid themselves interest and dividends on the stock of their holding companies with funds siphoned off from the operating companies as payments for advisory services, or dividends on the stock held by the controlling group. Some holding company promoters were probably sincere in believing that the economies they claimed resulted from their centralized management would justify the higher valuation of the assets of the operating utilities. But as it worked out, so much money was taken out of the operating companies to pay interest and dividends on the stocks of the holding companies that the utilities themselves were left in unsound condition. When the operating companies went under, as many did during the Depression, the pyramid collapsed like the flimsy house of cards it actually was.

Between 1929 and 1936, fifty-three utility holding companies with securities valued at $1.75 billion went into receivership or bankruptcy, while another twenty-three companies, with $535 million of securities, defaulted on interest payments while accumulating big arrearages on their preferred stock. The Public Utility Holding Company Act of 1935, which was directed at this situation, differed considerably from the previous reforms which had concentrated on forcing disclosure of information. It subjected gas and electric holding companies to SEC supervision as to capital structure and the acquisition or sale of subsidiaries, matters previously left to company management. Such broad authority gave the commission an important key to the cost of service to consumers, even though changes in rates themselves were put under the jurisdiction of the Federal Power Commission. In fact, the SEC's mandate was to regulate capital structure, not only in the interests of investors, but also in the interests of consumers.

The Holding Company Act also gave the SEC the authority to make sure utility holding companies were organized on the basis of geographical integration, forcing the divestment and even dissolution of outlying companies. The holding companies protested that this gave the SEC the power to impose a "death sentence" on them, and they fought hotly in the courts until the Supreme Court confirmed the SEC's control over them in the Electric Bond and Share case in 1939. This was also the year of the Trust Indenture Act, of 1939, which defined the responsibilities of corporate bond trustees in order that the rights of holders of securities issued under such indentures may be protected and enforced.

Investment trusts had also come in for their share of criticism in the Depression. These companies, as their name indicates, were primarily engaged in the business of investing in the securities of operating companies such as A.T.&T., J. I. Case Company, and G.E., much like today's mutual funds. The value of the securities issued by investment companies was frequently greater than the total worth of the securities they held. The difference apparently represented the promoters' capitalized brain power, and the faith that the market would go up indefinitely. Some investment trusts held their own securities, so that the financial genius of the portfolio managers was capitalized twice. All this, of course, was visible only after the Crash.

The investment trusts were born sometime around 1922, and they caught on so rapidly that 600 to 700 of them came into existence by 1929. Everybody got into the act from J. P. Morgan & Company to small-time shooters who cranked up a trust or two and hoped for the best. Investment trusts even sponsored other investment trusts, and toward the end of the bull market a trust of some kind was started nearly every day.

After the Crash, the securities in the investment trusts' portfolios slid to virtually nothing and the price of the trusts' own securities slid down with them. One investment trust stock that had been above $30 dove to 50 cents. Again the United States Congress stepped in to protect the investing public that was unable, or unwilling, to protect itself. The protection was called the Investment Company Act of 1940.

The 1940 act, as summarized by the Securities and Exchange Commission, which has the responsibility for administering it, requires, among other things, "disclosure of the finances and investment policies of these companies in order to afford investors full and complete information with respect to their activities; prohibits such companies from changing the nature of their business or their investment policies without the approval of stockholders; bars persons guilty of security frauds from serving as officers and directors of such companies; regulates the means of custody of the assets of investment companies and requires the bonding of officers and directors having access to such assets; prevents underwriters, investment bankers, and brokers from constituting more than a minority of the directors of such companies; requires management contracts in the first instance to be submitted to security holders for their approval . . ." etc.

In the 1951 edition of their book *Security Analysis,* Graham and Dodd said "In the ten years since passage of the 1940 Act, the investment funds have been almost totally free from scandals or objectionable practices. This is an excellent record, especially when it is considered that almost anyone is free to start an investment fund if he can raise $250,000 for the purpose, and that there are wide opportunities for malfeasance by the wrong kind of managers." This fine record continues up to the present time.

The Securities and Exchange Commission enjoyed esteem both inside and outside of government in its first decade of operation. The securities industry itself had been left a good measure of self-regulation under the laws, and, trying to redeem its public image, avoided any major conflict with the commission. On its part, the SEC found that informal discussions, persuasion, and an occasional appeal to public opinion was all it took to police the industry. When World War II came along, the SEC was forced into a back seat as production problems preoccupied the nation. The huge amount of capital necessary for war production was poured into industry by the government instead of being raised from the investing public, and there were those who thought Wall Street's best years were behind it.

The big post-World War II bull market took these pessimists by surprise. Again fabulous stories of making money in the market circulated, and small investors began to flock in. Activity on the exchanges accelerated as more and more issues were listed, and before long some of the legal restrictions began to prove burdensome. For example, during the interval between the time a new stock issue went to the SEC for registration and the time the application was granted or automatically went into effect after twenty days, broker-dealers were forbidden to offer the securities for sale. There was no approved way of circulating information to the hundreds of potential investors who were eager to find out something about the proposed issue so as to get in on the ground floor. An amendment to the Securities Acts was passed in 1954 to provide for issuance of a preliminary prospectus giving the basic information in summary form. It, too, had to be filed with SEC and bear a prominent statement in red ink across each page warning that the issue had not yet received final clearance. "Red herrings," as these prospectuses are called, soon came to be an important part of the securities sales machinery.

By 1961, when the number of share owners in the United States had reached 17 million, the Congress felt that a thorough review of the relationship of the securities industry to its customers was in order. Speculative fever was again in evidence whenever a new issue came out that fired public imagination. Stock prices on these issues would rise to dizzy heights only to drop again. There were two rather severe setbacks to the market that raised fears of a repetition of 1929, although industry and government authorities kept repeating, "It can't happen again."

In sheer size, the securities business was far different from what it had been when the original securities laws were passed in the early 1930s. There were 6000 broker-dealer firms, and some 100,000 registered representatives on the rolls of the National Association of Securities Dealers. The business of selling securities had spread out from a few large cities to the entire country. And the over-the-counter market, left unregulated in 1933–34 because it was relatively unimportant, now affected millions of stockholders.

The Congress decided to direct the SEC to undertake a massive study of the effectiveness of the laws and the rules of the industry in protecting today's investors. The Special Study of the Securities Markets, published in 1963, came up with 175 specific recommendations. Many people in the industry protested that the study distorted the generally good record of the industry. It also inspired a rash of unwelcome lawsuits against dealers, companies, and the exchanges themselves. The need for further reform, however, got an unexpected boost in the public mind by a purely fortuitous circumstance. Shortly after the voluminous SEC report was issued, a scandal—whose size and impact reminded many investors of the bad old days of 1929—hit Wall Street like an atomic bomb. The "great salad-oil swindle," as it came to be known, involved bank loans based on 900 million pounds of non-existent vegetable oil in New Jersey, forged warehouse receipts, and a good deal of bad judgment. One respected old Wall Street firm went into bankruptcy while another was saved only through merger. Thousands of small investors would have been burned had not the New York Stock Exchange put up $12 million to help out—the second time in three years that it had had to take such action. While the scandal had little to do with the reforms the SEC was suggesting, it shook public faith in Wall Street and made it easier for further legislation to pass. The exchanges and broker-dealers also voluntarily tightened up their own procedures.

New legislation passed in 1964 brought the over-the-counter companies into the SEC orbit. The special study had found that of the more than 1600 OTC companies surveyed, 25 per cent did not issue any financial reports at all to stockholders. Those which did issue them often failed to disclose important information or sent reports not fairly comparable to those of previous years. The new law required companies with assets of over $1 million and 750 or more shareholders (the number was cut to 500 in 1966) to make the same full disclosure of assets, profits, executive salaries, and so on as listed corporations. Even publicly owned banks, which had been notoriously reluctant to reveal financial information, were asked to file similar reports, although with federal bank regulatory agencies rather than the SEC.

The SEC study also objected to the custom of publishing "retail" prices of over-the-counter stocks that included a markup of some 5 per cent over what the broker had to pay to get the stock. Early in 1965, the industry yielded to pressure and started quoting "wholesale," or dealer prices.

One of the more interesting and exclusive breed of stock market tradesmen are the "specialists" who buy and sell a few specific stocks for other brokers and for their own account. Specialists work on the floor of the exchange—on the New York Stock Exchange there are some 350 specialists constantly on duty near the posts where their stocks are traded—and among other things the specialist is supposed to make an orderly market in his stocks. This means he must always be willing to buy or sell his stocks at a figure reasonably near the last price at which they were traded. The original draft of the Securities Exchange Act prohibited specialists from trading for others as well as themselves. The clause was discarded before the Act was passed, however, for the drafters came to recognize that the specialist could serve a useful purpose in creating an orderly market for a stock. But the 1963 special study found several examples of what it believed were failings of the specialist system. These findings were reinforced by a study the SEC did of the activities of a few specialists on the day President Kennedy was assassinated. After negotiation with the exchanges, the rules governing specialists were tightened up, and the SEC, for the first time, adopted a rule of its own governing the activities of specialists, although it still left the Stock Exchange the right to lead the way in taking corrective action.

The practice of floor trading also aroused the SEC's ire on the ground of potential conflict of interest. Floor traders buy and sell stocks on the floor of the exchange for their own account. They are members of the exchange, hence pay no commissions and can make a nice living by taking small speculative profits on a few transactions every day. The commission's special study found that about four hundred members of the New York Stock Exchange traded for themselves from time to time without paying normal brokerage commissions—and also executed orders for the public. The special study recommended the abolition of floor trading because it felt that floor traders were able to act on information the public didn't have, and because it believed that floor trading had a destabilizing effect on the market. This time, however, the industry reacted strongly. The stock exchanges vigorously defended the floor traders as a stabilizing force in the market, and talks initiated by the SEC to formulate more stringent rules were broken off in a deadlock. Finally, the New York Stock Exchange agreed to a compromise that would allow floor trading to continue, but under severe restrictions. The amount of capital required to be a floor trader, for example, was raised to $250,000, which alone reduced the number of these individuals to about three dozen.

Not unnaturally, the SEC study recommended a general enlargement of SEC powers; one specific idea was that SEC be empowered to review all Exchange rules and disciplinary actions, including those affecting nonmembers. The SEC argument got an unexpected and probably unintended boost from another government agency. The Justice Department had begun to show interest in the question of whether or not the "Big Board" (nickname of the New York Stock Exchange and the nation's largest auction market for stock) was subject to anti-trust law. Broker-dealers who were not members of the Exchange were objecting to certain practices they thought reduced competition in the industry. In the Silver Case, of 1963, the Supreme Court ruled that the Exchange was not exempt from anti-trust laws. It implied, however, that the areas of Exchange activity that were subject to SEC review might be exempt. The decision put the SEC in the position of having both a carrot and a stick, and it seemed likely that government policing of the securities business was going to be more vigorous than ever before.

The Securities and Exchange Commission, under its new chairman, Manuel F. Cohen, shook up the financial community in the waning days of 1966 with a 346-page report aimed squarely at the huge mutual fund industry. The SEC's summary of its eight-year study of this industry concluded that "the Investment Company Act of 1940 has substantially eliminated the serious abuses at which it was aimed, but that the tremendous growth of the industry, and the accompanying changes, have created a need for additional protections for mutual fund shareholders in areas which were either unanticipated or of secondary importance in 1940."

The report's major theme was that many mutual funds cost investors too much. The SEC had harsh words for the sales commissions charged by most funds which average about 9 per cent, and which the report felt should be no more than 5 per cent. The report also attacked the funds for their separate fees of one-half of 1 per cent for managing investors' money, a figure that's considerably higher than what banks charge to do a similar job. In addition, the SEC recommended the outright prohibition of future sales of one popular type of fund known as "front-end load" plans. Some one million Americans have opted for these funds whose shares they buy in small installments over a period of years, but pay most of their sales commissions in the first year. This commission usually amounts to 50 per cent of the first year's payment, and buyers are almost certain to suffer losses if they get out of the plan before the end of the fifth year. Finally, the SEC charged that funds which invest primarily in other funds are "particularly expensive," "of doubtful utility," and should be curtailed.

All in all, it was an impressive list of victories for the American stockholder, and for public opinion. For the first time since corporations began, corporate democracy could be made real—but only if stockholders themselves cared enough to exercise their rights.

Do today's 20 million stockholders care about their rights?

All the evidence we have examined suggests that—with a few well-publicized exceptions—they couldn't care less.

Let's look at the record.

Book Two

7

BEWARE OF

BARBERS, BEAUTICIANS, AND WAITERS:

THE FINANCIAL PRESS

On April 28, 1961, *Time* magazine printed a story lauding the outlook for a little-known company called Technical Animations, Inc., of Port Washington, New York, which owned rights to a process for adding animated material to film presentations. The company had never earned a penny's profit, yet rumors of the impending article boosted the price of its stock from about $6 to $9.25 a share before the story appeared, and to just over $15 a share following publication. By year's end, Technical Animations' shares had collapsed to $1.75 apiece, and the Securities and Exchange Commission had begun searching for shenanigans behind the stock's wild gyrations on the over-the-counter market.

This example of the influence the press can have on the fortunes of investors was cited by the SEC in a special report on the security industry, when it severely criticized *Time*'s business news editor for trading in the stock of Technical Animations and other companies he planned to treat in the magazine's business section. As in the case of Technical Animations, the price of the stock of these companies often would rise sharply following publication of favorable news in *Time*.

The SEC's investigation revealed that *Time*'s business news editor had purchased 2500 shares of Technical Animations' stock at an average price of about $6.25 a share before assigning a *Time* writer and researcher to the story. Not long after the article appeared, the editor sold out at a profit of some $3875—or a gain of roughly 25 per cent on his investment. According to the SEC, the editor had acquired stock in 64 different companies between 1957 and 1961, and stories about 27 of these firms had showed up in the pages of *Time*. The editor, who was eventually dismissed from *Time* for what the magazine said were other reasons, usually purchased his stock just before *Time* published an article about the company and soon after sold out at a "considerable profit," according to the SEC.

In describing the case, the SEC was careful to point out that the "publicity apparently was not generated by the issuer or its public relations man." Nevertheless, the SEC said, "It is clear that the *Time* article was the principal cause for the rise in the price of the stock."

This official testimonial to the influence a single widely read publication can have on the investment decisions of stockholders should be kept in mind by every capitalist careless enough to rely innocently on any one source of information in deciding which stocks to buy, sell, or hold.

The late Bernard M. Baruch, one of the most astute capitalists this nation has ever produced, recognized information as one of the bedrock ingredients of successful investing. He was particularly concerned about the origin, depth, reliability, and availability of data he relied on when making investment decisions—a fact which comes through loud and clear when reading Mr. Baruch's " 'rules' or guidelines on how to invest or speculate wisely," published in his autobiography:

1. Don't speculate unless you can make it a full-time job.
2. Beware of barbers, beauticians, waiters—of anyone—bringing gifts of 'inside' information or 'tips.'
3. Before you buy a security, find out everything you can about the company, its management and competitors, its earnings and possibilities for growth.
4. Don't try to buy at the bottom and sell at the top. This can't be done—except by liars.

5. Learn how to take your losses quickly and cleanly. Don't expect to be right all the time. If you have made a mistake, cut your losses as quickly as possible.

6. Don't buy too many different securities. Better to have only a few investments which can be watched.

7. Make a periodic reappraisal of all your investments to see whether changing developments have altered their prospects.

8. Study your tax position to know when you can sell to greatest advantage.

9. Always keep a good part of your capital in a cash reserve. Never invest all your funds.

10. Don't try to be a jack of all investments. Stick to the field you know best.

The ebb and flow of information is of such primary importance to the prudent capitalist that we examine the subject in some detail in the next four chapters of this book devoted to the press, the investment community, stockholder reports, and annual meetings. In doing this, we have gone behind the scenes whenever possible to report not only how information is communicated, but, perhaps of more significance, how this type of information is generated in the first place.

Information is food and drink to serious share owners. Opinion may vary, of course, as to what facts should be made known to the company's owners. Management, for example, may find that the immediate release of a certain piece of information, while of great significance to stockholders, may damage the company or hinder it in achieving its objectives, and therefore not serve the owners' best interests. Such is often the case in merger negotiations in which the market price of shares of the companies involved, or some other equally vital aspect of the deal, bears on whether the merger can be consummated. After Frank Freimann, president of the Magnavox Company, one summer morning told a news service reporter his company might complete a "very sizable acquisition" within the next thirty days, the price of his company's stock that day jumped by $3.125 to $42.875, and was the third most actively traded on the New York Stock Exchange. Mr. Freimann, however, apparently regretted issuing the news, because he and his public relations staff spent most of the afternoon frantically trying to stamp out the fire of speculative activity. In a series of official statements, the company said, "no merger in the immediate future is likely," and "no definite conclusion has been reached, nor has the matter been considered by the board."

In the meantime, the price of shares in the "sizable acquisition" Wall Street assumed Mr. Freimann had been talking about—General Precision Equipment Corporation—began moving ahead on the rumor. GP's stock that day rose $4.25 to $34.25 on the New York Stock Exchange, and its chairman, James W. Murray, gave the impression that he too was dancing barefoot on hot coals. He said he had spoken with Mr. Freimann about mergers in the past, but General Precision now "had no merger agreement nor tentative agreement with anyone and isn't discussing a merger with anyone."

The day closed with the busy Magnavox public relations department issuing its third statement of the afternoon confirming that General Precision was one of the companies Mr. Freimann had in mind. Whatever the facts, it is clear that at some point a merger between the two companies was under consideration, and both Mr. Friemann and Mr. Murray felt it was not in their companies' best interests to have this known—although the gyrations in the market place indicated that investors considered the news of serious import.

The premature disclosure of substantive information about new products may also work against the best interests of a company's stockholders. A classic example is the case in which Reporter John Williams of *The Wall Street Journal,* on the basis of some sure-footed investigative reporting, wrote a front-page article describing new model autos months before the major manufacturers were ready to announce them, and before dealers had emptied their showrooms of the current year's models. The auto companies were furious, and General Motors promptly withdrew a king's ransom in advertising from the *Journal.* The dealers and the auto companies claimed the story and accompanying sketches resulted in the public's holding off buying current year's cars, preferring to wait a few months for the intriguing new models portrayed on page one of the nation's most widely read financial newspaper. The controversy raged for many weeks, with the newspaper holding its ground and General Motors finally reinstating its advertising.

In every industry, certain information, if made public, might lend aid and comfort to competitors, or stifle sales. This accounts for the reluctance of most companies to publish breakdowns of sales of individual products or product lines, or detailed figures on production costs or sales expense. No company need fear criticism if it refuses to discuss publicly facts which, although not themselves detrimental to the company or embarrassing to its management, would harm the company's interests if disclosed.

Management, however, traditionally is closemouthed about its business, a carry-over from the days when even publicly held companies were operated as personal fiefs. This results in a peculiar and imperious reluctance on the parts of some managements to disclose publicly vital investment information which today's aggressive newspaper reporter can ofttimes easily uncover. Webb & Knapp, Inc., once filed with the American Stock Exchange and the SEC the detailed results of a widely publicized sale of its properties which took place in the second quarter of the year. Although its report was filed with the Exchange in September, it wasn't until October 25—three days after the company's annual meeting—that it was made known to stockholders, and only then through a newspaper story which was put together by an enterprising reporter who took the trouble to check the Exchange's files.

There is general agreement that publicity has its uses, and U.S. corporations maintain massive machinery to utilize press channels of communications to gain appropriate objectives, including that of keeping stockholders up to date on the status of their investments.

The Gentlemen of the Press

The most important media group in the press spectrum is the wire services, which produce most of the news you read in the financial pages of your newspaper. They include the Dow-Jones news service, the Associated Press, and United Press International. Each of these organizations is based in New York City but has offices in many other cities. Dow-Jones, the smallest of the three in terms of personnel, nevertheless, is of major importance because it is the only one which specializes in business news and is regarded by many in the financial community as a primary source of business and financial information. It has offices staffed with financial reporters in New York, Chicago, Los Angeles, and some dozen other business centers.

Both the AP and UPI have nationwide networks of offices staffed primarily by general assignment reporters, with financial staffs based mainly in New York. Most radio and television stations also subscribe to these news services. A major piece of business news sent out over the wires of these three major wire services can reach every interested investor in the United States in a matter of hours.

Daily newspapers in the nation's major business centers usually have at least one business news specialist on the staff. Some papers, such as the *New York Times,* Chicago *Tribune,* and Los Angeles *Times,* have good-sized staffs of business reporters. These big city newspapers cover business news on a national scale, some of it taken from the wire services, or from information mailed or delivered directly to them by the company. Business news of immediate local interest to a newspaper's readers, of course, will get a much bigger play than news farther from home. The Chicago *Tribune* will devote far more space to the closing of one of the city's major meat packing plants than it will to a new defense contract received by an aerospace company in Los Angeles. The Los Angeles *Times* will handle these stories in exactly the opposite way.

Financial periodicals comprise another major medium for the dissemination of business news. The leading publication in this category is *The Wall Street Journal.* This newspaper, which is published daily, Monday through Friday, has a national daily circulation of more than 1,000,000, and its market research indicates that at least one subscription is mailed to the headquarters of every one of the top 500 corporations in the U.S. *The Wall Street Journal* is owned by Dow Jones, which owns the Dow-Jones news service and *Barron's* magazine, a weekly business magazine with a circulation of about 150,000. All three of these media have their headquarters in New York City.

There is a host of other authoritative and widely read business publications serving the financial community. These may appear weekly, such as *Business Week, Financial World,* and *Barron's;*

fortnightly, such as *Forbes* and *The Magazine of Wall Street;* monthly, as is the case with *Fortune* and *Dun's Review & Modern Industry,* or bimonthly such as the *Analysts Journal* and the *Harvard Business Review.* The general-circulation news magazines, *Time, Newsweek,* and *U. S. News & World Report,* also provide a medium for business news and, as indicated earlier, exercise considerable influence in the financial community.

One group of publications whose importance to stockholders is often overlooked is the trade press. This group includes magazines and newspapers specializing in news about companies in specific industries. Examples are *Drug Topics, Electronics News, Oil and Gas Journal,* and *Chemical Week.* Serious stockholders would do well to subscribe to at least one publication covering each industry in which they have a major investment. Often these publications carry news of considerable financial significance long before word reaches the general public.

Among the most influential channels for financial news are publications issued by the big securities reporting services, the major stock exchanges, and large brokerage houses. These include Standard & Poor's and Moody's published services, Merrill Lynch, Pierce, Fenner & Smith's *Investor's Reader,* and the New York Stock Exchange's *Exchange Magazine,* and the American Stock Exchange's *American Investor.*

There are, of course, many market advisory letters published by investment banking and brokerage houses for their customers, on a daily, weekly, or less frequent basis. These can have an important influence on market prices, although in most cases corporations do not have direct access to their pages as they have to publications sold by public subscription. For many years, one of the most prominent market letter writer's pungent commentary was followed closely by a large and loyal corps of investors. His popularity fell off at least temporarily, when the SEC accused him of using his letter to tout stocks in which he and his wife held positions. He would sell his holdings, the SEC said, after publication of his own favorable comment had helped push up the price.

There is no question but that the daily press, for the vast majority of stockholders, is the major source of investment news and information. Unfortunately, space in business news departments of newspapers is limited, although papers such as the *New York Times* devote more columns of text to business news than to any other category, including foreign and national news. Many variables affect the coverage a specific company will receive. The four main determinants:

1. Geographic location of the company's operations in relation to the centers of readership of the newspaper.
2. The intrinsic interest of the company's product or service. Control Data Corporation, a Minneapolis computer manufacturer, attracts more interest in distant New York City than a company such as Kennecott Copper Corporation which is headquartered only a few blocks from Times Square.
3. Size of the company in terms of sales and profits.
4. The number of stockholders and the number of shares of stock outstanding.

It's easy to see, on the basis of this brief list, that small companies, and large companies in the older and more stable industries, stand less chance for space in the daily press, or in news media generally, than do larger companies in the glamorous industries. However, as we shall see, if your company has a sound press relations program it can help attract its fair share of attention in the press, and, in some cases, even more.

One of the first lessons that a corporate public relations man learns is that the most important single factor in a successful relationship with the press is recognizing that the newsman's greatest love is news—not booze. To be sure, the business luncheon, the fabled press cocktail party, and the holiday gift all have their purpose and their place. General Electric, for example, holds a "Guaranteed Annual Lunch" at Christmas time for New York labor reporters. It offers both the reporters and G.E.'s personnel department brass an opportunity to renew acquaintance and talk shop, cementing relationships which may become vitally important to the company later on in the midst of sensitive labor negotiations or a strike. G.E. hands to the reporters, as they leave the luncheon, a gift of a G.E. appliance, wrapped neatly in plain brown paper. The *New York Times'* labor reporters, who usually turn out for the occasion, invariably pass up the gift, primly preserving the paper's reputation for bending neither to fear nor favor.

The gamut of gifts offered reporters is extraordinary. The investment banking firm of Lehman Brothers handed out vicuña sweaters. Florida Power distributed baskets of citrus fruits. Magarete Steiff, Gmb H., the West German toy manufacturer, dispensed stuffed dwarfs. Merritt-Chapman & Scott gave away matched decks of playing cards. Other companies have plied newsmen with cases of free liquor, theater tickets, automobiles (on loan), air-conditioners, Havana cigars, and occasionally call girls.

One of the most popular gifts a company can present to a reporter is something euphemistically called the "junket." The junket is an expense-paid trip to some distant pleasure dome, ostensibly for the purpose of gathering news. Actually, the news is carefully prepared in advance and can be made available to the reporter right at his desk. The junket, however, is viewed by companies as a good way to ingratiate themselves with the press, thereby perhaps gaining more space and greater prominence for the news at hand. Reporters accept it as one of perquisites of the journalistic profession, while their editors, with few exceptions, benignly hand out junket assignments as they would bonuses.

The junkets range far and wide. The Hilton chain of hotels invites the press to attend the opening of each of its hostelries, even in such distant places as Istanbul and Caracas; the motion picture companies think nothing of flying a planeload of Hollywood and Broadway reporters and celebrities to Tangier or Tokyo; Trans World Airlines each winter flies a gaggle of reporters to Phoenix to publicize its flights to that winter resort.

Sometimes, the junket backfires. Such was the case with a four-day visit to Miami Beach one winter sponsored by the State of Florida. With the help of a public relations firm hired expressly for the purpose, Florida was attempting to publicize its plan to turn 1800 acres of swampland ten miles north of Miami into a year-round Western Hemisphere trade fair. The long-range goal was to make Miami the trade center of the Americas. This ambitious undertaking depended on the reporters' enthusiastic response to the trade fair project, and no expense was spared in making their trip pleasant and informative. Reams of data on the project were delivered in a neat package complete with engineering studies and the testimonials of prominent New York investment bankers, including Lehman Brothers, which was eager to sell bonds to finance the project to a panting public whose appetite was to have been whetted by the stories in the nation's business press.

The peak of the party occurred on a Saturday night in the ballroom of one of Miami Beach's plushest hotels, where the city's business and civic leaders turned out to add their blandishments to the big pitch. The story was set for release the following Tuesday, to enable the reporters to return to their offices and turn in their stories at their leisure.

Overlooked by the planners of the gargantuan shindig were the local Miami reporters, not invited to participate in the four days of fun and frolic, but who could hardly overlook one of the biggest local news stories of the year. Quite properly, the Miami papers ran the story in their Sunday editions on the basis of the public presentations made by the city fathers the night before, and the major news services picked it up and carried it the same day as a brief news item. The reporters who had been invited from afar lost interest in the story since it would be old news by the time they arrived home, although several glumly phoned in a few routine paragraphs to let their editors know they weren't asleep on the job. Unfortunately for its promoters, the trade center for the Americas is yet to be built and the alligators who call the swamp site home are still able to sleep on undisturbed by progress.

Whether a reporter accepts such largesse gracefully or declines with thanks on the basis of his publisher's policy or his own misgiving, his paycheck depends on his ability to keep his readers informed and his editor convinced he's doing that job in at least passable fashion. Anything a company can do to ease his task, within the bounds of good taste, good fellowship and good business, is not only justifiable but can be considered almost obligatory. The gift a good reporter appreciates most is a piece of publishable news.

Waltzing at the Press Ball

Only a fraction of each day's business news ends up in your daily newspaper. For every annual meeting reported in the financial press, a dozen are not. Thousands of new products are reported in trade journals, but only a handful reach the public through major news media. Scores of new factories rise each year, yet small notice is taken of these in the general press. The fact remains, however, that many meetings are covered, some new products do gain notice, and some new plants do make their public debuts accompanied by photographs in the *New York Times*. Within this favored group, of course, are the giants of industry, whose every corporate hiccough is covered breathlessly by the press.

This doesn't mean that small or unglamorous outfits must be corporate wallflowers. Any company has many opportunities throughout the year to waltz at the press ball. There are periodic earnings reports, dividend announcements, executive changes, plant expansions, and new products. There are speeches by top brass, price changes in product lines. Some of these occasions may call for a formal press conference, while others can best be handled by setting up a cozy meeting with one or more of the company's officers.

With a little ingenuity, a company may generate news that might ordinarily go unnoticed. Most corporations today are substantial contributors to a wide variety of eleemosynary causes, yet rarely do corporate gifts attract more than passing notice. One noteworthy exception was an American Export Lines, Inc., contribution of $135,000 to the Metropolitan Opera of New York for the scenery and costumes for a new production of the Italian opera *Aïda*. It was thought to be the first time a corporation, as such, had contributed directly to the Met. The sum, payable in equal installments over a ten-year period actually depleted the company treasury by less than $70,000, or $7000 a year, since it was a tax deductible item. If the $135,000 had been retained as profit it would have been subject to the stiff corporate income tax. For a relatively modest amount, then, American Export Lines received favorable notice in the press in the U.S. and in Italy and will continue to receive notice in the programs of every Metropolitan Opera performance of *Aïda*. One objective of the gift and the attendant publicity, as explained by American Export's chairman, Admiral John M. Will, was to gain favor with opera patrons here and in Italy. These persons, he added, are prime customers for the company's luxury liners steaming between the East Coast of the U.S. and Genoa, their principal port of call in Italy, and other European cities.

The basic mechanics of dealing with the press, or "servicing" the press, are rather uncomplicated, although press custom and reporters' temperament have created what some company officials view as a stylized mating dance resembling in some respects the courtship of peacocks.

The mechanics boil down to just a handful of items, according to battle-scarred public relations men. There is, first of all, the deadline, which varies depending on the frequency of publication, and, in the case of daily newspapers, the very hour of publication. The trick here is, where possible, to prepare and distribute a press release at least a day or two in advance of the time the news should appear in the daily press. Secondly, the company should make certain that its releases go to the proper person. Thirdly, it should provide for the speedy supply of information. Reporters usually want facts immediately, if not sooner, and it's important that someone be available to provide them at a moment's notice.

It's fair to observe at this point that some publications can be influenced or coerced into modifying a story, or even dropping it entirely. The SEC has severely criticized the financial press for permitting itself to be used to mislead the investing public, and the commission chronicled a number of specific cases of this in its monumental five-part study of the securities markets, published in 1963.

Although it may be tempting for a company to do so, pressuring a publication to change what it plans to print may at best result in unwitting distortion, and at worst expose the company to criticism and possible punitive action by the SEC, the stock exchange on which its securities are traded, and in serious cases intervention by the federal or state attorney general's office.

Seeking change or retraction of an error in a matter of fact is something else again, even if the company itself was responsible for the mistake. Most publications have a set format for printing corrections even though many variables are weighed before the decision is made to print a correction.

On rare occasions, an error may create havoc, or what feels like havoc, in the newsroom as well as the executive suite. One respected business publication, for example, printed an article erroneously stating that an appliance manufacturer had discontinued one of its product lines. No printed retraction could undo the damage it suffered, the company believed, and as a result it sued the publisher for $6 million.

A face-to-face interview with the press is one of the most effective means a company can use to pump information into the financial community's news pipelines. First, it provides the opportunity to clarify ambiguities or questions concerning the "news" the company hopes to see in print. Secondly, it enables company officials and reporters to become better acquainted, thus helping build a personal relationship which, indirectly, could lead to greater understanding between the company and its stockholders.

A good example of what a valid interview or press "conference" can accomplish for a company was that held by Joy Manufacturing Company, Pittsburgh, a mining equipment manufacturer. It was called to discuss the results of the president's tour of Joy's European operations and his trip to Russia. He told the reporters at a luncheon meeting that Joy received an order for over $10 million for potash mining equipment from the Soviet Union, adding that the company had not yet received the necessary U. S. Government delivery clearance.

Joy's president, James A. Drain, said the order would supply work for 725 men for a year at the company's Franklin, Pennsylvania, plant, and probably an equal amount of work for Joy's suppliers. The Russians, he told the assembled reporters, threatened to buy the equipment from European manufacturers if Joy wasn't permitted to fill the order. In this way, presumably, Mr. Drain was able to illustrate the effects on company operations of European competition. At the same time, he was able to demonstrate the benefits of the order in terms of U.S. employment. Not incidentally, the presentation helped offset possible criticism of the company's having done business with an unpopular customer.

Mr. Drain's meeting with the press gave him a forum at which he could discuss other matters of significance to the financial community. He estimated that despite a slight drop in sales for the fiscal year, Joy's profits would rise from 53 cents a share in the previous year to at least $1.75 cents a share. He explained this was due to a pickup in new orders for coal mining equipment, enabling the company to begin building its backlog of orders after having had to eat into it for some months.

A press interview often will be initiated by the press itself. Or a company will seek an interview with a representative of a specific publication, because the information it wishes to publicize fits its particular format. The business news sections of a number of large metropolitan dailies, for example, often carry brief profiles of chief executive officers. This may enable the company to have its president better known to stockholders and employees. Or it may help publicize a policy of special interest to employees or to customers who are also readers of that paper.

Regardless of who initiates the interview, it's important for both parties to have its purpose clearly in mind. It's up to the company, then, to gather pertinent data and either get it to the reporter in advance or, if this isn't feasible, have it ready for him at the interview or press conference.

But even a packet of printed data doesn't ensure that the reporter will know what a press conference is all about. He may choose not to read it until he returns to his office. If the press conference is in the late afternoon, and if the refreshments are particularly appealing, the press "kit" may not receive study until the following morning. One famed science reporter attended a General Electric press conference late one afternoon, arriving just after the formal portion of the meeting had been completed. He greeted several colleagues and G.E. friends, downed a few hors d'oeuvres, tucked a press kit under his arm, and dashed to catch his commuter's train home. He planned to read the G.E. material the next day. Late that night he learned something from a TV newscast: the press conference had been called to announce that G.E. scientists had discovered how to manufacture diamonds—one of the biggest business stories of the year.

Many reporters resent being asked to show their finished stories to the company before publication, and, in fact, some publications prohibit them from doing so. They feel such a request implies that the reporter's skills are lacking, that he is incapable of fair interpretation, or that the company is anxious to change the story to suit itself.

One reporter swore never again to permit a company to see an unpublished manuscript after his experience with a manufacturer of equipment for chemical processing plants. He had offered his manuscript for checking, on the basis that it contained a number of sections dealing with rather complicated manufacturing techniques. The effect was rather like throwing a feather pillow into an electric fan. The public relations director of the company fired off telegrams to the reporter and his editor insisting the story not be published until he returned the "corrected" manuscript. He sent a special delivery letter to the paper's advertising director asking him to use his influence to see that the corrections were made. The manuscript came in, with each paragraph numbered in sequence. Accompanying it, was a corresponding manuscript, with at least one change in almost every paragraph, each numbered to correspond to the original version. There was only one actual error in the entire manuscript, and that having to do with a minor historical point in a paragraph dealing with the company's development. The "errors" which occasioned such public relations hysteria were on this order: "You describe our Mr. Anderson as 'grey haired and bespectacled.' Actually he is steely-eyed and firm-muscled."

There is one area in which a company can express righteous indignation. That is the case where a reporter violates a promise to hold certain information in confidence. In the argot of the journalism profession, anything said "off the record" is understood not to be for publication unless the same information comes to the reporter independently—and unsolicited—from another source. It's wise for company executives, in the course of even the most casual conversation with a newsman, to be aware that anything they might say could appear in tomorrow morning's newspapers. To avoid embarrassment, the executive should either refrain from saying anything he wouldn't want the world to know or preface certain of his remarks with the clear statement that what follows is "off the record."

Should the executive, for some reason, wish to have the reporter include something in his story without naming the source, he then must preface the remarks in question by saying what follows is "not for attribution." The reporter, if he includes such information in his story, will attribute it to "an industry spokesman," an "observer," an "authoritative source," or some equally prescient and ubiquitous presence.

Of course, these techniques must be used sparingly, else the reporter becomes exasperated with the executive's reluctance and marks him and his company as an outfit to avoid. Another sound press relations technique that similarly can boomerang if overdone is the press conference. A press conference should be called only when the announcement is sufficiently weighty and so complicated that it requires detailed discussion before its implications can be grasped fully.

One sure way to enrage a reporter, his editor, and quite possibly many of his colleagues in the local journalism fraternity is to release a story promised him exclusively. A reporter treasures an exclusive story and his enterprise along these lines often is reflected in pay raises and job promotions. Stockholders, not incidentally, benefit from journalism's persistence in snatching from a duped public's eyes the wool occasionally pulled over them by unscrupulous managements. The press, imperfect an instrument though it may be, in a real sense stands watch over a large portion of the nation's economy. A reporter's exclusive story more often than not will concern a matter of only passing importance, but he and his publisher usually view it as a matter they're duty bound to publish. If it doesn't indicate violation of the law or stock exchange rules, involve deception, or isn't of vast or immediate public interest, the reporter might agree to suit the company's convenience as to the time of release of the story. He'll do this only in exchange for additional information and the assurance that when the company is ready his publication will still be able to publish it ahead of the competition.

If a second publication happens on the same story, then it's the duty of the company immediately to so inform the first reporter and release him from the agreement. Once published, of course, the story is up for grabs. If the company fails to follow these unwritten rules of the road, chances are that word will spread and the company for some time to come might find itself dealing with a rather unco-operative and even hostile local press corps.

Almost every company, it's safe to say, would like to see itself in print from time to time, provided that what appears is neither out of keeping with its image of itself nor so revealing as to damage it competitively. Such absolute control, however, is rather difficult to achieve, and impossible for companies listed on major stock exchanges. Companies listed on the New York Stock Exchange are required to publish widely, and as soon as available such data as annual reports, dividend declarations, stock splits, mergers and spin-offs of subsidiaries. Unlisted, publicly held companies generally aren't required by statute to publish this amount of information, although they must file it with the SEC.

The regulations of the SEC and the stock exchanges covering disclosure are varied and complex, but the rule of thumb followed by industrial corporations determined to keep within the bounds of law and sound practice is to release to the press, as soon as physically possible, any information which, in the words of the New York Stock Exchange, "may affect security values or influence investment decisions, and in which stockholders, the public and the Exchange have a [direct] interest." This rule, it should be said, covers favorable as well as unfavorable information.

One of the most vexing and potentially destructive problems a company may face is unfounded rumor. This can directly affect the stockholder's investment and the company's welfare. Such a rumor can cause stockholders to panic and sell at a loss, or it can create undue optimism, causing them to buy at an unduly high price. It can cut a company's credit rating with its banks and suppliers and ruin the sale of a new stock or bond issue. Even if a rumor temporarily benefits the company, the reaction to the disappointing truth sure to follow can adversely affect management's reputation for integrity, with all that implies in terms of the company's relationship with suppliers, customers, bankers, and stockholders.

Among the most widespread rumors in modern corporate history was one in which Teflon, a product produced by E. I. du Pont de Nemours & Company, was thought to give off poisonous fumes when heated. Teflon is a plastic resin which, when bonded to metal or ceramic cookware, enables the housewife to cook without grease. Eggs, for example, can be fried on a Teflon fry pan without using butter, bacon fat, oil or anything else. Du Pont and other companies in the U.S. and abroad have spent untold thousands of dollars in laboratory experiments proving Teflon's safety, and thousands more attempting to dispel the rumors about Teflon, which for some still unknown reason kept popping up unexpectedly. The company finally published a special fourteen-page booklet which frankly acknowledged the rumors and refuted them point by point with scientific thoroughness.

Rumors concerning mergers, acquisitions, or tender offers may send stock prices soaring, or, on the reverse side of the coin, rumors about dividend decreases will surely send stock prices into a downward spiral.

The best policy for companies to follow in squelching harmful or embarrassing rumors, if false, is to refute them promptly. Supervisors are informed of the facts so they can respond immediately when questions arise. If a rumor has gained wide currency, and appears to have staying power, informational memos are sent to the press, and perhaps also to stockholders, employees, customers, and suppliers.

If the company's stock is listed on one of the nation's major exchanges, the exchange staff will almost certainly swing into action whenever it hears the first rumblings of a rumor. G. Keith Funston, president of the New York Stock Exchange, tells the story of how fast his staff can move when the need arises. "Shortly before noon one morning," Mr. Funston says, "the Exchange staff was informed of a rumor on the trading floor about a tender offer for the capital stock of Emerson Radio & Phonograph Corporation. Within minutes, the Exchange obtained confirmation from the Emerson chairman that such an offer was indeed in the works—but that the company making it, not an NYSE-listed company, did not wish to be identified until the details were set. At 12:20, the Exchange halted trading in the stock, pending an announcement—an action which, the company agreed, was appropriate under the circumstances. The last sale before the halt was at 15⅜, up ¾ from the previous day's close.

"At about 3:15, the company advised the Exchange that no announcement would be possible before the 3:30 close of the market. Shortly before the close, the Dow Jones broad tape carried an item indicating that an announcement was expected before the next day's market opening. And at 9:45 A.M. the next day, the broad tape carried the details of the offer—at $18 a share—being made by National Union Electric Corporation. Trading in Emerson was resumed later in the morning and the stock opened at 16¾.

"This particular situation had two most unusual aspects. First, it involved a rumor which proved to be true. And second, this was a very rare instance in which trading was halted and not resumed on the same day. But the important point is that prompt and full cooperation between the listed company and the Exchange avoided the possibility of uninformed trading being based on the unconfirmed rumor—and thus helped safeguard the interests of the investing public without premature disclosure of the facts."

Fast and accurate information is the lifeblood of successful investing. Yet it's amazing how few stockholders take even five minutes to investigate before they invest, or know more than yesterday's closing price of their company's stock once they've purchased it. The press is the fastest communications channel between your company and you, and if you ignore it you do so at your peril. But the press by itself isn't enough, because it cannot provide you with official company data in depth, or give you a chance to meet personally and question your company's management. If you want this kind of information you must read your company's reports, and attend its annual meetings. This information is there for the taking, but today's careless capitalists simply aren't interested.

8

THE HIGH COST OF IGNORANCE:

CORPORATE REPORTS

At a black-tie dinner held in New York each fall, *Financial World* magazine presents a gold "Oscar-of-Industry Trophy" to the corporation that has published the year's outstanding annual report to stockholders.

Some 5000 companies compete for this trophy, and within recent years it has been accepted with obvious pride by the heads of such major corporations as General Motors, Standard Oil (New Jersey), Pennsylvania Railroad, and General Electric.

A good many of today's annual reports are designed by famous graphic artists such as the brilliant Paul Rand and Erik Nitsche, illustrated with beautifully reproduced color photography done by men whose work hangs in the Museum of Modern Art, and written by professional journalists who have learned their trade at *Fortune* and *The Wall Street Journal*.

The modern annual report is also being revolutionized by an upsurge of research to determine exactly what stockholders want in the way of financial data, photographs, charts, graphs, and statistical summaries. Still other studies have probed the average stockholder's understanding of commonplace financial terms such as "working capital," "subsidiary," and "paid-in surplus."

Morgan Guaranty Trust is so eager to keep its stockholders informed that it prints its annual report in French, Italian, German, Spanish, and Japanese for the convenience of its overseas owners, while A.T.&T. makes its report available in Braille and on phonograph records so its sightless share owners can keep pace with their company's progress.

Corporations are making an all out effort to keep their stockholders informed. Yet America's careless capitalists, taken as a whole, prefer to remain in blissful ignorance about the status of their billions. One of the most fascinating investigations of this remarkable situation was conducted not long ago by a nonprofit investors' organization called the United Shareowners of America. This group surveyed 2000 common stockholders throughout the nation, nearly 75 per cent of whom had a college education. Just over 50 per cent of those interviewed could not name a single product made by any company in which they owned stock. "In other words," said Benjamin A. Javits, president of the group, "more than half the investors have no idea of what they are buying or what they own."

Those who claimed a knowledge of what they owned were then asked "From memory, name the products made by the corporations in your investment list which have produced substantial profits for these companies during the past year." Six per cent gave ludicrous answers such as Bell & Howell Company makes most of its profits from aircraft; General Motors from gasoline; Sterling Drug, Inc., from silver, and Swift from trucks.

If these stockholders had spent only five minutes a year glancing at nothing more than the pretty color pictures in their companies' annual reports, they would have been able to rattle off the fact that Bell & Howell makes a substantial dollar from cameras, G.M. from automobiles, Sterling Drug from pharmaceuticals, and Swift from meat.

All of which raises a fundamental question. Do stockholders read the annual and interim progress reports their companies send to their homes at considerable expense?

No, says Reynolds Girdler, vice-president for public relations and advertising at the Sinclair Oil Corporation. In a *Saturday Review* article entitled "18,000,000 Books Nobody Reads," Mr. Girdler bemoans the fact that "Some $9,000,000, countless hours of grueling and exasperating work, and miles and miles of good intentions have gone into the making of these many books. But for all the cost, and for all the earnest endeavors of those who wrote, edited, and approved these publications, and for all the importance of the subject matter, nobody—or almost nobody—will read them."

While the situation is not really as bad as Mr. Girdler suggests, it's bad enough. Readership studies made by quite a few of the nation's largest corporations provide an excellent insight into what happens to an annual report when it arrives at a stockholder's home.

The single most significant fact unearthed by this sleuthing is that about one-third of all stockholders never read their annual reports. Among those stockholders who do read them, roughly 40 per cent will spend only from two to twenty minutes glancing through the report, another 40 per cent will look at nothing more than those few sections that interest them, and a mere 20 per cent will invest the hour or so it takes to read the report from cover to cover—even though they may have invested their life's savings in the corporation's common stock. When stockholders are questioned about their lack of interest in their company's annual report they offer such answers as "I don't have enough time," "I don't understand it," "It's too complicated," "I'm not well educated," or "I have confidence in the company: they know their business, so I don't have to read about what they're doing." The Kendall Company, in an effort to improve this situation, has inserted a supplement in its report which stockholders can use to improve their understanding of what they've read. Holders who return this quiz to the company, along with their comments on the report's design, receive a free box of Kendall's Curad bandages in return.

A corporation's annual and interim reports represent the main channel of communication between the company's management and its owners. Stockholders who ignore these reports—as the majority do to all intents and purposes—are throwing away their precious right to know what their company's management is doing with their money.

If the company is a small, little-known firm, reports and letters from the chairman are the only way stockholders have of keeping themselves informed on a regular basis. News about these small corporations—which number in the thousands—is rarely given even a passing mention by the nation's press unless they do something cute or spectacular. *The Wall Street Journal,* for example, normally prints very little about Philadelphia's smallish Jerrold Corporation. Yet it gave the company a six-line mention on its front page when it "distributed red-ink ball point pens to stockholders at the annual meeting because the company won't be using red ink any more, according to Milton J. Shapp, chairman and president. . . ."

While the press will print columns of news about America's corporate giants, it cannot hope to carry all the vital information packed into the pages of their annual reports. Any stockholder who relies completely on the press to keep himself informed about the affairs of corporations even as large as G.M. and A.T. & T. is short-changing himself. All he'll get from the press is the most obviously important news, i.e., this year's financial results compared with last year's. What he won't get is such highly significant material as the full chairman's report, the full balance sheet and income statement, the full ten-year report on growth trends, as well as the photographs of the company's products, plants, and personnel which can often say more about the company than its latest statement of earnings per share.

To capitalists who really care about their investments, annual and quarterly reports are the fundamental source documents on which decisions to buy, sell, or stand pat ultimately rest. These investors will study their reports thoroughly, use the financial data they contain to work out ratios which shed light on questions such as whether or not the company has enough working capital, a sensible inventory position, or a good profit margin, and, finally, file the reports away for future reference.

The Securities Act of 1934 provides that "Every issuer having securities listed and registered on a national securities exchange shall file an annual report. . . ." with the commission.

Corporations do not have to mail a copy of this report to their stockholders, the SEC says, unless they plan to solicit proxies relating to an annual meeting at which directors are to be elected. If management wants to do this, then its proxy material "shall be accompanied or preceded by an annual report to such security holders containing such financial statements for the last fiscal year as will, in the opinion of management, adequately reflect the financial position and operations of the issuer."

The New York Stock Exchange goes further than the SEC by insisting that "Every company having securities listed on the Exchange is required, by its listing agreement with the Exchange, to publish and to submit to its stockholders, annually, a balance sheet as of the end of the previous fiscal year, and an income statement and surplus statement for such previous fiscal year." The Exchange adds that these annual financial statements must "be published and submitted to stockholders at least fifteen days in advance of their annual meeting, but not later than three months after the close of the company's fiscal year."

As far as interim financial reports are concerned, the Exchange "merely requires . . . a statement of earnings; it does not require that such statement be sent to stockholders." The Exchange "does not fix a specific time limit for publication of interim statements, but it is assumed that such statements will be published as soon as available. While there is, of course, some variation, the majority of listed companies publish their interim figures between four and five weeks after the close of each period."

Credit for today's attractive, readable, and highly informative stockholder reports belongs to enlightened American management —prodded by a handful of crusading American stockholders and the New York Stock Exchange. (In addition to providing stockholders with more information than required, many companies see that they get it far faster than required. IBM, for example, has its annual report in the mail about one month after the close of its fiscal year—even though it must consolidate financial data from more than a hundred countries around the world.)

New York Stock Exchange President G. Keith Funston had this to say about annual reports when he addressed the *Financial World* Annual Awards Banquet on October 26, 1965, at which the magazine's gold "Oscar-of-Industry Trophy" was awarded to the Copperweld Steel Company. "The main purpose of an annual report, it seems to me," Mr. Funston said, "is to inform the share owner— not necessarily to entertain him or to provide a monument to the accomplishments of management or to demonstrate the technical ability of attorneys. Economic sophistication among share owners is on the increase today. A great many of the nation's 20 million investors are now equipped to understand and evaluate significant corporate data—if it is presented in clear, layman's language. Certainly they are entitled to know what's going on in the companies they've invested in. And, acknowledging this, many companies are working hard to make their reports more meaningful.

"We have pointed out to Exchange-listed companies that annual reports can stress content and readability without sacrificing visual appeal—without being unduly technical or verbose. We have urged the inclusion of more material on general economic matters and, where it is relevant, the relation of company activities to these broader economic developments.

"On the accounting side, we have strongly encouraged the publication of statements of source and disposition of funds. A recently completed Exchange survey shows that more than 700 listed companies did include such statements in their 1964 annual reports.

"We are also carefully studying the question of comparability of financial statements of companies within the same industry. Now this is admittedly a highly controversial area—and the mere mention of it is like waving a red flag at some corporate officers. But when two similar companies use different financial reporting techniques, the non-expert investor inevitably is going to have a difficult time evaluating them on a comparative basis. At the Exchange, we believe that it may be possible to develop a specific approach to this problem—at least on an individual industry basis —that will prove feasible."

Quite a few companies these days are scientifically investigating exactly what it takes to seduce their owners into reading their reports. General Electric, for example, has found such surveys to be well worth their cost in improving the readership of their annual report, according to Raymond J. Dodge, G.E.'s consultant on investor data collection and analysis. "As a result of detailed readership data," Mr. Dodge notes, "features that had been traditional were dropped for lack of interest, features that were too long were shortened, items of special interest to share owners were amplified, and new features were added."

An illustration of how G.E. puts its readership studies to work can be seen in the way the company used its chairman's photograph to lure share owners into reading his "Comments" on the year's results. "The first time our Chief Executive Officer's picture was included on the page with his comments," says Mr. Dodge, "the readership of this feature jumped 69 per cent from its previous level of even below 50 per cent. The following year the picture was omitted and readership dropped back to 52 per cent, so we've used the picture ever since."

One reason stockholders are so eager to see what management looks like was suggested by a phone call United Industrial Corporation president Bernard Fein once received from a worried share owner in Arkansas. "You look 100 pounds too heavy in the picture in the annual report," the investor said. "Are you in good health? It's important."

Stockholders can most easily be drawn into reading an annual report if it has a visually exciting cover. Not many covers rate more than a perfunctory glance. A few rare ones do, however, and they usually—but not always—generate their eye appeal by using dramatic color photographs. One exception is Kennecott Copper which used eight lines of bold printing on its cover to trumpet new highs in earnings, net income, and sales—a gimmick guaranteed to excite the most blasé investor.

The most fortunate corporation in the land, when it comes to creating dramatic annual report covers, is the Eastman Kodak Company, whose business is photography. There is practically no limit to the kinds of pictures Kodak can use, be it Switzerland's Lake Lucerne viewed through a bower of spring blossoms, or the setting sun silhouetting windmills on a Dutch landscape, or a three-dimensional photograph of two attractive American teen-agers. Kodak management, incidently, offers stockholders free color reprints, suitable for framing, of the best photographs in its annual report.

The cover of a Merck & Co., Inc., annual report featured a photomicrograph of a new product used for treating hypertension which resembled a Kandinsky painting. Chrysler succeeded in making one of its new models spinning around a test track look like a misty Japanese watercolor. The Anaconda Company pictured an actual work of art consisting of five tons of varying length sheets of polished Anaconda brass which had been transformed into a space sculpture called *Orpheus and Apollo*. The work decorates the grand promenade of Philharmonic Hall at New York City's Lincoln Center for the Performing Arts.

Company studies reveal that stockholders, even if they don't pay much attention to their company's reports, have very definite ideas about what kinds of facts and figures they want to see in them. In a nutshell—the more this report has to do with profits the greater its chances of winning share owner interest.

The best read sections in most reports deal with subjects such as financial information about the company's progress, research and development advances, new products and services, acquisition and merger plans, and indications of the company's prospects for future growth. One of the most delightful long-range predictions of future growth prospects was contained in an annual report of the Bergstrom Paper Company of Neenah, Wisconsin. It read as follows: "The Lord's Prayer has 56 words; Lincoln's Gettysburg Address has 266 words; the Ten Commandments have 296; the Declaration of Independence has 300; a recent Government order setting the price of cabbage has 26,911 words. And it would probably take 26,911,000 words for the Federal Trade Commission to prosecute the U. S. Government for price-fixing on those same cabbages! And so, paper use grows. . . ." Some corporations go out of their way to satisfy this passion for peering into the future. The Glens Falls Insurance Company's report, for example, features a table of "goals" for the year ahead including such key financial forecasts as the dollar amount of "premium writings," "investment income per share" and "life insurance business in force."

Bell & Howell, and Chas. Pfizer & Company, Inc., help stockholders understand the meaning of accounting terms used in their reports by defining them on the spot. Guardsman Chemical Coatings, Inc., of Grand Rapids, Michigan, includes a glossary of accounting and financial terms "for the non-professional investor," and accompanies its report with a copy of Merrill Lynch's pamphlet *How to Read a Financial Report*. The Glens Falls Insurance Company goes a step further and provides stockholders with "A Brief Definition of Selected Insurance Terms" used in its annual report. An insurance policy, for instance, is defined as "A contract by which a company assumes specified risks for a stated period of time."

Stockholders particularly savor reading about corporate events which have received major attention in the press during the year. Examples of this would include General Electric's conspiracy with other manufacturers in its industry to fix prices, rig bids, and divide markets on electrical equipment, which resulted in the biggest criminal case in the history of the Sherman Act; and General Motors' contretemps with auto safety critic Ralph Nader.

The caliber of a company's interim reports to its stockholders bears a close family resemblance to the quality of its annual report. Quarterly reports normally contain all the basic elements of the annual report, only presented in a far less voluminous and spectacular fashion. Four-color photography, for example, is infrequently used, financial figures are obviously less comprehensive, promotion outlays average from one-tenth to one-quarter of the cost of the annual report, and the report itself almost always plays second fiddle to the dividend check which often accompanies it. (A major oil company discovered that a majority of its share owners were so interested in their dividend checks that they discarded the quarterly reports without even realizing they received them.) Corporations are not required to report on what took place at their annual meetings, yet a growing number of firms are doing so through reports ranging from a simple one-page summary which Du Pont sends to stockholders who request it, to the elaborate booklets distributed to all share owners by such companies as Radio Corporation of America, Texaco, Inc., Ford, Columbia Broadcasting System, Inc., and others. These reports normally contain results of the voting on business matters before the meeting, the chairman's address, remarks by other corporate officers, and the highlights of the question and answer period.

While management reports represent the main channel of communication between companies and their owners, they are augmented by a steady flow of letters on everything from welcoming new stockholders into the family to telling investors that their company is in the process of being taken over by outside interests.

Many of these letters are intended to give stockholders important company news that management feels they ought to have without delay. United Air Lines, Inc., used this type of special letter to inform stockholders that "your company [has] contracted for the purchase of 20 Caravelle jet airliners." Du Pont used a series of letters to keep stockholders up to date on the court order to divest itself of 63 million shares of General Motors stock. Swift & Company wrote to stockholders suggesting that they might wish to express their views on the proposed repeal of dividend tax credits, and the introduction of a withholding tax on dividends, "to your Senators and Congressmen." Libby, McNeill & Libby wrote to stockholders telling them that two European companies had offered to buy 20 per cent of their company's outstanding common stock and that "it is management's belief that the purpose of this purchase is useful and constructive."

The most common type of stockholder correspondence is the "welcome" letter sent to new investors, which is almost always signed by the president or chairman and usually includes a copy of the annual report. Other popular items sent to new stockholders include copies of the company's house organ, credit cards or applications for them (oil firms almost always include these), and booklets describing the company's history and business such as "This Is Du Pont," "An Introduction to General Electric," Chain Belt Company's "The Shape of Tomorrow is Formed Today," and "A.T.&T. Your Business." Occasionally samples of the company's products are included such as the kit of tapes, ribbons, sandpaper sent out by Minnesota Mining & Manufacturing, or the box of toothpaste and other products distributed by Bristol-Myers.

A few venturesome companies, usually those with their shares listed on the New York Stock Exchange such as Standard Oil (New Jersey), The Borden Company, and Gulf Oil Corporation, send "good-by" letters to departing stockholders. Most of these letters simply express regret that the investor is leaving "our shareholder family" and assure him he will be most welcome should he decide to return to the fold. Some companies ask the departing stockholder to tell them if he is dissatisfied with their policies, products, or program for keeping him informed.

In rare instances, companies will send stockholders personal form letters during the time they are active share owners. Standard Oil Company of California, for example, sends investors a note of congratulations when they celebrate their twenty-fifth anniversary as a stockholder. Another company does the same thing whenever a stockholder buys more shares. Still other firms send "thank you" letters to stockholders acknowledging receipt of their proxy.

Running parallel to this flow of special stockholder correspondence is the steady stream of routine letter writing. Large corporations such as A.T.&T., Du Pont, and General Electric receive hundreds of letters each working day from their stockholders. The bulk of this correspondence involves requests to change a stockholder's address, transfer his shares to a new name, replace a lost dividend check, and so on.

Letters questioning the operation of the business are distinctly in the minority, but if stockholders become alarmed they will write. At the 1963 annual meeting of the Kratter Corporation, for example, Chairman Marvin Kratter devoted a major portion of his speech to answering what he called a "barrage" of inquiries from shareholders about the real estate investment company's position. The queries came in the wake of widespread press reports dealing with financial troubles in the real estate business which had contributed to a sharp decline in the price of the company's stock.

Management takes this kind of stockholder criticism very seriously —perhaps because it is so remarkably rare. One chairman, for instance, interrupted a meeting with his top executives to show them a quarterly stockholders report which had been returned with the words "When are you going to stop making excuses and start making profits?" scrawled across it in red ink. A large oil company even wrestled with the most diplomatic way to answer a stockholder's complaint consisting of the word "humph" written on his proxy card.

Up until several weeks after a report to stockholders has been mailed out, the executive responsible for preparing it lives in constant terror of receiving a telephone call which begins, "Please turn to page nine of your latest report, right hand column, sixth line from the top." The call normally heralds a setback for the poor chap's career because it means the report contains an error, something which makes the company's chairman look careless at least, and a damn fool at worst.

To avoid mistakes, corporations often go to extraordinary

lengths. Several years ago, for example, one company decorated its report with the flags of the nations in which it does business. The executive in charge of the report personally checked the flags' accuracy against every available guidebook, then took the finished artwork over to the United Nation's flag expert for a final approval. As he passed the row of flags fluttering outside the UN, the executive noticed that the banners of Saudi Arabia and Morocco didn't match the guidebooks. He broke this calamitous news to the UN's man as gently as possible. Undaunted, the UN's flag authority walked over to an ancient metal filing cabinet and pulled out two drawings of the Saudi Arabian and Moroccan flags that had been personally sketched and signed by the heads of state of these two countries.

Despite the most elaborate routines for checking and double-checking every word, number, chart, graph, and picture that go into stockholder reports, mistakes still occur. Perhaps the most famous struck a nationally known company in the transportation industry. This firm had just opened a new sales office in a major city on the West Coast. The company decided to feature the office on the cover of its annual report, and it wasn't until copies were already in the mail that it discovered with horror that two of man's best friends were enjoying a romantic interlude in the lower right hand corner. The company desperately attempted to call back those reports already mailed, but by that time they were collector's items.

9

THE PROFESSIONALS:

THE INVESTMENT COMMUNITY

Ralph W. Michaud is a Maine native who as a child played with wood chips left from logging operations in the great forests surrounding his home. After college, he carved out a Wall Street career and today is a senior analyst of paper company securities for Dean Witter & Company, one of the Street's most prominent investment banking houses. In that capacity, analyst Michaud's recommendations each year influence the purchase and sale of millions of dollars of securities by Dean Witter's customers throughout the U.S.

Mr. Michaud and thousands of other security analysts, investment bankers, brokers, dealers, and stock exchange specialists are members of the professional investment community. These are the "middlemen" of the world of finance, the group through which the investment dollars of the nation are placed at the disposal of companies requiring capital.

Because of their special knowledge and the crucial role they play in maintaining an orderly and active securities market, they are by all odds the best source of investment information. More significantly, their latest thinking is available, usually without charge, to any stockholder or prospective stockholder who takes the trouble to ask for it. The best advice a small stockholder can follow is to get a good broker, for it is through the broker (sometimes called a "customer's man," or, more elegantly, a "registered representative") that the information and opinion amassed by the professional investment community is made available to the public at large.

Step into any office of Merrill Lynch, Pierce, Fenner & Smith, for example, and you can have, usually within minutes, the latest report on the securities of almost every actively traded, publicly held corporation in America. If a printed analysis doesn't happen to be available for a particular company, the broker can pick up the phone and get the information directly from the Merrill Lynch security analyst who specializes in that company's industry group.

Large houses such as Merrill Lynch, Dean Witter, and Bache & Company will provide such service to almost all who seek it. Smaller brokers, naturally, must of necessity limit such service to their own customers.

For most of the nation's stockholders, the professional investment community is represented mainly by the broker or mutual fund salesman. The vast and complex machinery supporting their activities is usually unseen and likely unperceived. A close look at this machinery and the people who make it work can be instructive for those stockholders seeking to invest more intelligently, and more profitably.

Individuals or institutions such as mutual funds, banks, and insurance companies seeking to invest in the securities of publicly held corporations, as a practical matter, can do so only through the services of the professional investment community. Conversely, companies seeking to raise money by issuing stock or bonds usually can accomplish the task only through the same group of middlemen. The relationship is not unlike that between a manufacturer and his wholesale distributors.

There are, to be sure, profound differences. Major among these is that the securities industry, if it may be called an industry, is one of the most closely regulated in the United States. Federal and state law, judicial decrees, and regulations of the various stock exchanges and distributor organizations such as the National Association of Securities Dealers shape the character and day-to-day behavior of every segment of the business.

If a single word can be said to characterize the mountain of rules governing the issuance and trading of securities in the U.S., that word is "disclosure." But such are the complexities of business and the vagaries of securities values that even experts, with access to all the facts, are hard put to plot the future of any particular investment. Examples are legion. However, in deference to their expertise and strategic position as middlemen, a company has to reckon with Mr. Michaud and his colleagues. That is, if it is interested in having its stock and bonds sell at fair prices and in keeping its stockholders informed. These two principal goals, as we shall see, are closely related, and in fact are matters of profound personal importance to many corporate managements as well as to stockholders themselves.

It may be well, at this point, to sketch the professional investment community. Its address is Wall Street, and one should understand that Wall Street crosses the main business district of every city of consequence in America. It is composed basically, of 1. distributors of securities, 2. holders and traders of securities and, partly overlapping these two areas, 3. advisers on the purchase and sale of securities.

Dean Witter, headquartered in California but with large, bustling offices in New York and forty-nine other U.S. cities, is as typical as any firm in the first category—the investment banker and broker-dealer. This is the selling group, and it includes such national marketing giants as Merrill Lynch, and Bache, as well as smaller local firms such as Courts & Company, of Atlanta. Courts, like many firms of its kind, has a modest New York office, though it specializes in the securities of Atlanta companies, viz., Delta Airlines and Coca-Cola.

The professional holders and traders, our second category, may include wealthy individuals such as showman Billy Rose, who was, until his death in 1966, the largest single share owner in American Telephone & Telegraph and one of the largest share owners in the New York Central Railroad. Or they may be those hardy types who make their living buying and selling small amounts of stocks, eyes glued to the ticker in their favorite brokerage office. Some are of modest means and some wealthy, but all love the excitement of the game and take covert pleasure in tossing off the phrase "trading for my own account" in response to the query from old business associates as to how they spend their time these days.

There are also the broker-dealers, those firms which handle the trading of America's twenty million individual share owners. Some broker-dealers, like Merrill Lynch, with its nationwide chain of

168 offices, engage in retail as well as wholesale business. They sell to other broker-dealers and large institutional buyers, just like wholesale merchants, and they sell also to individuals, like retail stores. Other broker-dealers prefer to operate exclusively as either wholesalers or retailers.

The distinction between a broker and a dealer, incidentally, is that a broker is an agent who works for a commission under the instruction of his customers. The customer's man is a broker. He never owns the securities he's handling. A dealer does. He'll buy here and, as owner, will sell there. If he buys low and sells high, he makes money. The tireless, quick-witted stock exchange specialists, who man the trading posts on the floor of the New York Stock Exchange and other stock exchanges around the country, are dealers. Most of the nation's listed securities are traded through them, and some specialists have been known to end a hectic trading day a quarter of a million dollars poorer or richer than when they got out of bed in the morning.

Among the least colorful but most important professional buyers of securities are the institutions. These include mutual funds, banks, insurance companies, college endowment funds, pension plans, and philanthropic foundations. The investment managers of these institutions deal in incredibly large sums and as trustees of other people's money were tagged by economist-writer Peter Drucker as "the new tycoons."

You can get a sense of their formidable financial influence by looking at a few figures. Institutional investors' holdings of stock accounted for 12.7 per cent of the market value of all stock listed on the New York Stock Exchange in 1949, the year the big postwar bull market began. By the close of 1966, this share rose to 21 per cent of the total.

The dollar value of institutions' Big Board holdings was a thundering $101.1 billion at the end of 1966, against only $9.7 billion in 1949. A large portion of the gain, of course, stemmed from the big increase in value of many stocks in the intervening years of the bull market.

In a special survey of market activity on March 10, 1965, the New York Stock Exchange found that institutions accounted for 31.4 per cent of the Big Board's total volume for the day. This was the highest percentage ever and compared with the previous record of 26.2 per cent, set in September 1961. Transactions by individuals accounted for 48.5 per cent of the total in the latest study, the first time it fell below the 50 per cent mark.

Brokerage houses are putting more and more effort into institutional sales. Mr. Michaud of Dean Witter, for instance, devotes himself to lengthy, detailed analyses, running up to fifty pages in length, of companies whose stocks may interest his firm's institutional customers. Some firms that have long catered to individual investors are setting up separate departments to grab their share of the lush and fast-growing institutional accounts. Bache opened an institutional department in 1962, after almost a century of business. In 1963, Delafield & Delafield, G. C. Haas & Company, Orvis Bros. & Company, and Moore & Schley, Inc., did the same. Other firms, including the big wire houses that do most of their business with the public, like Francis I. du Pont & Company, are expanding their institutional departments. It should comfort the small investor to know that he has access to substantially the same information and advice as does his large fellow stockholder.

There is even a new breed of research-oriented brokerage house springing up lately that specializes entirely in institutional sales. These relatively small new firms, such as Donaldson, Lufkin & Jenrette, and Faulkner, Dawkins & Sullivan, seem to be competing successfully against the established giants, which while doing a broad-based business, have many institutional clients.

Some firms consider this aspect of their business so important they reserve their major research studies for institutional customers. One goes so far as to monitor the daily trades of its "retail" salesmen and woe betide any customer's man who shows activity in one of the stocks recommended to institutions within the previous six months.

It should be pointed out that the Securities and Exchange Commission takes a dim view of this practice. Later distribution to the public of the same recommendation, usually in abbreviated form, may drive up the price of the stock, thus benefiting the institution which had already acted on it.

The firms, on the other hand, feel their institutional customers might lose part of any potential gain during their usual drawn-out deliberations over analytical studies if word of the recommendations were distributed to individual buyers. This might antagonize the institutional customer. It might also ruffle the feathers of the management of the company that was the subject of the report, thus jeopardizing future underwriting business from that source. And customers who did not hear of the advice might get sore as well. However, should a customer happen to call seeking information covered by a detailed institutional analysis, the facts would be made available to him.

Among institutions, the fastest growing group is the corporate pension funds. Originally started around the turn of the century as an informal way through which companies could help retired employees, at the end of 1965 their portfolios accounted for 30 per cent of all Big Board stocks held by institutions, the largest share of any of the others. Their slice was only 5.2 per cent in 1949.

The pension funds' total assets of $71.4 billion cover some 26 million employees. By 1980, predicts the National Bureau of Economic Research, pension fund assets will swell to $234 billion and the number of workers covered will reach 41 million.

The banks manage most pension fund portfolios, although the insurance companies are showing interest since the SEC in 1962 enabled them to enter the field in a serious way. Now they are permitted to manage pension funds invested in common stocks by placing the funds' assets in accounts segregated from general insurance assets. Previously, the Government severely limited the amount of reserves they could put in common stocks.

One of the characteristics of the institutions, of particular significance to publicly held corporations, is that the largest portion of their stock is directly controlled by the professional investors, and not by the people whose interests are served by the ownership of the stock. Owners of mutual fund shares and employees covered by bank-trusteed pension funds fall in this category. The power of investment decision on the part of the institutions then is far greater in relation to the number of shares they hold than the marketing segments of the professional investment community—such as brokers—whose influence must filter out to many large and small individual customers.

The third and final category of professional investor, the security analyst, helps guide the investment decisions of the rest of the entire financial community, including millions of small investors who are brokerage-house customers. There is probably no single individual in the professional investment community more important to the small stockholder than the security analyst whose reports are transmitted to him through his broker.

There are almost 11,000 security analysts in the U.S., organized into societies in more than three dozen cities and affiliated in the Financial Analysts Federation. Some company presidents wait months to address the larger analysts groups, especially the New York Society of Security Analysts. Others never quite make it; the New York Society has only about 250 luncheon meetings a year and there are some 1300 companies listed on the New York Stock Exchange alone.

The analysts weren't always so popular. "Back in the 1930's, we were little more than statisticians," recalls Pierre R. Bretey, a partner and top analyst at Hayden Stone & Company. In those days, small investors were nowhere near as numerous as today. The little fellow was usually looking for a speculative killing, and he neither sought nor received much real investment information. Institutions in those days invested chiefly in "safe" bonds and mortgages. Big speculators in common stocks often depended on tips from friends inside the company. However, analysts and other outsiders had difficulty prying information out of management which traditionally kept company facts close to its vest. The market, prior to 1933, was lightly regulated and could be manipulated by the large operators, and the public shied away.

Since then, stock ownership has broadened, and the many years during which yields on bonds and other fixed-asset securities were held down helped drive the institutions into stocks. Today, by legal requirement and by choice, management is more inclined to see that the analysts know about their companies.

There are four major classes of these securities experts:

1. Analysts with major institutions who have the greatest investment responsibility.

2. Analysts at institutional brokerage firms or investment counseling firms. They also often wear the hats of salesmen. For example, Donaldson, Lufkin & Jenrette's highly paid researchers all

handle selling chores—the firm has no salesmen as such. But they're on a salaried basis and receive no commission. Other firms, though, pay commission on sales generated by the research staff.

3. Analysts with the smaller institutions who rely almost entirely on institutional brokers and investment counselors for their information—their operations aren't large enough to justify lengthy personal investigations.

4. Finally, there are the analysts working for brokerage houses and investment advisory services, most of whose customers are individuals. These analysts cover the most ground, and each may keep tabs on hundreds of companies. As a group, they provide most of the advice going out to the army of small investors in the U.S.

There is much to be gained by a company conducting an aggressive program of communications aimed at the professional investment community. In some cases, as described later in this chapter, the gain to the company can be measured in dollars and cents. Thomas W. Phelps, partner in charge of research at Scudder, Stevens & Clark, cautions, however, "Important as communications are, of course, they are no substitute for having something good to communicate about." But many companies fail to cash in on good news simply because the professionals never learn of it. And if they don't, neither do stockholders or prospective stockholders.

The Importance of the Pros

Companies are becoming increasingly aware that one immediate benefit deriving from a soundly conducted communications program aimed at professional investors is a fairer evaluation of its stock. Market price is based, among other variables, on facts, or the lack of facts. It's reasonable to assume that if the pros can see elements of value they didn't see before, they'll pin a higher price tag on the stock. The professional's estimate is often widely published, tending to drive the price of the stock upward as buyers are attracted to it. This, obviously, bears on the terms of a merger or acquisition for stock and on the market price of a new issue of securities. A gain in price of an eighth of a point, in even a small offering of, say 200,000 shares, means $25,000 more in cash to the company seeking additional equity capital. If a merger or acquisition is contemplated, an increase in market price affects the terms of the deal. It goes without saying that the sword cuts two ways. The process would, theoretically, reverse if the pros turn up information which would lead them to place an evaluation on the stock lower than that indicated by its current market price.

The price of a stock in the market means considerably more to a company than a tribute—or lack of it—to management's stewardship. A higher ratio of price to earnings permits a company to raise a larger sum of money in the form of equity capital. A well-regarded growth company with earnings of $1 million can support new equity capital of well over $20 million. A less exciting name, selling at a lower price earnings ratio, would need $2 million or $3 million in earnings to raise that much additional capital.

A company the pros think well of is ahead of the game if it wants to add more stockholders to its roster, thus easing the way for any new offering of securities. Prospective stockholders look to their brokers as a major source of information and advice. Through the medium of the security analyst, then, a company can create a reservoir of knowledgeable potential buyers. He serves as a supplementary channel of communications, too, between the company and the share owner—and the only direct channel to the beneficial share owner whose stock is held in brokerage firm names. All this tends to broaden the market for the company's stock, thus enhancing its marketability. This also is translatable in dollar terms.

Take, for example, the case of Aeroquip Corporation, now listed on the New York Stock Exchange. In 1966 it had more than 6600 share owners. Sales for the year ended September 30, 1966, were $113 million with earnings of about $6.3 million, or $3.92 per common share on 1,606,490 common shares outstanding.

Aeroquip's first public stock issue came out in 1950 and it put the stock in the hands of about 900 stockholders who paid $4 a share. The underwriter's commission in the offering was 13.75 per cent. A little over two years later, a larger offering was sold, at $7 a share, at a 10 per cent commission, and the stockholder roster increased to 2500. Says Peter F. Hurst, Aeroquip's president: "The officers and directors are convinced that this could not have been accomplished had it not been for our continuing, well planned financial community and stockholder relations program."

In even a small public offering, say $1.5 million, a 2 per cent difference in underwriters' commission means $30,000 to the company.

The fair evaluation of a company stock in the market can be crucial to its ability to raise capital. Nationwide Corporation, an insurance holding company traded over-the-counter, felt obliged to call off what was to have been originally a $26 million common stock offering in early January 1964. When Nationwide filed its registration statement in November 1963, for 1.75 million shares, its common was trading at over $15 a share. It planned to use $9 million of the proceeds of the sale to repay a bank indebtedness incurred in an acquisition earlier in the year; about $2 million for a proposed joint venture with Greyhound Corporation, and the balance for future acquisitions.

Shortly after the filing, the price of the stock started to slip, and Nationwide cut back the number of shares in the offering to 1.2 million. It appeared the market demand wasn't strong enough to absorb the larger amount, and so was depressing the price. But the downward pressure continued. By December 10, the day scheduled for the offering, the stock was being bid at $14. Nationwide pulled it back hours before it was to come to market. A month later, the company canceled the offering altogether with the stock bid at $14.75. Louis E. Dolan, vice-president, said the directors thought the stock was selling at too low a price "in relation to the value of the stock."

Recognition by the professional investment community is essential to almost any form of private financing, whether by way of bank borrowings or other debt, sale-leaseback, or private placement of securities. The last mentioned has been gaining popularity in recent years. In 1963, corporations seeking cash offered more securities privately than publicly for the first time on record. Private placements normally cost less than public offerings.

Companies keep in close touch with the professionals, especially the analysts, also as a defensive maneuver; to prepare for a setback in a company's fortunes. Unlike many individual investors, the institutions normally study a company in great detail before buying its securities, and aren't frightened into selling if it falters. And the retail brokers and dealers, if they have the facts, can more soundly advise and calm small individual stockholders anxiously seeking counsel during a time of market travail.

From the company's point of view, a particularly good man with whom to maintain communications during such periods is the stock exchange specialist, the broker-dealer on the floor of the exchange through whom all trading there is conducted. It's his job to maintain an orderly market in the issues for which he is responsible; to match buy and sell orders and to make sure price fluctuations are gradual. In the course of his activity he may have to do considerable trading for his own account and his confidence in a company whose stock he handles will influence the enthusiasm with which he will commit his own funds and will communicate itself to the floor brokers around him. Simply stated, the specialist can do a far more effective job if he knows what's going on.

In sum, if the analysts and other pros, and the investors who rely on them for advice, are convinced the company is basically sound and its long-range prospects are bright, the market's reaction to a temporary decline may be softened. Stock prices may merely flutter instead of plummet.

The institutions' ability to gulp down quickly large quantities of stock, and their tendency to hold stock for long-term investment purposes, also prevents undue weakening of the price and of the marketability of a stock. This is especially helpful if a large secondary offering suddenly hits the market. A secondary is a large block of already issued stock offered for sale by the owner through a broker who sells it to buyers directly rather than through the auction market. Secondaries must be registered in advance with the SEC. A secondary that isn't quickly grabbed up may be a sign that something's lacking in a company's relations with the institutions. Of course, there may be some other explanation such as poor timing by an unwise seller. Or, perhaps, the stock may be out of favor and there just aren't enough interested buyers to take up the entire offering.

The more impressed the army of share owners is with a company, the faster and more anxious it will be to buy up any shares it can put its hands on. So heavy was the demand for Ford Motor's first stock offering back in 1957, that some brokers had to allocate shares, limiting distribution to their best customers. Even those so privileged were allowed no more than 100 shares apiece. A.T. & T. uses its own shareholders as a prime source of fresh capital. "Telephone," as it's referred to on Wall Street, has over 3 million stockholders, and the company makes it a practice to give them an exclusive first crack at any new offering at a price below the market. In 1964, for example, it raised $1.2 billion in this way. It was the largest amount of money ever raised by any company in any type of financing venture.

Widespread ownership, as against concentrations of stock in the hands of institutions, is a goal sought after by some companies who see in it a superior means of stabilizing the market for their shares. Aeroquip is one of these. About 64 per cent of Aeroquip's registered stockholders own 100 shares or less, with another 31 per cent owning from 101 to 500 shares. Only 5 per cent own more than 500 shares, and many of these are brokers who represent a substantial number of the 2000 Aeroquip stockholders who are beneficial owners and have their shares held in brokerage firms or "Street" names.

It's hard to say which is better for a company; to have its shares distributed widely among small owners, or to have it held in the "strong" hands of institutions and large stockholders. Each school of thought has its proponents. Whatever the philosophy, the security analyst is a key figure. In most large companies one or more top executives are assigned the task of dealing directly with the analysts on a day-to-day basis. Often the chairman or the president will meet with a visiting analyst, and the visit is a first-priority item on their agendas for that day. Although the analyst usually cannot ferret out facts that would not be available to any stockholder who takes the trouble to ask for them himself, the interpretation he may place on them before passing them along to the investing public enhances their value to the stockholder.

Many companies have developed special information programs for analysts alone, on the theory that they require more detailed and comprehensive data on a company than does the amateur investor. Such a program will, of course, include everything that stockholders normally receive. But it may also include a special statistical supplement to the annual report that the average stockholder would have little interest in seeing. Analysts will also be sent announcements that are generally released to the press but that may not be sent to stockholders. These may include announcements of capital expenditure programs, new financing, important new product developments or changes in selling prices. Some companies prepare special comprehensive reports bringing together in a single volume the trends, statistics, history, facilities, and other factual material that could be valuable in understanding a company's operations. These studies are available, on request, to stockholders. Similar ones are issued independently, on a regular basis, by a number of stock market analytical services, such as the Value Line Investment Survey, Standard & Poor's, and Moody's, which are available to the public on a subscription basis.

In addition to talking with analysts individually and in groups, company executives will occasionally take them on field trips to their plants or laboratories. It would be impractical, if not impossible, for many companies to do the same for stockholders. But stockholders can benefit indirectly by way of the analysts' reports.

Lately some companies have taken to inviting analysts to attend the annual meeting. This gives analysts an additional opportunity to keep themselves current on the activities of the company, and gives stockholders the direct benefit of the open exchange. Chances are, too, that the questions put to management by the professional would elicit more information than those asked by the average stockholder attending the meeting.

You as a stockholder should expect management to do everything possible, within ethical and legal bounds, to assure that your investment will receive a fair market evaluation. If for no other reason, therefore, part of management's responsibility is to maintain close and effective relations with the professional investment community. And you should make every effort to enlist the aid of the stock market professionals in helping you keep tabs on the activities of the managements of the companies whose shares you own. Careless capitalists don't bother.

10

"MY PILOT LIGHT LEAKS":

THE ANNUAL MEETING

Some years ago, *The New Yorker* magazine published a cartoon that in its own acerbic way summed up what the average stockholder thinks of his once-a-year opportunity to interrogate his company's chief executive officer. The cartoon pictured a sweet little old lady standing up at a gas company annual meeting to inform her chairman that "My pilot light leaks."

Farfetched? Not by any means. At a National Tea Company session a real lady stockholder asked the chairman to stop selling a brand of butter she disliked. Another investor wanted to know why National Tea stores were held up more than competing shops. One female stockholder asked the chairman of the Frank G. Shattuck Company, operator of the Schrafft's restaurant chain, to do something about customers who dawdle all afternoon over a cup of coffee. An American Express share owner complained to president Howard L. Clark because he couldn't cash one of his company's traveler's checks in an Automat.

The caliber of share owner inquiries at annual meetings has reached such a low that General Electric recently felt obliged to invite some security analysts to its meeting in the hope that they would ask some intelligent questions. A total of fifty-four analysts showed up and four asked questions about the effects of a tax cut on G.E.'s profits, changes in the economic climate of the European Common Market, G.E.'s work on the Apollo moon vehicle and other space-exploration projects, and the trend of the company's prices. G.E.'s top brass called the question and answer period "penetrating, illuminating and interesting."

While stockholders have a propensity for asking annual meeting questions that verge on the inane, they have an even greater propensity for ignoring their companies' meetings altogether. A corporation that gets 1 per cent of its owners to attend its yearly get-together is doing well, and it's not unheard of for a company to attract no stockholders at all, as happened at the 1964 annual meeting of the Standard-Thompson Corporation in Waltham, Massachusetts. President Harry P. Neher, Jr. had an optimistic report to give his company's owners, and he went ahead and gave it anyway even though the only share owners present were members of the firm's top management. "I'll be darned if I was going to throw away my notes after I'd gone to the trouble to make them," said President Neher.

Few stockholders have any conception of the amount of work and worry that corporations invest in luring them to their companies' annual meetings, entertaining and informing them once they've arrived, and making sure that everything goes as smoothly as a White House reception.

"Annual meeting day," says the stockholder relations director of a major manufacturing company, "is the one time of the year our Chairman really sweats."

At first glance, of course, he has nothing to worry about. Days before the meeting, enough stockholder proxies have been received to more than guarantee the re-election of the chairman and other directors.

The company has also invested hundreds of man hours to make certain the meeting will go like clockwork. A hall has been selected and attractively decorated. Exhibits have been set up. Lunch arranged. Plain-clothes detectives hired in case some stockholder gets overly obstreperous. The chairman's speech written and rewritten. Scouts dispatched to other meetings to find out what kind of questions professional stockholders such as Lewis Gilbert and Wilma Soss are asking this year. And possible stockholder questions have been fired at the chairman for two or three hours without interruption.

But still the chairman worries, and for good reason, even though the company may have an excellent sales and earnings record. This is the day the chairman is totally exposed. Maybe someone will ask him about that relative who's had such a meteoric rise within the corporation. Maybe someone will crucify him because of that new product that flopped. Maybe he'll get caught flat-footed by a tough question, or flustered by a stockholder demand that everyone rise for a silent tribute to the firm's long-departed founder.

The question and answer period is a decided ordeal for most chairmen because it's the one thing from which even the mightiest organization cannot protect him. He's on his own and his every word and action are being observed, not only by the stockholders, but by his fellow directors, corporate officers, rank-and-file employees, and possibly the press.

Dun's Review summed up management's feeling about its yearly appointment with stockholders in a story headlined "What's the Annual Meeting Worth?—The men who run them make a sweeping reassessment." The magazine polled the 300 members of its Presidents' Panel, learned "that a full two-thirds of the panel presidents believe the annual meeting is a truly worthwhile executive exercise."

"The greatest value of the annual meeting," said Koppers Company chairman, Fred C. Foy, for instance, "lies in causing us at least once a year to consider in advance the questions which a stockholder might ask. And in turn usually forces us to focus on aspects of the business which are different from our normal operating figures." "The meeting," said Union Oil Company of California's president, A. C. Rubel, "requires us to make a critical review of possible subjects of discussion, and this sharpens up the whole organization." "It is like an annual final examination—for which it is well to be fully prepared," said Pennsalt Chemical's president, William P. Drake.

The average chief executive is usually pretty well prepared to handle stockholder questions on annual meeting day, although it's not unheard of for the chairman to get burned at least once during the hour or so he's on the griddle.

The sharpest stockholder barbs, obviously enough, are aimed at the heads of companies with less than dazzling performance records at annual meeting time.

A Raytheon stockholder at one recent annual meeting, according to press reports, expressed the wish that president Charles F. Adams would resign along with the rest of his management team. Another stockholder asked Mr. Adams "what thought is being given to merging with a company with good management?" Still another share owner reminded the beleaguered Mr. Adams that "Year after year you have told us dead wood was being eliminated and the company was making progress. One of those who left was Mr. Geneen [Harold S. Geneen, now president of International Telephone & Telegraph] and he took the company he went to—which was a sleeping giant—and made a billion dollar company out of it."

A Tower Universal Corporation stockholder blasted Chairman David B. Chase for acquiring, and subsequently selling, five money-losing subsidiaries in the travel business, and later acquiring a swimming pool concern. Mr. Chase was taken to task for acquiring subsidiaries "that depreciate year by year" and have a habit of turning into "everything but money."

Nepotism is a favorite target of irate investors, such as the Twentieth Century-Fox Film Corporation stockholder who criticized president Darryl F. Zanuck for making his son Richard Zanuck head of the company's Hollywood studio. "You put in young Zanuck who's 28 years old," the share owner complained, "to replace another man at $1,000 a week." Replied the elder Zanuck quietly, "It's very difficult for a father to defend his son."

Donald W. Douglas, chairman of the Douglas Aircraft Company, was asked to explain why he sold 5000 of his 10,000 Douglas shares just two days before the government canceled the company's Skybolt missile contract, which depressed the market price of the stock. Mr. Douglas at first replied that the sale was "his own business." He later amended this reply, however, with the explanation that the sale was prompted by the death of a close friend, and the realization that he himself was past seventy years of age and should pay more attention to his family's financial future.

The main attraction at any annual meeting, at least from the stockholder's point of view, is the chairman's report on the state of the business. Most companies attempt to give their stockholders a solid, fact-filled progress report, although there are exceptions. "The only thing we'll give stockholders," says Myron Bantrell, president of Los Angeles' Filtrol Corporation, "is the financial information; if they like it, swell, and if they don't, that's too bad."

An excellent summary of the kind of basic information you have every right to expect from the chairman of your company's annual meeting was published several years ago by the New York Stock Exchange. The summary applies to all publicly held corporations, and not just those listed on the Big Board. The list covers the following ten broad areas:

1. The current trend of sales and earnings.
2. Any major operating problems that may be facing management.
3. The prospects of any non-recurring profits or losses.
4. Management's plans for expanding its plants and product line.
5. The company's dividend policies.
6. Research and development policies and programs.
7. Any major litigation that is pending by or against the company.
8. Any unusual financial matter that the company's independent auditors may have brought to the board's attention in the past six months. (Stockholders are entitled to have a representative of the auditing firm present at the meeting and available for questioning on such matters.)
9. Any pending moves importantly affecting the corporation's executive personnel, and the status of its labor relations.
10. The management's intentions, if any, to seek new financing.

There are instances where management not only refuses to give its stockholders this kind of informative report, but turns around and insults the intelligence of the share owners attending the meeting by giving these facts to newspaper reporters after the meeting is over. This is particularly true as regards "the current trend of sales and earnings," and it puts the stockholder in the position of having to buy a paper to learn what management should have told him at the meeting.

Annual meetings are a trial (General Aniline & Film Corporation president Jesse Werner called the experience "a travesty"), yet practically every corporation of any size is obliged to hold one, and management has long since learned how to make the best of a difficult situation. The management of CIT Financial has gone so far as to send its stockholders a free calendar with the date of the annual meeting carefully marked in full color.

Stockholders who succumb to management's siren song are often warmed up for what's to come by displays and exhibits located in the foyer directly outside the annual meeting hall. Western Union once demonstrated a bomb alarm system, Merck exhibited a monkey under the influence of a new drug, United Aircraft Corporation periodically fired off a small rocket motor encased in glass, and American-Standard Sanitary Radiator Corporation showed off the latest in toilets.

On the more human side, Pfizer once recruited four male employees, dressed them in straw hats, blazers, and bow ties, and had them serenade arriving stockholders with versions of famous Barbasol radio commercials and other selections.

Unabashed entertainment is even creeping into the business part of the annual meeting with the chairman himself occasionally playing the role of top banana. Chairman McGregor Smith, of Florida Power & Light, usually favors stockholders with a harmonica solo of "You Are My Sunshine" or other noncontroversial tunes, and Chairman Milton G. Holme, of Thorofare Markets, has been known to regale investors with bits of poetry and other sayings including "Middle age is a state of life, most men first notice in the wife."

A *Wall Street Journal* reporter covered a Warner-Lambert Pharmaceutical meeting where they showed color movies illustrating the effect of the company's new drugs on an ulcer patient's stomach and a hog's heart. "The spotlight then focused on a slim brunette model," the story continued, "whose hair was dripping wet. In a few seconds, a hairdresser applied a creamy, orange-colored substance called Color Foam. The lights went out, came back in a few seconds, and showed the model with a lustrous hair-do. It was all a trick, an announcer explained. The girl with the finished hair-do is a sister of the girl who used the Color Foam. But the second girl used Color Foam that morning, he said."

G.E. injected a bit of show business into its first annual meeting held in California by introducing stockholders to Mr. Duane Ostrom, the company's 500,000th share owner who, as luck would have it, worked for G.E. and lived in California. Westinghouse

Electric interrupted one of its meetings while a shapely employee walked up to the podium and handed Vice-President John K. Hodnette a glass of desalted sea water from the company's desalting plant at Point Loma, California. Sometimes stockholders themselves get in the act, as happened at a Continental Can annual meeting when, as the company's post meeting report put it, "A 12-year-old shareholder surprised everyone by singing 'Happy Birthday' to General Clay."

Another entertaining feature at some annual meetings is the gift to stockholders. Stockholders have received one-pound boxes of "Candy-by-Wire" sweets from Western Union, cigarettes from P. Lorillard, ashtrays from Raytheon, chewing gum from Warner-Lambert, a pound of coffee from W. R. Grace, a Brownie Bullet II camera from Eastman Kodak, a plastic bag full of Prestone upholstery cleaner, Smooth-On MT-13 resin repair cement, an eight-inch Eveready flashlight from Union Carbide, and a twelve-inch long-playing record from CBS.

One particularly off-beat gift was a coloring book distributed to stockholders of Season-all Industries, Inc., an aluminum building products manufacturer. One page of the book showed a "typical" aluminum products dealer who "used to make lots of money, but now he just cuts prices." Stockholders were instructed to "Color this fellow good and blue." The next page showed a Season-all dealer, and stockholders were advised to "Color him green for lots of profit dollars."

Perhaps the most memorable gift ever distributed at an annual meeting went to the more than one hundred stockholders attending the SFC Financial Corporation's 1963 get-together. President Theodore H. Silbert gave each of these lucky people two free shares of their company's stock from his personal holdings in honor of his thirtieth year with the corporation. Among the least memorable gifts was an empty canister given to loss-plagued United States Hoffman Machinery owners.

No rundown on corporate largesse would be complete, of course, without mentioning the complimentary corporate lunch. This festivity reached its zenith during the decade just past. This period witnessed such marvelous stockholder repasts as creamed lobster à la General Motors, fresh strawberries and pecan pie served up by the Chesapeake & Ohio, a buffet and all the beer investors could drink from Jacob Ruppert, Inc., buffet and cocktails at American Research and Development Corporation, and boneless squab and wild rice—topped off by cigars for the gents and orchids for the ladies—courtesy of Western Air Lines.

Enlightened management, in some instances aided by changes in state laws permitting locally incorporated firms to hold their annual meetings outside the state's borders for the first time in history, is making it possible for many stockholders to attend their company's meeting who never really had the opportunity before.

Avco Corporation, Johns-Manville Corporation, Lockheed Aircraft Corporation, United Fruit Company, and W. R. Grace are but a few of the companies who rotate their annual meetings about the country. In 1965, for the first time in its history, General Motors left Wilmington, Delaware, and traveled to Detroit. ACF Industries' 64-year record of New Jersey annual meetings was ended by its journey to St. Louis, which Chairman William T. Taylor said enabled "our officers and directors to exchange views with a broader cross-section of persons interested in the company."

Closed-circuit television has permitted such corporations as General Mills and American Machine & Foundry to meet with stockholders in several cities simultaneously. RCA has been doing this since 1964 via color TV, and one major company even gave serious thought to holding its annual meeting over open-circuit television via the ABC-TV network. This would have enabled every TV set owner in America to sit in on the proceedings.

A relatively few companies such as Westinghouse, General Mills, and Middle South Utilities hold regional stockholders' meetings throughout the year in addition to their annual get-together. Middle South goes still further and meets with investors in Great Britain, Holland, Belgium, West Germany, and Switzerland. "We view our European investor relations as something of a trail blazing effort which turned out to be eminently worthwhile for Middle South," said the company's late president, Edgar H. Dixon, who originated the idea.

Corporations are not only bringing their annual meetings to a wider geographical distribution of stockholders than ever before, they are also holding them in some marvelously pleasant surroundings. American Machine & Foundry, which manufactures pin-setting equipment, for example, held one of its annual meetings in a bowling alley where stockholders were permitted to bowl free of charge. Brunswick Corporation, which makes golfing gear, held a meeting at Chicago's South Shore Country Club, where share owners were given free golf balls and professional instruction on how to hit them. White Motor conducted its meeting in a service and parts center, and the Matson Navigation Company traditionally holds its annual meeting aboard the luxury liner *Monterey,* berthed in San Francisco Harbor.

Chief executive officers, with increasing regularity, are capitalizing on their companies' annual meetings by using them as vehicles for local publicity and frequently national publicity on major issues of the day. Ford Motor chairman Henry Ford II, for example, spoke out in favor of tax cuts to stimulate consumer spending and increase the economy's growth rate.

Occasionally, of course, an attempt at the profound can collapse into pompous nonsense. An illustration of this, taken from an annual meeting report to stockholders made by the president of a pharmaceutical company is worth quoting at length. The president informed his company's owners:

> It is impossible, to foretell the precise nature of the problems that will confront us or the specific skills and capacities which these problems will demand.
>
> But there are no signs that as a company we will be spared any of the problems arising from containment, on the one hand, and global expansion, diversification and product discovery through research and development, on the other hand.
>
> But, even if we are called upon to face a still greater challenge, do not underrate our capacities, our energies, our potentialities or our zeal for greatness.
>
> For the moment we must keep pace to a different drum, but unlike the ocean we can and will hasten our tide.
>
> We know the value of stern discipline and vigorous unremitting effort.
>
> We know that high qualities and achievements are not matters of chance, but the product of long, hard toil.
>
> We know we are, more than ever, masters of our own fate—for

we have the will to translate knowledge into action and to gain further knowledge from action.

We know we can face and meet the travail of uncertainty and the unknown.

These are things we know!

Now, there is something I want you to know.

It has been said "that no single principle can answer all of life's complexities". I propound, however, that the challenge of the future lies in the human heart, in the realm of the spirit. Sustained by a high faith we call upon ourselves, as did our forebears, to transmit challenge into triumph.

I have publicly stated that it is the avowed objective of this Company to be great. I pledge to you that this generation of superb organization, endowed with a determination as strong as the coil of life itself, will meet its commitment.

For we believe:

"The woods are lovely, dark and deep

"And we, too have promises to keep

"And miles to go before we sleep."

The moment of truth for all annual meeting chairmen, even the poets, comes when their formal report is finished and the meeting is thrown open to questions from the floor.

As a stockholder, you have the right to begin cross-examining management from the instant the meeting is called to order. It's customary, however, to permit the chairman to say a few words of welcome, introduce the company's directors and officers, and describe the plans for lunch—if any—before unleashing the questions.

This usually begins when the chairman turns the meeting over to the company's secretary, who formally opens the meeting by announcing when the proxy statement containing the items of business to be acted upon was mailed to stockholders. This agenda is outlined in the proxy statement's notice-of-meeting section, and the first tip-off that a storm is brewing often comes when a stockholder leaps to his feet and says, "Mr. Chairman, I rise to the Notice of Meeting."

This bit of strategy enables owners to question immediately any item of business scheduled to be discussed at the meeting, and more than one annual meeting has come to grief at this early point in the game.

Once the chairman has navigated this reef, he must attempt to sail a peaceful course through the other phases of the meeting preceding his formal report. The first of these are usually routine, such as the announcement that a quorum of stockholders is present in person or by proxy so that business can be lawfully conducted, the motion to dispense with the reading of the minutes of last year's meeting, and the naming of inspectors of election to police the tallying of ballots on matters to be voted upon at the meeting.

The chairman then gets down to the items of business on which the stockholders have been asked to vote. This is the point at which every responsible owner of the company can make an important contribution, provided he has troubled himself to understand the issues. In fact, management can often profit from such a survey of stockholder sentiment, obtained on the spot and free of charge.

These items vary from one company's meeting to the next, but they include management requests that stockholders approve proposals involving employee pension plans, selling shares of the company's stock to employees at slightly below the market price, giving key executives options to buy the stock over a period of years either at or below the current market price, paying bonuses to top management, approving the appointment of the independent auditing firm selected by management, amending the company's certificate of incorporation so as to increase the amount of its total authorized capital stock (owners usually approve this proposal automatically, as it permits management to split the outstanding stock), election of directors, and transacting any other business that may properly come before the meeting.

Stockholders themselves, thanks to the Securities Exchange Act of 1934, can also propose items of business for share owners to approve at their company's annual meeting. These matters, just like those proposed by management itself, are spelled out in the proxy statement. The only difference is that management can use the statement to present its arguments against or for stockholder proposals, while you as a stockholder are denied a similar right to present your views on management's proposals. The only way you can register your disapproval of management's intentions is to vote against them.

The only opportunity you have to do this is at the annual meeting, and by that time management's proposals have almost always been approved.

Stockholder proposals usually have to do with such fundamentals as rotating the site of the annual meeting, limiting the amount of executive compensation and pension benefits, requiring executives who get stock at cut-rate prices under option plans to hold their shares for several years before selling them, and eliminating the stagger system of electing directors, which prohibits stockholders from replacing their company's entire board in any one year. Under SEC rules, a stockholder's proposal may not be repeated two years in a row unless it received at least 3 per cent of the votes cast in the first go-round. If it does not receive that much of the vote, two years have to elapse before it may be brought up again. The second time the proposal is made it must receive a 6 per cent vote and the third time a 10 per cent vote to allow it to appear the following year.

In a story on annual meetings published in *Fortune* a few years ago, a public relations counselor was quoted as saying that "the purpose of annual meetings is to adjourn." In American industry today, only the most antediluvian managements are buying this outdated point of view. Most modern corporations take extraordinary pains to hold reasonably informative meetings that are easy to get to and have been most carefully planned for the benefit of both share owners and management. The best way to appreciate the extent of this planning is to go behind the scenes and examine what your company's management has done to prepare itself for your arrival at the hotel in which its annual meeting is likely to be held.

The moment you've passed through the hotel's revolving doors, you should see the first of a series of signs pointing to your company's annual meeting. If you get lost and need directions, just ask a desk clerk, bellboy, or elevator operator, who will be happy to point you in the right direction.

As you near the meeting room, you'll probably see a coatroom with a sign saying "No Tipping Please." The management of your company has taken care of all gratuities, and has told the hatcheck girls to be ready for anything. At one A.T. & T. meeting, for instance, a lady walked up to the coatroom and without blinking an eye checked her eighteen-month-old baby, a bottle of milk, and the child's dolly.

After you've checked your coat, you'll begin noticing attractive people standing around wearing name tags on their bosoms. These people are company employees, many of them secretaries, whose job it is to make you feel comfortable and wanted. Each of them has been carefully briefed so they know the location of the nearest rest rooms, how to summon a physician if a stockholder feels faint, how to handle stockholders who try to smuggle battery-driven bull horns or other disruptive devices into the meeting, how to operate the microphones given to share owners during the question and answer period, and what to do when two or more stockholders threaten each other with physical violence—a not uncommon occurrence.

Before being ushered to your seat, you'll most likely have to stop by a registration desk. This is management's front-line command post, and it's used to determine who gets into the meeting and who doesn't, to handle last-minute voting by stockholders on issues before the meeting, to answer share owner questions, and to provide the chairman of the meeting with a card index containing the name of every person in the auditorium at the time he walks up to the podium and gavels the meeting to order.

If you're a registered stockholder of the company, or if you hold the proxy of such a stockholder, you'll be automatically admitted to the meeting. There's every chance that your husband, wife, or children will be admitted too if you request it. Newspaper reporters, security analysts, and representatives of other firms who are curious to see how your company handles its stockholder meeting will also undoubtedly be welcomed.

The people sitting behind the registration desk, just like the hosts and hostesses with their name tags, have been drilled within an inch of their lives on how to get you into the meeting without ruffling your feathers. The people with the easiest jobs are those assigned to the desk marked "Guests and Visitors Register Here." All they have to do is get each outsider to fill in a small card with his or her name, company name if any, and address. The people with the tough jobs are those sitting at the tables marked "Stockholders and Holders of Proxies Register Here." This assignment is nerve-racking because it involves dealing with the company's owners, and with their proxies, who ultimately determine everything from the size of the chairman's retirement pension to the men and women elected to serve on the company's board of directors.

Most stockholders fill out their proxies when they receive them at home, and mail them back to the company weeks in advance of the meeting. When the proxies are received at corporate headquarters they are checked, and then processed—often by computers—so that management knows from one day to the next how the voting stands on each question before the meeting.

Stockholders attending the meeting in person, however, can turn in their proxies when they register, and change their vote right up to the minute the polls are officially closed following the question and answer period. If you decide to hand your proxy in to the people manning the registration desk, they must first make certain that it's not invalid because it's undated, contains a stamped or typed signature, is not signed on the signature line, is a joint-tenant proxy with both names signed in similar handwriting, and so on.

If you've already sent in your proxy, you'll simply be asked to fill out a stockholder-registration form with a space for your name, the name or names in which your stock is registered, and a check mark showing that you've sent in your proxy and have thus already voted on the issues before the meeting. If your shares are held in the name of your broker, you'll be given a proxy or paper ballot and allowed to vote your shares any way you wish. The normally insignificant number of votes cast on annual meeting day will be combined with the votes already cast and the totals announced at the conclusion of the proceedings.

As you leave the registration desk, walk past the lobby displays, and are ushered to your seat, you may notice a few things that require an explanation. The first are the "Reserved" signs on the choice seats in the first rows near the stage. These are usually put aside for members of the press, who must see and hear everything that happens so they can write their stories, for the company's officers and directors, who will be introduced during the meeting, and for stockholders who are hard of hearing.

Between the front row of seats and the stage you'll probably see a solitary chair and a funny-looking gadget that looks like a skinny typewriter standing on a thin steel tripod. This setup is for the stenotypist who will attempt to take down everything that's said during the meeting. Few stenotypists can catch every word that's spoken or mumbled by people in various parts of the hall, and because of this you may see a tape recorder or two at work as a backstop so that the official transcript of the meeting can be as faithful as possible to what actually took place. This is so even though microphones are used to amplify the voices of all those participating in the meeting. Microphones are also used to deamplify the voices of stockholders whose antics, in the opinion of the chairman, threaten to disrupt the meeting. Many an obstreperous stockholder has found himself shouting into a dead mike right at the height of his oratory.

The central point of all annual meetings is the speakers' table, from which the chairman and his lieutenants attempt to guide the meeting to a smooth and successful conclusion. The chairman is almost always accompanied by the company's secretary and general counsel, who have important roles to play in the proceedings, as you'll see in a moment. These three men, incidently, have not arrived at the speakers' table alone. They are accompanied by a pile of documents and binders including the company's bylaws, certificate of incorporation, affidavit of mailing of the notice of meeting, minutes of the last meeting, stockholder list, latest annual report, proxy statement, and what one company calls "the fat book," containing answers to all the questions that management figures may be asked during the meeting. The chairman, of course, can handle most questions himself, but he'll occasionally be tossed one on which he needs some help. The distinguished chairman of one giant corporation, after being thrown a particularly vexing query, told the stockholder "I don't know the answer to your question, sir, but I'll be very much surprised if someone doesn't hand me a slip of paper with the answer on it within sixty seconds." The paper arrived in forty-five seconds, thanks to the well-indexed thoroughness of the fat book.

Celanese Corporation once tried to take a little pressure off its chairman Harold Blancke by setting up a machine inside the entrance to the annual meeting that could answer 100 stockholder questions automatically. Investors eagerly interrogated the machine and received answers to everything from the cost of the company's annual report to the dividends from its foreign operations. Yet according to a Celanese executive, the number of stockholder questions fired at Mr. Blancke were "about the same" as the year before.

No two annual meetings are exactly alike. But there is a certain similarity to them, and if you would like to know what a typical stockholders meeting is like you can find out by reading the following amalgam of meetings held by corporations both large and small. They all begin when the chairman bangs the gavel and says:

Ladies and gentlemen, it is now 10 A.M. The meeting will please come to order.

As provided by the Bylaws, I, as chief executive officer of the Corporation, will serve as chairman of this meeting, and Mr. Harry Smith our General Counsel, will serve as Secretary.

On behalf of the Board of Directors, the officers and employees of the Corporation, I want to welcome you to this annual meeting of stockholders.

Before the formal portion of this meeting begins, I should like to introduce to you the directors and officers of the company. I imagine it would be best to withhold our applause until all of them have been introduced. (*Directors and officers are introduced.*)

I asked that the secretary present to this meeting a complete list of stockholders of record at the close of business April 15, arranged alphabetically, as prepared by the First National Bank, transfer agent of the Corporation and by Mr. Smith, our General Counsel. This list, throughout this meeting, will be open to inspection of any stockholder or person entitled to inspect it who might be present. The list has been open for inspection for the past 30 days at company headquarters.

SECRETARY:
Mr. Chairman, I present the list you speak of to the meeting.

CHAIRMAN:
Mr. Smith, will you please report on the Notice of Meeting.

SECRETARY:
Mr. Chairman, each stockholder of record on March 12, the record date for this meeting, was mailed, addressed to his record

or designated address, a Notice of Meeting, Proxy Statement and Proxy Card. This mailing was accomplished on March 25.

The material mailed to stockholders complied with the laws of New York where the Company is incorporated. I present to the meeting the original affidavit as to the mailing of the Notice of the Meeting and other materials to the stockholders. They read as follows: (*reads affidavit of mailing and Notice of Special Meeting*).

CHAIRMAN:

The affidavit of mailing, Notice of Meeting, and Proxy Statement will be filed in the minute book of the Corporation immediately following the minutes of this meeting.

If there is any person present who has not turned in his Proxy and now wishes to do so, will he please raise his hand, and his Proxy will be collected.

All the proxy cards that were sent in before the meeting have been tabulated. On the basis of this preliminary count, we can determine whether the necessary quorum prescribed by the Bylaws is present. I'll call on the Secretary for a report as to the quorum.

SECRETARY:

Mr. Chairman, the number of shares of stock of the Company issued and outstanding and entitled to vote at this meeting are————.

The tabulation of the Proxies received and processed so far shows there are present at this meeting, either in person or by Proxy, the holders of at least————shares of stock, constituting more than 50 per cent of the outstanding shares entitled to notice of and to vote at the meeting. Under our Bylaws, a quorum is a majority of the outstanding stock.

The original proxies are at the entrance to the meeting room and will be open for inspection at this meeting.

CHAIRMAN:

A quorum is present. Therefore, the meeting is lawfully convened for the transaction of business.

The minutes of the last meeting of stockholders, which was last year's annual meeting, may be dispensed with, if we have a motion to do so.

MR. BROWN:

I move that the meeting dispense with the reading of the minutes of last year's annual meeting.

CHAIRMAN:

Thank you.

MR. GREEN:

I second the motion.

CHAIRMAN:

Thank you. It has been duly moved and seconded that the reading of the minutes of last year's annual meeting of stockholders be dispensed with. All in favor please say, "Aye." Those opposed please signify by saying, "No." The motion is carried and the reading of minutes will be dispensed with. We will now proceed with the business of the meeting. The first item is the appointment of two impartial Judges of Election for the purpose of conducting the vote. The two judges are Mr. Edwards and Mr. Murphy, who have subscribed an oath to execute faithfully their duties as prescribed by law and our Bylaws. Will Mr. Edwards please read that oath.

MR. EDWARDS:

(*Reads oath.*)

CHAIRMAN:

Thank you, Mr. Edwards. Will you please file the oath with the Secretary.

This meeting has been called to consider: (*election of Board of Directors and other matters*).

In a moment, I will call for motions addressed to these purposes. I believe some stockholders will want to discuss the motions to come before they are taken to a final vote. We will follow a procedure designed to help us conduct this meeting in an orderly fashion without prolonging it unduly and still be democratic and fair. Therefore, I am going to suggest we handle the discussion this way: The counting of votes is a time-consuming process. To save time, we will proceed with the voting directly after the motions are made and seconded. At the conclusion of the voting, the Judges of Election will commence counting. I will leave the polls open while I make a report on Company operations. I will then open the meeting for discussion. Following the close of discussion, I will give stockholders who wish to do so an opportunity to change their vote as a result of the discussion.

Stockholders will have this opportunity to change their votes before the polls are finally closed. In this way, we can keep the meeting moving ahead while preserving the principles of democracy and fairness.

I now call for the moving and seconding of motions.

MR. PORTER:

Mr. Chairman, I move the adoption of the following resolution:

Resolved, that assuming the incumbent Directors are up for re-election, Mr. Goldman, Mr. Longacre, Mr. Walters, etc., each be continued in office as a Director until the next annual meeting of stockholders and until a successor shall have been duly elected and shall qualify.

CHAIRMAN:

Thank you.

MR. REDMOND:

Mr. Chairman, I second the motion.

CHAIRMAN:

Thank you.

Are there any other motions?

(Note: The meeting's official business is restricted to those items listed in the Notice of the Meeting. Therefore, resolutions may be declared out of order by the Chairman, on advice of Counsel, unless they match those listed on the ballot. In the event an out-of-order motion is made, the Chairman may say:

"Sir, I am sorry, but the Bylaws of this Corporation and the laws of the state in which it was incorporated, require that any resolutions deal directly with the purpose for which the meeting was called. That is: [list items of business] as set forth in the Proxy material mailed to you. Therefore, I am required to rule your motion out of order.")

(*If a proper motion is made*)

CHAIRMAN:

Thank you. Is there a second?

MR. BLUM:

(*Motion is seconded*)

CHAIRMAN:

Is there any other motion?

(*Remaining resolution is moved and seconded*)

There being no other items of business, I declare the floor closed to further motions. The polls are declared open for the reception of votes. I might say at this time there is no need for anyone who has turned in his Proxy to do anything. His Proxy will be counted as his vote. However, if someone wishes to change the vote on his Proxy, please raise your hand and an usher will give you a ballot. Or, if you wish to hand in a Proxy at this time, please give it to an usher.

I would like to say again that there is no need for any stockholder to vote by ballot if he has already mailed in or turned in his Proxy—unless he wishes to change his Proxy vote. Will those who wish to receive a ballot or turn in a Proxy vote please raise their hands.

(*Ushers distribute and collect ballots and Proxies.*)

As I mentioned earlier, there will be full opportunity for discussion before the polls close. And following discussion, stockholders will have this opportunity to change their votes before the polls are finally closed.

Do we have all the votes?

We apparently have for the present. Since there is to be some discussion, I will not declare the polls closed. However, the Inspectors will canvas the vote thus far and will retire to prepare their report. In the meantime, I want to bring you up to date on operations of the Company.

(*Report to stockholders*)

And now, I would like to open the floor for discussion. The ushers will please come into the aisles with their microphones.

If you will indicate your desire to ask a question, an usher will come into your aisle with a microphone. Please give your name so we may have it for the minutes of the meeting.

The meeting is now open for questions.

(*Full Discussion*)

I think we have all had the opportunity to discuss the issues at hand, and we are now ready to resume the business of the meeting.

Does any stockholder present wish to change the vote which

he has already cast? If so, will you please raise your hand so that the ushers may give you a ballot.

I believe that anyone who might wish to change his vote as a result of the discussion has had an opportunity to do so.

Therefore, I now declare that the polls are closed and will ask the Election Judges to submit their report.

MR. MURPHY:

I hereby present to the Meeting the Certificate of Inspectors. It reads: (*Reads Certificate of Election*)

CHAIRMAN:

I declare that Messrs. Goldman, Longacre, Walters, etc., have been duly elected as Directors of the Corporation, each to serve until the next Annual Meeting of Stockholders and until his successor has been duly elected and shall qualify.

I want to thank all of you again for coming. I will now entertain a motion to adjourn.

MR. BROWN:

I move the meeting be adjourned.

MR. GREEN:

I second the motion.

CHAIRMAN:

All in favor please say, "Aye."
All opposed say, "No."
The Meeting is adjourned.

That's what the average annual meeting is like.

What you need to know to get the most out of attending your company's meeting is another question, which different experts answer in different ways.

One of the most provocative answers was supplied by the late Charles E. King, of Chicago, who was in a unique position to speak out on this subject. On the one hand Mr. King was the president of two stockholder-owned rubber companies, and on the other hand he was a tub-thumping believer in stockholders rights who regularly preached the gospel to groups of investors on topics such as "How to Attend a Stockholders Meeting."

"Why is it," Mr. King asked one group of share owners he addressed in Skokie, Illinois, "that if you own real estate investments instead of stocks the chances are that you visit the property every couple of months and talk to the manager and tenants? In fact, you watch that real estate investment pretty closely—and you do it personally.

"But why, when you buy stocks, do you take such an indifferent attitude? Many of you ignore the Annual Report and give it a perfunctory glance . . . and the Proxy Statement upon which your proxy vote is solicited is tossed aside as you sign your name to the proxy which returns the same gang to office year after year whether they are knaves or honest men, whether they are capable or bunglers. . . .

"Fortunately, following the example started in New York, more and more Midwest investors are watching their investments by going to the Stockholders Meetings of the companies in which they have invested, and asking questions about management's stewardship of their investments. DO NOT FORGET THAT THE MANAGEMENT'S INTERESTS ARE NOT THE SAME AS YOURS AS A STOCKHOLDER."

With this off his chest, Mr. King then turned to specific action that stockholders can take to get more out of their companies' annual meetings:

1. Having decided to go to the meeting of the company in which you have sunk your money—for better or worse—let's hope it is where you can get to it. A favorite trick of company management is to hide out someplace where you can't find them.

If your company does not meet in a place convenient to stockholders, write the company President and ask why, and if you don't get results use the Proxy Statement under the proposal rule available to small stockholders to make their views known to your fellow owners.

2. Now, when you get to the meeting where do you sit? Get up front where you can hear and be heard for you should participate in the meeting. Often, the meeting is packed with employees or management stooges who boo or jeer anyone who dares to speak not on the signal of their boss. Remember, this is the meeting of stockholders and YOU ARE THE BOSS.

3. Don't be cowed if the Chairman asks you to state how many shares you own. Don't be ashamed if you own only five

or ten shares because large or small your investment is important to *you*. If you get this question I suggest you reply, "Mr. Chairman, the number of shares that I own is contained in the stockholders list before you and you may consult it if you wish. But I want to assure you that the shares I own are important to me and I have every right to address this meeting of Stockholders and I do not intend to be cowed by your question."

Mr. King then goes on to list several "con man" stunts some managements use to prevent stockholders from fully airing their views:

1. Equipping the chairman of the meeting with a powerful microphone system and then denying similar communication to the stockholders.

2. Running a long movie about some phase of the company's operation so that everybody's patience is exhausted when the question and answer period comes.

3. Scheduling the meeting for noon, when everyone is hungry and wants to go to lunch. This makes for a short meeting.

4. Failing to schedule a time for shareholders' questions.

5. Arranging for a management stooge in the audience to call for adjournment while some stockholder is left talking on his feet.

"I don't want to paint a picture that all managements act this way," Mr. King said in wrapping up his remarks. "On the contrary, progressive companies with smart managements welcome participation of their shareholders in the Annual Meeting."

OUR MAN IN THE BOARD ROOM:

THE CORPORATE DIRECTOR

When the pipe-puffing young professor of Business I sets out to initiate his students into the mysteries of corporate organization, he usually starts by drawing a little square box on the blackboard to stand for the stockholders, and then some vertical chalk lines running down from that box to a smaller one representing the board of directors. He then takes a contemplative pull on his briar and explains that ownership of stock has become widely dispersed, and 50,000 stockholders, or even 500, cannot run a company efficiently. The company's owners, therefore, elect a small group of representatives called directors, and delegate to them the authority to manage the company's affairs. The directors make all major policy decisions, and see to it that the company is run for the glory and profit of the stockholders. The directors elect the officers—another little box on the blackboard—who then operate the company with the authority delegated to them by the board.

All this, as the professor knows, is theory. In real life, it doesn't quite work that way. Close observers of the corporate scene know that in the majority of companies, the board of directors identifies far more with management than with ownership.

It would be well, therefore, if stockholders understood a little bit more about the responsibilities of corporate directors, who come from all levels of society and include college professors, lawyers, Wall Street tycoons, in-laws of company presidents, scientists, movie stars, as well as an ex-astronaut and an ex-Vice-President of the United States.

The more than 70,000 directors who sit on thousands of boards legally have all the powers of the corporation and commensurate responsibilities. The fundamental legal responsibility of the board of directors is to manage the company in the interests of the shareholders. American Telephone & Telegraph's nineteen directors, for example, have to look after $33 billion worth of assets on behalf of over 3 million shareholders. The fifteen directors of Standard Oil (New Jersey) are responsible for $12 billion in assets, 40 per cent of them located outside U.S. borders.

Managing these assets can mean anything from bringing out a new product or acquiring a new subsidiary to fending off a bid for control that the directors think is not in the company's interest. It even includes approving major contributions to charity. (Evelyn Y. Davis, one of the inveterate annual meeting attenders, habitually charges that such contributions are a waste of assets unless the cause is directly related to the company's business. When she was told by A.T.&T.'s chairman, Frederick Kappel, that A.T.&T.'s annual donations exceeded $10 million, she exclaimed, "I'm about to faint." "It would be helpful," Mr. Kappel replied.)

Although directors are not legally trustees, they are fiduciaries who must use diligence, honesty, and prudence in running the company's affairs. The exact degree of their responsibility is still evolving through court decisions. They can be held personally liable for harm done the corporation, but generally the courts have not punished them for what turned out to be honest mistakes of judgment. The courts have not even held that an inactive director who misses board meetings is culpable, unless it can be clearly shown that the company was thereby harmed. When the directors do not perform their duties to the satisfaction of share owners, they are supposed to be replaced by better men. That's what the professor's chalk lines mean.

State laws and corporate bylaws spell out many of the powers of stockholders and directors. Generally, stockholders have to consent in basic matters like mergers, dissolutions, and recapitalization plans. Directors are in charge of borrowing money, floating stock, approving budgets, and deciding how much of the year's earnings will be retained and how much paid out in dividends. At least once a year, under most state laws, share owners have to be convened to receive a financial report on their company and to elect the board of directors. While the states fix the minimum number of directors a corporation must have—three in New York State—the average board of a publicly-held manufacturing company numbers eleven. Among nonmanufacturing companies the average is fourteen. Nine out of ten manufacturing companies elect a full slate of directors annually; the rest use a stagger system, electing three or four directors every year to serve for longer terms. Some states do not allow the stagger system because it can mean retaining part of a board that has lost the approval of the electorate—rather like "lame duck" senators.

In drawing his organizational chart the professor really knows that his neat lines of authority embody a certain amount of corporate folklore. Widely scattered share ownership, with no individual or group holding a large block of stock, has created a void at the top of many big U.S. companies which is filled by the directors or officers. Share owners have become a backstop group that has the ultimate power to protect its own interests, but is rarely willing or able to take the initiative.

While shareholders elect directors, they do not nominate them as a rule. A subcommittee of the board draws up a management slate; it is usually accepted without challenge. The board is thus able to perpetuate itself almost indefinitely, provided it keeps stockholders happy. Barring a radical change of control, a director, once elected, generally serves for as long as he cares to. Only one company in four has a mandatory retirement age for directors. That is why three companies out of four can tell of some time or other in their history when they had an elderly director who would snooze quietly through meetings until his favorite subject was mentioned, when he would instantly snap to attention and catch everyone else off guard. The 1965 edition of Poor's Register of Corporations, Directors and Executives lists 1402 directors over eighty.

There is no machinery by which thousands of scattered stockholders can propose candidates for the director's job with hope of success, unless they have organized leadership. After a management representative reads off the management slate of nominations at the annual meeting, the chairman may, pursuing the model of corporate democracy, ask if there are any additional nominations from the floor. A lone shareholder will occasionally get up and nominate someone else. Usually it is only a gesture of protest. Unable to find a well-known figure who will lend his name to the occasion, the stockholder often has to nominate himself, amid groans and boos from his companions. In spite of the assemblage of notables nominated to the first board of directors of Communications Satellite Corporation, one small stockholder arose at the first meeting and tossed in his own name as a candidate. Such rebels seldom poll more than their own votes. At a meeting of Briggs Manufacturing Company in 1963, when the company had had only one profitable year since 1956, stockholder Edward J. Capper, who with his wife owned 725 shares, did a little better when he nominated himself. He got over 10 per cent of the vote cast, indicating that many share owners agreed that something new was needed.

This nominating system has been likened to that in U.S. politics, where most candidates for office are selected by party leaders. No ordinary voter far down the line, enrolled in the party but not active in its top echelons, can put up his next-door neighbor as a candidate and expect to get many votes. A provision for write-in votes, existing in many states, is so insignificant that the press seldom even reports the results.

In politics the system is well understood. The voter, in the end, can express disapproval of his party's candidates by voting for a rival slate. There is no such two-party choice in corporate elections, unless there happens to be a major fight for control going on. To put a rival slate before all the voters, a dissident stockholder has to file Form 14B with the Securities and Exchange Commission, obtain approval to solicit proxies, get a stockholder list from the company—usually disgorged only after a court battle—and then mail out publicity material calculated to discredit the slate of the incumbents and boost his own. Obviously, this costs money. Such fights are usually—but not always—led by men who have the funds to pay for them. These proxy fighters are aiming higher than does the average discontented stockholder, who merely wants things better run so he will get bigger dividends or a higher price for his stock. They aim at control, and if they obtain it, they can generally get the board to vote to reimburse them from the corporate treasury for the costs of the battle.

Despite the costs and headaches involved, it's a rare week that doesn't see a proxy fight launched for either representation on a board of directors or, less often, for control of the board and thereby control of the corporation. Few of these fights end up with a showdown vote by stockholders. More likely, the insurgents back off, or a settlement of some sort is reached. Of those proxy wars that carry to a conclusion by ballot, the insurgents do occasionally win, despite the odds stacked against them. The knowledge of this possibility creeps into the mind of every chief executive when there's a sudden and unexplained rise in the volume of trading of his company's stock.

When the board's committee on nominations is drawing up its slate, the company president, as administrative head, is given a stronger voice than he would have merely as one director. He is the one who has to "get along" with the board. At a panel discussion among one hundred corporate presidents reported by *Dun's Review,* the presidents maintained that they should not only have an important part in selecting directors but should be given a final veto power. "Boards are shaped by management," says one New York director. "Naturally this tends to keep the same executives in power. If a director were brought in that the president didn't want, it would be tantamount to a vote of no confidence. The Board wouldn't do that unless things were in a terrible mess. They'll go along with the president's wishes. Let's face it, corporate management is autocratic."

"Management, as long as it's successful and things are going well, is more than likely to have reversed the flow of authority from the boards to management so that it runs from management to boards," a speaker told a group of executives not long ago. "The corporate executives are in the drivers' seats nowadays," says another director. "Just compare the amount of material published on how to be an executive with what's published on directing. About all that's written on directors is how the chief executive can make better use of them."

In practice neither investors nor investment companies give much weight to the composition of the board when deciding to invest in a certain company. "We make up a list of points considered important in studying a specific company, mostly related to the industry it's in," says the head of a huge investment firm. "The make-up of the board is fairly far down the line." To banks and potential lenders, however, a "strong board" is a factor in their esteem. "If one or more board members are nationally known businessmen it would certainly make us more inclined to lend the company money," says one banker.

As large corporations evolved from privately owned, owner-managed firms, the founder often invited his friends and relatives to fill out the board although he remained the boss. Some corporations are still run by the original owner's family or representatives. Such companies tend to have boards made up almost entirely of officers of the company—"inside" boards—and are likely to defer to the wishes of the founding family even though its actual control may have been much diminished by public stock offerings. There is little doubt that Peter Grace runs W. R. Grace & Company even though his family ownership is less than 10 per cent and there are more than 40,000 other stockholders.

The tradition of a closely knit board pervades whole industries. None of the big tobacco companies, for example, had even one outside director until 1961, when Liggett & Myers put a member of its legal firm on its board. American Tobacco did not acquire an outside board member until 1964, and even then selected the president of its management consulting company who, after all, had to be careful not to do or say anything to upset the client relationship.

According to the National Industrial Conference Board, there has been a trend in recent years toward more outside directors. About 60 per cent of manufacturing companies, and 90 per cent of non-manufacturing companies, have boards on which outside members outnumber the inside members. Nevertheless, among quite a few large, well-established corporations, such as Du Pont, the tradition of an inside board, built up over the years, remains strong.

The shareholder who wants to form an opinion about whether his company would be better off with an outside or inside board finds that there is no real standard for measuring board performance. No one has found enough cases where he can definitely assign credit or blame for a certain decision on the board, as opposed to the executives, to make a good comparison. A study by Professor Stanley C. Vance, of the University of Oregon School of Business Administration, attempted to compare companies with inside and outside boards according to the way the companies fared in eleven categories—growth of sales, net income, employment, etc., and various kinds of productivity. He concluded that companies with inside boards outperformed those whose boards were dominated by outsiders. On the other hand, the American Institute of Management, using a ten-point weighted evaluation system of its own devising, decided that outside boards were more effective.

The difficulty that faces outside directors was expressed at a Columbia University symposium:

> It's commonly said that you're going to have a lot of outside members on the board to check and double check on what management's doing. Now I don't know how you check what a man is doing unless you're able to evaluate it on knowledge you have yourself. I mean, it's not to easy to sit down and say, "I'm going to check the general manager of this company." You've got to know first what to check, what to look for, what kind of standards to apply, and what kind of results to judge by. So that this business of checking people, unless you know very much about what you're going to check, is to me just a lot of words and not very much substance . . . There are an awful lot of areas where what we commonly call judgment, or intuition, or whatnot, isn't good enough.

The case against an inside board was put by another speaker at the symposium:

> In comes the vice president in charge of production, who hates the guts of the man who created the Board. Yet he happens to be on the board also. He disagrees with his chief's philosophy of management. He possibly disagrees with his board of directors' philosophy. Yet, he has put in thirty years of his life with the company, it's the only company he really knows. He is dependent for his livelihood, and his family, his wife and children, on the income that he gets from that company; he's not particularly in-

terested in trying to go outside and get himself a comparable job. How can he stand up before the stockholders and say, I "endorse everything the board has done." He can't. Yet, the poor fellow can't afford to say, "I quit, because I disagree."

The board chairman of one of America's great corporations agrees with this latter view, though he expresses it in somewhat different terms. "All the inside directors do is keep the chairs warm at Board meetings. They don't mean a thing. It's the outside directors who count."

Before the Securities Exchange Act of 1934, share owners did not have to be given much information about the men nominated to be directors. Now the proxy material sent out by management before the election must list the chief business connection of the nominee, any relationship in which he deals with the corporation—such as lawyer, supplier, consultant—and the nominee's salary provided he's one of the three highest paid officers and earns above $30,000 a year. The amount of stock a director owns must also be disclosed. Some states require a minimum number of shares—one in New Jersey—to qualify as a director; corporate bylaws also sometimes specify minimum amounts. Most directors feel this is unnecessary. "If a man does not already feel identified with the interests of stockholders, no ten, twenty or even 100 shares is going to make him different," says one company chairman.

To most share owners it may seem that the board of directors acts as smoothly as a well-programmed computer—a fallacy that management is usually anxious to preserve. The management of the S. Klein Department Stores, Inc., for example, took the unusual step of opening its annual meeting with a denial of rumors of policy differences within the board room, calling them "so much fiddle-faddle."

A startling glimpse behind the board room door was offered when Curtis Publishing Company's perhaps overly articulate executives and directors fell to squabbling in public in 1964. Despite its respected position as the publisher of well-known magazines, such as the *Ladies' Home Journal, Holiday,* and the venerable *Saturday Evening Post,* Curtis had been losing ground for a decade. New banking interests came to the rescue, and a new chief executive named Matthew J. Culligan was hired. But the methods of this flamboyant ex-advertising salesman famed for his black eye patch aroused so much opposition at hidebound old Curtis Publishing that two inside directors soon brought charges to the board that Culligan was mismanaging the company. What followed was a custard-pie comedy fit for the pages of the Curtis kiddies magazine *Jack and Jill*. First the two directors were forced to resign. Then an investigating committee of the board cleared Culligan of financial mismanagement, but upheld charges that he had committed errors of judgment—whereupon Culligan resigned. After a fruitless search for a strong outside chief executive the directors elevated an inside man to the job. Amid the furor of discharges and resignations that followed, a notable group of artists and writers took an ad in the *New York Times* to salute four of the men who had left in a huff. "It only proves," said one director privately, "that temperament is one thing directors can't direct."

Certain well-established conventions often influence the selection of directors. Banks, for example, seek solid local businessmen whose presence will attract commercial banking business and impress depositors. Real estate firms recruit astute lawyers versed in the complexities of real estate deals. The value of "influence" has been recognized ever since the days when Jay Gould decorated his boards with Boss Tweed of New York City and assorted state legislators. Nowadays companies that like to have prestige in Washington get former generals, admirals, cabinet members, or socially well connected Washingtonians to fill out a "big name" board.

General Electric's board was graced by two ex-Secretaries of Defense at the same time, Neil McElroy and Thomas S. Gates. General Lucius Clay, now a senior partner of Lehman Brothers, sits on nine boards. Former Vice-President Richard Nixon got two board memberships as soon as he went back to law practice. Robert Roosa, Undersecretary of the Treasury for Monetary Affairs, joined the board of Prudential Life when he left Washington, as did former New Jersey Governor Robert A. Meyner when he retired from office. The most active Washingtonian in a business sense is George E. Allen, who rose to prominence during the Truman administration; by 1966 he was sitting on boards of thirty-two companies. Despite his popularity as a director, Mr. Allen is overshadowed by Boston financier Ralph Lowell, who is listed as an officer or director of forty-three corporations. Mr. Lowell, who is seventy-six, is chairman of the Boston Safe Deposit & Trust Company.

Professors and college presidents have been popping up to give weight to boards. Donald K. David, former Harvard Business School Dean, for instance, sat on nine boards at once.

There are more than 1000 women directors of American companies, and the Federation of Women Shareholders never misses a chance to suggest there should be more. The youngest is probably Miss Catherine Hohenlohe, great-grandaughter of William Boyce Thompson, who founded Newmont Mining Corporation, who was elected to Newmont's board at the age of twenty-two.

Companies in keen competition for consumer favor sometimes select national heroes to help their image with the public. When Spyros Skouras was fending off a bid by Charles Green to control Twentieth Century-Fox, he nominated General James A. Van Fleet, a recent hero of the Korean War, to his slate of directors and had Van Fleet circularize the stock owners on behalf of management, a move that may have helped Skouras win. Astronaut John Glenn, after retirement from the Marine Corps, joined the board of the Royal Crown Bottling Company.

When an English insurance company elected Lord Ogilvy, Princess Alexandra's brother-in-law, to its board in 1963, the big-name appeal backfired. "I just can't understand it," Lord Ogilvy said. "My family's record is simply appalling in the question of insurance claims. Without doubt we are first-class smashers of motor cars. As an insurance director, I am the perfect example of how to succeed in business without really trying."

Businessmen agree that there are not enough good directors to go around. "If you find an able fellow, he's not on one board, he's on six," says one top executive.

The chairman of another large company says: "We can get all the bankers or lawyers we want—they'd never turn me down because they figure sooner or later they'll get some business out of it. But try and find a good marketing man—it's next to impossible."

While Sidney Weinberg, partner of the investment banking firm of Goldman, Sachs & Company, and member of numerous boards of directors, says the most important quality of a director is independence, it is not a trait given much weight when a man is being considered. "Directors are not picked for their known ability to criticize," says one old-time board member. "You don't see John Kenneth Galbraith at the directors' table."

After studying the difficulty of getting first-rate board members, *Fortune* magazine came to the conclusion that the choice had to be made by intuition. "When it comes to choosing a board, one can throw all the books away," *Fortune* said.

Practically speaking, many directors often come onto a board because a large block of shares has been acquired by them or their firms, and it is understood that they are spokesmen for those interests. The point at which a shareholder puts out feelers for a board seat varies according to the distribution and number of shares outstanding. In a company with very widely dispersed ownership, 2 or 3 per cent of the stock is a significant amount. When Robert Young made his first bid for a seat on the New York Central board, he and his associates controlled only 3.1 per cent of the railroad's stock. He was refused, and didn't get one until he had won a bitter and costly proxy fight. But the late Billy Rose, the largest individual holder of A.T. & T.'s widely scattered stock, was given a board seat in 1965 though the ex-showman owned probably less than 1 per cent of its shares.

Where sizable blocks are owned by executives and directors, a larger amount is required to rate a board seat if you're a rank outsider wanting in. Norton Simon, of Hunt Foods, had acquired a potential 22 per cent of Canada Dry Corporation through common and convertible debentures before Canada Dry finally invited him to the board in 1964, acknowledging that "The election of Mr. Simon to the Board gives consideration to the ownership interest of Hunt Foods." Two foreign companies that held 17 per cent of Libby, McNeill & Libby were given seats on its board, as was the Nestlé Alimentana, S.A., of Switzerland, which also had an 18 per cent block. To prevent undue influence from such acquisitions, a board can always enlarge itself, as Libby, McNeill did. Conversely, when a fight for control looms, a board can fend off its opponents by reducing its size, leaving only directors who stand a good chance of re-election. The board of Boston & Maine Railroad, facing a bid by Patrick B. McGinnis for three board seats in 1965, rejected his approach and reduced its size from twenty-one to fourteen.

Members of brokerage firms are frequently found on corporate boards as watchdogs for the stock they and their customers have taken. A survey by the SEC in 1962 found that out of 4964 registered broker-dealers who replied to the questionnaires, 476 reported directorships in one or more listed companies, and 995 had representation on boards of one or more over-the-counter companies. Lehman Brothers, for example, had directors in fifty-eight listed and twenty-three over-the-counter companies; Kidder, Peabody & Company in twenty-three listed and twenty-nine unlisted companies.

The idea of having the underwriter represented arises before a public issue of stock is made, when he can be of special value in guiding the company through the requirements for registering and issuing stock, and can take large positions in the stock for himself and his customers. The underwriting agreement usually provides that the company will use its best efforts to get the underwriter elected to the board, which means nomination and almost certain election. Naturally, presence on the board puts the broker-dealer in a good position to obtain any future securities business the firm may have.

Utility companies are forbidden to have brokers on their boards, and the potential conflict of interest has perturbed the SEC for many years. In the SEC survey a few brokers reported that they were reluctant to have board membership. As a director, a broker may get inside information that would affect the price and value of the stock. Many underwriters have a close enough relationship with the companies they launch to obtain inside information anyway, but when the broker is actually on the board, there is a chance of conflict between his responsibilities to the general stockholders and to his firm and its clients. The SEC reported a case where a broker on a corporate board had advance knowledge that the company was going to reduce its dividend and used the knowledge in trading for discretionary accounts for his firm. In another case, a broker found out that the company was going to buy back its own stock at a favorable price, and purchased it for his wife's account and for customers. In the first case, the SEC prosecuted under the antifraud provisions of the Securities Act; in the second, the New York Stock Exchange fined the broker under an Exchange rule.

The stockholders or even the management itself may, however, be unaware of the use the broker is making of his inside knowledge. If a director trades for his own account, he must report his transactions to the SEC monthly and any profits made within a six-month period are recoverable by the company under Section 16 of the Securities Exchange Act of 1934. Not only by law but as a matter of business ethics it is pretty well recognized that when a broker serves as a director he has an obligation not to use inside information for his personal benefit. His duty with regard to disclosing information to customers is a more difficult problem. The Stock Exchange has tried to set standards for its members. In 1962 one of its circulars said:

> Every director has a fiduciary obligation not to reveal privileged information to anyone not authorized to receive it. . . . Any director of a corporation who is a partner, officer or employee of a member organization should recognize that his first responsibility in this area is to the corporation on whose board he serves. Thus a member firm director must meticulously avoid any disclosure of inside information to his partners, employees of the firm, his customers or his research or trading departments.

Despite such advice, some brokers told the SEC that they saw nothing wrong with using inside knowledge of favorable future developments to benefit their customers, since the customers, knowing the broker was on the board, expected that kind of service from him.

Although directors are responsible for the conduct of the company, the presence of able, experienced, and honest men on the board is no guarantee of smooth sailing. This has been proved time and time again by corporate disasters, such as the one that befell General Dynamics in 1961. The company had been put together by the brilliant, autocratic John Jay Hopkins, using the Electric Boat Company as a nucleus for a vast complex making nuclear reactors, motors, concrete products, and planes. In the course of numerous mergers the board was enlarged to thirty-two, even though Hopkins continued to call the tune. When General Dynamics' Convair Division in California, which functioned with a good deal of independence, wanted to go into the intermediate-range jet airliners business, the question never came before the full board, but was decided by its twelve-member executive committee.

Shortly before he died, in 1957, Hopkins pruned the board down to fifteen personally selected members, and hired Arkansas Lawyer and ex-Secretary of the Army Frank Pace to replace him as chief executive officer. In the spring of 1960, Pace told shareholders that the jet program would be one of General Dynamics' most successful ventures. The following September losses were serious enough to necessitate a dividend cut. The company plowed ahead with its jet program until, in July 1961, it became clear that the company was going to lose over $400 million on it. Seven directors took over as an executive committee to deal with the crisis, but nothing could repair the damage already done.

How much responsibility for the disaster belonged rightfully to the board? *Fortune,* in its story of the events, gave it a full measure of responsibility, indicting the whole top management: "It failed to recognize that the new age of advanced technology demands advanced management techniques. It failed to establish the intelligence system that would have given accurate and timely warning of danger. It failed to limit divisional programs to those that would not imperil the whole enterprise and failed to call a halt on one such program even when it appeared to be in grave danger. . . ." Among the directors at the critical time were R. C. Patterson, Jr., former U.S. ambassador and director of a dozen other big companies; H. A. Anderson of the First National Bank of Chicago; R. F. Windfohr, a prominent Texas oilman; and various other respected and seasoned businessmen. It is not uncommon for management to deliberately keep directors in the dark about matters of the first order of magnitude, fully confident that they will approve management's actions when it is brought to them almost after the fact. In late 1965, for example, merger negotiations between Worthington Corporation and I-T-E Circuit Breaker Company hit a snag when Worthington wanted to make public its offer. I-T-E's management balked. As it turned out, most of I-T-E's 14 directors weren't aware of the offer until they were called by reporters checking a Worthington press release, or until the proposal was delivered to their homes the night the press release was issued. At least one

I-T-E director didn't know anything about it until he read the details the next morning in the newspapers.

When in 1960 the Justice Department showed that General Electric had been involved in a massive price-fixing conspiracy, its directors included not only Sidney Weinberg, dean of American directors, but Donald K. David of Harvard; George Humphrey, former Secretary of the Treasury; R. W. Woodruff of Coca-Cola; Neil McElroy of Procter and Gamble; H. S. Morgan of Morgan, Stanley; George Love of Consolidation Coal; R. T. Stevens of J. P. Stevens & Company, T. B. McCabe of Scott Paper, Henry Ford II— in fact, a blue-ribbon collection of American businessmen, many of whom had served or were serving as directors of Federal Reserve Banks. In its original bill of particulars the Government blamed not only G.E.'s top officers but the Board. It modified its charges before the case went to court. No director was ever shown to have known about or condoned the activities that sent lesser G.E. people to jail. The question was, should they not have known how business was being done in the electrical industry?

Said Henry Ford II: "I believe these recent happenings should alert outside directors to the need to be aware of the pertinent codes and policies of the companies on whose boards they sit. Normally, the outside director has only a broad picture of the business and cannot be completely familiar with the day to day operating details. But, when serious improprieties occur, all companies, whole industries, and individuals, whether legally responsible or not, suffer the consequences of an inflamed and properly outraged public opinion. . . . There is really only one thing for top executives to do at such a time as this. It is to forget the alibis and the explanations and have the fortitude—the plain guts—to stand up and say, 'This is our failure. We are chagrined and sorry. It will not happen again.'"

In trying to fulfill their duties, directors sometimes speak as though they were impeded by the traditions attached to the job. Discussions may be lively, but there is a point beyond which no gentleman must go. "It's surprising how much the decor—the walnut paneling, the picture of the founder on the wall—tones down the heat of a Board room discussion," says one director. "If directors met in Charlie's Bar and Grill the history of American business might be different."

"I know of no place where an eager beaver is less popular than on a Board," says a big company chairman. "You have to strike a balance between being completely subservient and being too curious, niggling about details. Unless you represent a take-over bid, you're not supposed to go on a Board unless you have confidence in the company and its management. So when you get there it isn't good manners to pry."

Accepting these rules of behavior can be said to mean the director abdicates his responsibility as the stockholders' representative. He behaves as a proper member of a very proper club, rather than as the representative of ownership interest. In fact, when an independent stockholder has the temerity to write or call a director for information about his company, the reaction is frequently one of surprise and occasionally even resentment and the inquiry is promptly turned over to management.

Outside directors are usually paid flat fees for attending meetings. The median fee is $200 among manufacturing companies and utilities, and $100 among banks and insurance firms, according to a National Industrial Conference Board survey taken in 1962. There is a trend toward putting outside directors on an annual retainer basis. The median retainer in 1962 was $2500. Some companies go much higher—General Mills pays $10,000 a year. Nearly half the manufacturing companies compensate directors on the dual basis of retainer plus fees for meeting attendance. In banking and insurance, such retainers are still relatively rare.

Even directors who are officers may get a fee for each meeting. First National City Bank gives $200 for each meeting to every director, including its chairman, James S. Rockefeller, who gets $216,000 a year as regular compensation. Two-thirds of manufacturing companies, however, do not give extra compensation to employee-directors. A director seated on a "working" board may spend anywhere from four or five hours to an entire day preparing for a meeting. Meetings are held once a month, except in the summer, in about half of all American companies.

In advance of the meeting the director gets the agenda, along with recent financial and operating information and background reports on questions scheduled to come up. When he wants supplementary material he can ask for it, though it is not customary to contact the operating personnel directly. If a big decision is to be made, it will usually come as no surprise to the director. He has already been unofficially approached over lunch or by phone by the company president, or by a fellow director, who described the situation and sounded out his attitude. Directors prefer this informal contact. "It gives us a chance to get an oar in before things have gone very far," one explains. The president, too, prefers informal consultation; he does not want to bring a question to the board unless he is pretty sure of getting approval for what he proposes. He may modify it to meet objections, but he does not like to be turned down.

"I used to rush things to a vote," says one company president and director. "I'd be satisfied if the majority supported a proposition and the rest abstained. Then I found the ones who abstained felt free to criticize and gripe. Now I try to get all unspoken opinions pulled out. I direct the conversation so that every director has at least to grunt. I can tell by the grunt whether he is in agreement or not, and keep on until I'm sure I have a consensus."

Without fairly consistent support for management policies, a serious breach between top brass and outside directors is apt to occur. After one president and chairman was ousted from his posts, a director of the company commented, "Basically you had two different philosophies of management; he wanted to expand and invest, and the board was more conservative." The final break came after a squabble over the company's money-losing European subsidiary.

It should be made clear that many boards, perhaps most, are not so actively concerned. They are not thought of as working boards. Meetings are perfunctory and the directors have little to do in the way of advance preparation. A few resolutions are offered and voted on, some operating statistics are presented and the session is adjourned after an hour or two.

The area of a director's responsibility has grown over the years. The stockholders' interest is only one among several within his concern; there are customers, creditors, employees, executives, and

something loosely defined as "community interest." Even national
interest may be involved, in international operations.

At a Columbia University symposium, one director explained:

> You've got to be sure that you're going to be able to keep on
> living as a corporation, and I'm just as sure as I can possibly
> be that that involves acquiring the approbation of the majority
> of the voters in the United States. If the majority of them be-
> lieve that the corporation as we know it in this country is the best
> thing for the country as a whole, taking everybody's interest
> into consideration, why, we're going to keep on having corpora-
> tions. But if the majority of people don't believe that, why, I'm
> damned sure that our politicians are going to change that.
>
> Now the things that will make the majority of the American
> people think that the American business setup is the best thing
> for the country, as compared to some other form of activity, is
> a composite picture; it's how you treat your employees; it's how
> you live in your community as a corporate citizen; it's how
> your management people conduct themselves, how you cooperate
> with government, what kind of product or service you give your
> customers—a composite of all those things. And you can't go
> overboard in any one of them but you try to achieve the maxi-
> mum total effect from all of those that you can, weighing and
> harmonizing all these various interests. And I think that a person
> that has that kind of a concept about corporation management
> responsibility is definitely looking after the interests of the stock-
> holders.

Beardsley Ruml once suggested that the responsibility to these
varied interests be formalized by having one director deliberately
assigned to act as "trustee" for the interests of customers, one for
suppliers, one for the employees, and possibly others, depending on
the business. It would be up to each "trustee" to see that the
interest he was protecting was given proper consideration when a
decision was made. One director would also be explicitly charged
with the ownership interests, the shareholders. These director-trust-
ees would be expected to do more work than usual, and be paid
accordingly:

> The board of directors would then consist of four paid director-
> trustees, the chairman and the president, and such other officers

and directors as the needs and traditions of the company dic-
tated. . . . Since these . . . special directors would be interested,
even from the standpoint of their special interest, in the growth
and prosperity of their corporation, and would be individually
and collectively only a minority of the board as a whole, it seems
improbable that the decisive interest thus deliberately built into
the board at a low level of power but a high level of articulate
responsibility would be harmful in any way to a clear-cut and effective corporate program.

To date no one has adopted this plan, at least publicly, and some
lawyers feel it might conflict with the responsibilities directors bear
to stockholders under law.

When the federal government chartered the Communications
Satellite Corporation in 1964, it acknowledged the desirability of
interests not connected with share owning having representation on
the board. COMSAT's charter provided for fifteen directors. The
communications companies, 161 of whom purchased a total of
50 per cent of COMSAT's stock, were assigned six places on the
Board. A.T.&T., by far the largest share owner in the group,
was limited to three of the six seats. International Telephone &
Telegraph, the second largest stockholder, got two, and the other
communications companies, one. Six other directors, according to
the charter, were to be elected by the individual public shareholders
in the normal manner. They turned out to be the management slate
—the original board members appointed by the late President John
F. Kennedy to incorporate the company, who renominated themselves. To represent the public itself, the President was empowered
to select three U.S. citizens; he picked Frederic G. Donner, chairman of General Motors; George Meany, head of the AFL-CIO, and
Clark Kerr, president of the University of California.

Although legally responsible to the stockholders, directors do little direct communicating with them. There is all the difference in
the world between an elected political representative, who takes
care to cultivate his constituents although he is not legally responsible to them for anything, and directors, who bear legal responsibilities to stockholders but are never seen out campaigning except
in an emergency. Many directors do not even attend stockholder
meetings; nothing requires them to do so. Since professional stock-

holders like the Gilberts and their supporters have been demanding that directors become more visible, some companies have adopted a policy of urging directors to turn out on annual meeting day, to be formally introduced.

"It is not necessary for directors to communicate with stockholders directly," says Donald Cook, head of American Electric Power Company and former SEC chairman. "A company should have only one voice, that of the chief executive officer. What he says must be acceptable to the Board or they should get rid of him. By seeing to it that what he says is accurate, fair and adequate, the directors collectively fulfill their obligations to report to stockholders."

A director who has had wide experience in fights for corporate control puts it a little more pragmatically: "If you have 100 shares a director will speak freely to you, if you can get past the public relations department," he says. "He knows you aren't going to upset the applecart. If you have 500,000 shares of course he will open up; you are important and may soon be his colleague at the director's table. But when you have something in between—a sizable block, not big, not small—then you won't get a scrap of information from a director. He doesn't know where you stand. You might be dangerous."

Book Three

12

THE POWER OF YOUR PROXY

Meshulam Riklis is an ex-schoolteacher who, in his short financial career, has dazzled even the sophisticates of Wall Street by putting together a retailing empire called the McCrory Corporation —a half-billion-dollar-a year complex of department, variety, and specialty stores.

Along the way, though, Riklis's retailing complex has become so complex that from time to time he has needed some quick cash to cut his company's rising indebtedness. For example, in 1963, he planned to sell off McCrory's biggest asset, Lerner Stores, a 326-unit chain of women's and children's apparel stores. He had a buyer: the Glen Alden Corporation. And he had a price: $35 million in cash and $15 million in notes convertible after two years into Glen Alden stock. All he needed was the necessary approval of the deal by McCrory's stockholders.

Riklis was confident that this was the least of his troubles. About the only opponent of the Lerner deal was a small stockholder named Leonard Marx, a little-known Manhattan real estate man. And Marx admittedly opposed the sale initially only because McCrory leased several outlets from his real estate enterprises. He was fearful that McCrory could not pay the rent if money-making Lerner were sold.

Thus Riklis was virtually convinced that he had the necessary votes in his pocket when he arrived in York, Pennsylvania, for the special meeting of McCrory's stockholders: proxies for some 1.5 million of the some 2.6 million shares eligible to vote on the Lerner sale. He was so confident in fact that on the eve of the balloting he sat down to a friendly game of bridge with Marx, who already wore the air of the graceful loser. Marx had even brought his golf bags to York as if he were just in town for the ride and some fun.

But Riklis's confidence and Marx's casualness soon evaporated. After the votes were counted the next day, a stunned Riklis announced to the noisy meeting that Marx had won. To his dismay, Riklis learned that the innocent-looking Marx had quietly politicked among McCrory stockholders. Marx got enough of them to reverse their proxies by signing new ones in his favor and not Riklis's, perfectly legal and proper under proxy solicitation rules.

Marx's victory, however, adds up to something more than probably the most shattering reverse suffered by "Rik" Riklis in his comparatively short career. As Marx himself later told a reporter from the *New York Times,* "It proved that unorganized stockholders, when they see their interests are jeopardized, can defeat entrenched management which has all the advantages of organization, of proxy solicitation and the use of corporate funds to influence stockholders' votes."

Even more important, the McCrory case reflects the potential power of even the lowliest stockholder. Most stockholders, of course, belong to the vast army of collectors of dividend checks and rubber-stampers of management decisions. But as Leonard Marx has proved, it would be foolish to write off all stockholders as faceless and transitory figures whose only recourse is to sell their stock when the going gets rough. Stockholders determined to use the power available to them, can be a decided force in shaping the destinies of the corporations in which they have invested their capital.

And woe be it to almost any management of a publicly held company which holds the theory that its power over corporate affairs is both self-perpetuating and well-nigh absolute. This idea only invites a comeuppance, according to no less a veteran of major proxy wars than Richard S. Nye, Sr., senior partner in Georgeson & Company, professional proxy solicitors. "Stockholders," as Nye sees it, "will rise in wrath against management just often enough— when someone leads them—to bring home their power to management of the companies whose shares they own."

Not that the sound of the stockholder's protesting voice is something altogether new. It was heard in such resounding proxy battles in the past as Jay Gould's and Jim Fisk's Erie Railway attack against

Commodore Vanderbilt in the 1870s. In W. C. Durant's capture of General Motors in 1915. It was called upon in the famous 1929 victory of the Rockefellers over Colonel Robert Stewart for control of Standard Oil of Indiana. And it was particularly loud and clear in A. P. Giannini's ouster of Elisha Walker from Transamerica Corporation (which controlled the Bank of America) in 1932.

But there are basic and radical differences in the stockholder's role then and his role today. In those early struggles for control, the emotions and votes of most stockholders were marshaled by former managements who could call on substantial stockholdings of long standing and important sympathizers within the existing managements they were out to unseat.

Today's stockholder rebellion can start anywhere at almost any time. It may spark with dissident directors, who, in good conscience, believe that management policies are not producing the potential of which the company is capable. It may be one stockholder who fans the flames, such as Detroit attorney Sol Dann, whose criticism helped bring about a significant change of management in the Chrysler Corporation. Or it could be a smallish firm like Fanny Farmer Candy Shops, Inc., of Rochester, New York, whose board was bounced; or, a regional bank like New York City's Meadow Brook National, where minority stockholders successfully sought representation on the board.

In the ebullient 1920s and the depressed 1930s, uprisings among stockholders were few and far between. It's not that way today. In the last ten years, there have been an average of more than thirty proxy fights a year among companies whose shares are listed on stock exchanges, and the trend shows no signs of diminishing. Incalculable as well are the scores of contests in unlisted companies whose fights for stockholder control do not come under SEC rules and regulations and where no holds are barred.

Why have so many stockholders felt inclined to take action to protect their capital investments? The basic reason, of course, is the historic shift that has taken place in the ownership of American enterprise.

Even as late as the early post World War II years, many a major business still was either family-owned or at least very closely held. When top management sat down to talk with the stockholders, it was talking to itself, its relatives, and a few close advisers. A company's secrets were its own and no one else's. But death, taxes, and the need for equity capital have all but laid this unity of ownership and control to rest. It is even rare for any one stockholder, or small group of stockholders, to hold the majority of the voting stock of any substantial corporation, thus retaining "absolute" control of who sits on the board.

Today, control of a large corporation usually is based on "effective" or "working" control. The key to keeping it is the ability to obtain the support of the holders of sufficient stock, which, when added to the holdings of the control group, will carry a corporate election its way.

Thus, it is not surprising that such broadly held corporations as A.T. & T., G.E. and Standard Oil (New Jersey) today give high priority to stockholder relations. And the more broadly held the company, the more sophisticated it seems to be about maintaining as many pipelines as possible to its investing public.

Take Standard Oil (New Jersey). It is owned by over 735,000 shareholders of record and an estimated additional 150,000 shareholders whose stock is registered in nominee or broker names. And 90 per cent of these are individuals, not institutional investors. As a result, the Jersey board has established a Relations Division in the corporate secretary's office. Its job is to assist individual directors and officers of the corporation in their relations with stockholders. In all, some 15,000 to 20,000 individual shareholder contacts per year are handled through the company's offices, according to Matthew F. Kane, manager of shareholder relations.

This, however, is not just an answering service. It is what Kane calls "a total investor relations program." Thus, Jersey's Relations Division is charged with everything from direct correspondence with stockholders to handling all the arrangements for annual and special meetings.

The division maintains contact through company publications, assembles information about Jersey shareholders, and keeps up with what other companies are doing to improve their shareholder relations programs. Such an operation, says Kane, acts as a two-way avenue of communication. Shareholders can readily get more information about the company if they want it, and the board of directors readily can identify trends in stockholder thinking and areas of concern.

Such a formal and careful shareholder relations setup as Jersey's is important from another major standpoint.

Some observers of business life are rather pessimistic about the evolution in corporate control from the few to the many. As they see it, the rising class of professional managers in control of things, and the increasing dispersion of stock ownership, has only widened the gulf between manager and owner. This is hardly a new view. It was clearly expressed by Messrs. Berle and Means in their 1932 book *The Modern Corporation and Private Property*.

Their main point is that the professional manager of today is a more uncommitted soul than the owner-manager of the past. Profit for the stockholders is not his prime motive. What counts is perpetuation of the enterprise. This means closer immediate concern with customers, suppliers, workers, etc., than with stockholders.

Conversely, runs the argument, the larger the body of stockholders, the more inert the mass. The wider the participation in ownership, the lower the level of stockholder knowledge and education. The result: in the clutches of the unscrupulous manager the stockholder is no less than a helpless pawn.

Certainly the stockholder lives in something less than a perfect "corporate democracy." And since not every stockholder desires, or is equipped, to dash into the executive suite to take matters in his own hands, the field is clearer for those capitalists who do care about protecting their investments. Since most of those in control usually have relatively small holdings themselves, they must put a large premium on the support of other stockholders. And when the chips are down, every vote counts. In the battle for control of Fanny Farmer, to mention one example, management retained power by a margin of only 308 votes.

What has really made even the smallest stockholder a potential force, however, is a new breed of business personalities who appeared on the scene in the early 1950s. These are the rank outsiders, often called "raiders," who set out to capture some of America's biggest and oldest companies.

The dispersion of stock ownership set the stage for their arrival. A favorable tax rate, encouraging these "money men" to play for capital gains, attracted them. Their special talent for finding "special situations" told them where to strike. And driving them on was an insatiable yen for control or their visceral need to be on the inside of a deal.

The pacesetter of them all was the late Robert Young, the wheeler-dealer from Palm Beach, Florida. He was the financier who upended the old management of the New York Central in 1954 by rallying stockholders in a massive proxy campaign. It was fights like Young's, too, that put into the headlines such epithets as "raider," "corporation destroyer," "proxyteer" and "pirate."

But success like Young's only indicated how important almost any stockholder could be as an agent of change, readjustment, or rehabilitation of a company. For the outsider gave the stockholder a choice between leaders.

And a pattern began to emerge indicating the kind of company which might (and still does) become vulnerable to a proxy fight. David Karr, a public relations man and proxy fight specialist who became president of Fairbanks, Whitney Corporation after guiding insurgent stockholders in a successful fight for control, has outlined the conditions that might lead stockholders to follow an outsider against management.

Karr's criteria are based on a study of eight different proxy fights involving as many companies: Transamerica Corporation, the New York Central, Twentieth Century-Fox, Twin City Rapid Transit Company, Decca Records, Inc., United Cigar-Whelan Stores Corporation, Minneapolis & St. Louis Railway, and Montgomery Ward & Company. And, as expressed in his book, *Fight for Control,* they are worth the inspection of anyone concerned about the value of his holdings. There are at least six basic considerations to be drawn from Karr's conclusions:

1. First, no matter how old a company is, is the management "conservative"? That is, is it more concerned about possible bad times ahead than the opportunities for future profit through expansion?

2. Has management made the company rich in terms of assets but poor in terms of its annual earnings and its dividend payments to the stockholders?

3. Is it a company whose competitive position has been declining

over the past few years, or, in a growing market, a company content to maintain past levels of production and profit?

4. Is it a company whose sales and profits have increased through acquisitions but whose earnings per share have been diluted by new issues of stock to make those acquisitions?

5. Has management failed to keep stockholders informed of the company's goals, prospects, and achievements?

6. Are managerial salaries and expense accounts out of line in comparison to those of competitors or the earnings record of the company?

By taking such grievances and issues directly to stockholders, outside challengers have often unseated a complacent board of directors. In many cases, their mere potential as insurgents has put pressure on management to move dividends up as soon as possible, or, to develop a plan for insuring greater profits and dividends in the future.

In any event, few stockholders have been hurt by the very fact that a big outsider becomes interested in a company as a new addition to his corporate collection. It usually causes an immediate rise in the market value of the stock. Take Louis Wolfson's unsuccessful attempt to unseat the management of Montgomery Ward. Not only was the increased sale price of the company's stock sufficient to cover the expenses of his abortive campaign, it also turned a profit for any other stockholder who chose to sell.

If an outside "money man" wins, he also may seriously seek his capital gains by improving management to the benefit of all the stockholders. A good example is the closemouthed West Coast industrialist Norton Simon. In recent years, and with little or no general publicity, Simon has strung together an impressive empire that ranges from Hunt Foods to Wesson Oil, from the cerebral *Saturday Review* to mass-circulation *McCall's* magazine and includes the Ohio Match Company. He also has made substantial investments in Wheeling Steel, the Northern Pacific Railway, and American Broadcasting-Paramount Theatres, Inc.

Characteristically, Simon, like other outside money men, will first buy a "position" in a vulnerable company where a possible change in management is indicated. Then he carefully appraises management's strength before closing in to get full control or abandoning a project completely.

Once in control, though, Simon sets out to rebuild a company into a profit-making organization, jacking up the price of the stock in the long run. For example, in 1943 Simon took over the Hunt Brothers Packing Company, a small West Coast food processor in the San Francisco Bay area. He steadily rebuilt the company into one of the biggest food companies in the business. Its Hunt catsup now gives the makers of H. J. Heinz catsup a run for their money. Simon simultaneously has merged other companies into Hunt's operation, such as can-making facilities. Hunt also has a portfolio of investments in other firms. In the process, Hunt's sales and the price of its stock have multiplied many times.

Generally the would-be "raider" heads a group of speculative investors since he cannot always finance out of his own pocket an attack that may run into the millions. Such a leader, for example, is the controversial Victor Muscat. In the past several years, the "Muscat group," also known as "the three Muscateers," has put together a small financial and industrial empire comprising everything from banking and insurance interests to paint and auto parts, with annual sales of more than $75 million. The Muscat group, whose individual members may decide to stay out of any given deal, includes Robert L. Huffines, Jr., a plantation owner and a former textile executive, and Edward Krock, a financial expert from Worcester, Massachusetts.

Like other outsiders, the stock-in-trade of the Muscat group is to pyramid its holdings in one company into control of a succeeding company. For example, Muscat *et al* first got working control in 1959 of the ailing Serrick Corporation, an Ohio maker of industrial stampings and screw machine parts. In 1960, they changed Serrick into a new company, Defiance Industries, and have since pushed Defiance into control of radio and electronics firms, a maker of electric dryers, and even a bank, Chicago's Guaranty Bank & Trust Company. Their most important coup: purchasing 30 per cent of the stock of New York's wobbly B. S. F. Company, which has holdings in everything from cameras to body-building salons.

But corporate collectors like Muscat no longer just level their sights on money-losing companies that can stand rehabilitation. They are just as liable these days to affect the fortunes of stockholders and careers of managers of sound ones as well. For example, the possibilities of Republic Corporation, an already lucrative appliance manufacturer and operator of a movie-film processing laboratory, appealed to the Muscat group so much that it took full control of its board in 1964, after first buying 10 per cent of its shares in 1963. But the former management, led by Victor M. Carter, fought back and regained control. By the close of 1966, Carter was fully in command and had purchased from the Muscat group the block of shares they had held. As an added fillip, stockholders of the company had voted to reimburse Carter for $365,215 of expenses incurred wresting control back from the Muscat group.

Similarly, it does not just take a proxy fight or the threat of one for the outsider to move in on a company. Muscat, in fact, has studiously tried to avoid proxy contests ever since he was rebuffed in an attempt to buck the entrenched management of American Hardware Corporation in 1962. Like many another outsider, he now counts on making a tender offer to stockholders. This is a promise to pay a fixed price for a specified amount of stock, generally a bit above the market price.

"They [proxy fights] aren't worth the trouble," Muscat once told a reporter from *The Wall Street Journal.* "Tender offers are easier. At least the money is going into stock and not such things as proxy solicitations and court suits."

Apparently Muscat's view is shared by a growing number of businessmen. The tender offer came into full flower in 1965, when the SEC counted twenty-nine cash take-over bids involving companies on the New York Stock Exchange, and fifteen involving companies listed on the American Exchange. By contrast, in 1960, there were only eight cash take-over bids involving stocks listed on both exchanges.

In 1966, the pace seemed to quicken before sources of financing dried up in midyear due to a general tightening of the nation's money supply. Few individuals or corporations have sufficient cash on hand to gain a controlling interest in a company whose shares are worth, say, $100,000,000 in the auction market. Before the money well ran dry, the financial press was dotted with reports of tender offers at prices set attractively above the market. The bidding companies included such names as W. R. Grace & Company, BVD Company, Glen Alden Corporation, American Electric Power Company, Pennzoil Company, Gamble-Skogmo, Inc., Sunshine Mining Company, American Financial Corporation, Tung-Sol Electric, Inc., Genesco, Inc., and Sun Chemical Company. Occasionally, an individual would enter the arena; S. T. Scheinman, a former director of Art Metal, Inc., offered to buy 125,000 shares of the company at $25 a share. The list goes on.

In some cases, the offers were successful. Tung-Sol, for example, offered to buy 954,062 shares of Wagner Electric Corporation at $35 a share. Prior to the offer in early June, the 1966 range for Wagner stock was 30⅞ high and 24 low. Tung-Sol already owned 73,600 Wagner shares, which with the stock it was offering to purchase, would give it more than 50 per cent of the 2,056,841 shares outstanding. Wagner stockholders went for the offer and subsequently both boards approved a consolidation of the two companies.

In other cases, the bid failed. Gamble-Skogmo failed to receive tenders for the minimum of 500,000 shares of First National Stores, Inc., common stock it had sought to purchase—first at $35 a share and later at $38 a share—and elected to return all shares tendered. The 500,000 shares sought amounted to about 30 per cent of the supermarket chain's 1,631,404 outstanding shares and, together with what Gamble-Skogmo already owned, would have given it working control of First National, whose stock was selling at a low for the year of $29 prior to the offer.

In practically all instances, managements whose companies are the subjects of cash take-over bids are taken by surprise, are mightily offended, resist fiercely, and strongly advise stockholders to hang on to their shares.

It is not uncommon for a management to learn of a tender offer at the same time stockholders do. The element of surprise is important to the offering group, which hopes to attract a considerable number of tendered shares before the subject of its affection can gather its wits. Pennzoil Company, for example, devoted a year to secretly buying 275,000 shares of United Gas Corporation and lining up financing through twenty-five banks, some of which had no idea how the money would be used. United Gas management was indeed astonished when the tender offer was made public and despite its most strenuous efforts—including buying stock in the open market to push the price above the tender offer—Pennzoil ended up with 42 per cent of the outstanding stock and effective control.

At first blush, a stockholder would find it difficult to turn his back on an offer to purchase his holdings at a price substantially above the market—usually 20 per cent higher. This is especially true when his company's shares have been in the doldrums for a long time, a characteristic which is attractive to individuals or groups seeking take-over candidates. Here, for example, are the key paragraphs of an ad by Genesco in the *New York Times* of March 11, 1966, announcing an offer to purchase, via tenders, the stock of Julius Garfinckel & Company, a Washington, D.C., department store, and its subsidiaries, Brooks Brothers and the A. De Pinna Company, both of New York:

> Genesco Inc. offers to purchase at $43.50 per share net, in cash, 575,000 shares of the common stock of Julius Garfinckel & Co., Incorporated. This offer is good until 5:00 P.M. (Eastern Standard Time), March 25, 1966.
>
> This offer is subject to the terms and conditions specified in the formal offer and form of Letter of Transmittal, copies of which may be obtained from:

> Genesco Inc.   Morgan Guaranty Trust
> 730 Fifth Avenue   or   Company of New York,
> New York, 10019   Depository,
> Telephone: 212-582-9090   Corporate Trust Dept.
>   23 Wall Street
>   New York, 10015

> or may be obtained through your own bank or broker.
>
> Genesco Inc. is obligated to purchase 575,000 shares. If less than 75,000 shares are tendered, Genesco Inc. may, but is not required to, purchase all the tendered shares.
>
> Genesco Inc. will pay to members of the National Association of Securities Dealers, Inc. or any member of a national security exchange, a commission of 82¢ per share for each share purchased which was solicited through such members. It will also pay any transfer taxes.

The price of $43.50 was well above the $34–$36 range which existed before Genesco made known its interest in Garfinckel, and 575,000 shares represents 53 per cent of Garfinckel's outstanding stock. At a press conference held the day before the ad appeared, W. Maxey Jarman, Genesco's chairman, severely criticized Garfinckel's management for what he considered an unwillingness to expand and a lack of aggressiveness in its merchandising. About Garfinckel's of Washington, he said, "It is a sleepy store today." Of its management, Jarman said, "The directors only own about 7 per cent of the stock and seem to be interested only in themselves."

The arguments and blandishments are those of the outsider wanting in. In a letter to stockholders, Willard O. Bent, Garfinckel's president, said the board of directors felt the offer was "definitely not in your best interests" and strongly recommended that it be rejected. His letter made these additional points:

1. Garfinckel's management owns more than 110,000 shares and had no intention of tendering any of it.

2. Sale of the stock would be a taxable transaction, the exact amount of the tax depending on the original cost of the stock and the stockholder's tax bracket.

3. Ultimately, each stockholder would have to decide whether he would be better off to continue his investment in Garfinckel, or accept Genesco's offer and invest the net proceeds, after taxes, in some other manner.

4. After outlining Garfinckel's sales and earnings history, the trend of its price in the market, and its plans for the foreseeable future, Bent concluded, "It seems obvious that Genesco recognizes the basic values underlying our shares, as well as your company's potential and is seeking to acquire your shares for these reasons. Does it make sense to turn over your growth and profit opportunities to Genesco rather than to retain your stock and share in the bright future of your Company? It is my personal belief that it does not."

Garfinckel's 5500 stockholders agreed with their president and turned down Genesco's offer. Genesco failed in its bid despite a promise to pay a commission of 82 cents per share to brokers for each share tendered through them. This bounty of about 2 per cent of the purchase price more than doubles the standard broker's commission, which the stockholder need not pay in this instance. It would be fair to say the average broker would be hard put to remain wholly objective in the face of this opportunity.

Another factor tending to stack the cards in favor of the bidder is that some brokers will, immediately on learning of a tender offer, start buying stock of the sought-after company for themselves and their customers, and tendering it. They not only profit on the basis of the substantial commissions but also on the basis that the price of the stock in the market usually doesn't rise to the tender offer level until a few days have passed. Therefore, there's profit for the alert investor in the early spread between the market price and the tender price. The decision to act, in this case, obviously is not determined entirely by the fundamental merit of the offer.

Stockholders might keep in mind, too, that the would-be new management may use the acquired company's own credit to carry the substantial loans required to purchase the tendered stock. In fact, there's really no way of learning very much of the new group's intentions or its own record, unless it wishes to volunteer information or the stockholder takes the trouble to drop everything and do some fast research before the offer expires. The tender offer is designed as a blitzkrieg—move in fast, give an all-powerful appearance, keep up a steady barrage, and establish a solid position before anybody has a chance to think.

All this is deeply disturbing to SEC Chairman Manuel F. Cohen, who, in a talk before a meeting of the American Society of Corporate Secretaries, contrasted the cash tender offer with an offer made by one company to exchange its shares for another. The latter must be registered under the Securities Act of 1933, which requires that the shareholder must get a prospectus explaining all material facts about the offer. He must be told who the purchaser is, what plans have been made for the company, etc., so that he will be in the position to make an informed decision either to hold or exchange his shares. The disclosures, as in the case of a proxy contest, are filed with the SEC and are subject to specific SEC requirements and sanctions.

The situation with regard to the cash tender offer, Chairman Cohen says, is quite different, although the investment decision is similar. "The choice whether to retain the original security or sell it is, in substance, little different from the decision made on an original purchase of a security, or on an offer to exchange one security for another," he said. In many cases of cash tender offers, he added, "the public investor does not even know the identity of the purchaser, much less what the purchaser plans to do with the company if the takeover bid is successful."

Cohen told the group of proposed legislation which would require disclosure by bidders of their backgrounds, sources of funds to be used in the acquisition, and, if funds are borrowed, the names of the lenders and any additional matters the SEC finds may be necessary for the protection of investors.

Whether or not such legislation is enacted, the investor must make a careful decision based on more than the price he gets for his shares. "How can an investor," Cohen asks, "evaluate the adequacy of the price if he cannot assess the possible impact of a change in control?" The task is anything but easy, and the careless capitalist is likely to make his decision on the basis of arguments that wouldn't stand up under close scrutiny. Managements, therefore, must respond to unwelcome tender offers and proxy solicitations with strategy and argument at least as sophisticated as that of the opposition. From the serious stockholders' point of view, he has to watch out for the fancy footwork of both sides and concentrate on the fundamentals.

Whatever the stratagem, of course, the ultimate test for the battler for corporate control, at least as far as most sophisticated stockholders are concerned, involves more than just an ability to win. For can the dissidents' chosen leader follow through as a manager or the key man behind a new management?

Even their sternest critics no longer question the proven record of a Norton Simon or a Victor Muscat as corporate in-fighters. But how will they perform once they win control? Do they have a new set of experienced managers on tap, or can they obtain them, to replace the executives they are out to unseat? Are they entering product fields new to them? What does the outsider stand to get out of such an attack? Is he in this deal for quick capital gains to bail himself out of another financial adventure?

Unless the stockholder can answer most of such questions satisfactorily, he may lose more than he hopes to gain by putting his proxy votes in the hands of an outsider or by falling prey to the immediate blandishments of a tender offer. Consider, say the skeptics, the contracting empires of such corporate collectors as realtor William Zeckendorf, whose ambitious expansion plans once were the rage of the business press and the delight of investors. Zeckendorf's Webb & Knapp realty company attracted much investor attention with his free-wheeling ideas and dreams, such as exploiting the air rights over Manhattan's Grand Central Terminal. But Zeckendorf only ended up mortgaging the company out of business and into bankruptcy.

Yet almost any management would be more than foolish to dismiss airily and complacently the existence of big outside investors who swim shark-like through the business community. In fact, the most experienced managements have already learned the value of offsetting these outsiders by tightening up heretofore haphazard communications with their stockholders through more informative reports, better annual meetings, and more enlightened relations with the press and the financial community, as discussed in detail elsewhere in this book.

The simple reason is that stock participation in today's corporations is so broad that it is becoming increasingly difficult to keep all of the stockholders happy all of the time—no less fool all of the stockholders any of the time. On one hand, many stockholders will remain quiescent through thick and thin if they believe management's reputation for integrity is justified, if it makes full and frank disclosure of its intentions, and if it makes a continuing effort to improve the company.

On the other hand, almost invariably there is a small vigilant minority ever ready to pounce on almost any managerial indiscretion. And, given time, money, and a little leadership, this "loyal opposition" can blow a single abuse or shady-looking transaction into a full-fledged stockholder war, particularly when those major guarantees of management tenure—good earnings and dividends—aren't there.

Take, for example, the touchy subject of executive stock options, whereby shares of stock are set aside at a given date for later purchase (at higher prices and no risk) by selected executives. No management can ever be quite sure, even when things are improving, that some stockholder will not raise the roof when he hears about this kind of executive incentive plan.

A stockholder of ten years' standing took violent exception to a stock option plan put forth by the management of the General Baking Company, for example. He was Patterson Branch, a Richmond, Virginia, broker with 3700 shares of General Baking common stock and 10 shares of preferred, who launched a proxy fight to defeat management's stock option plan. In a close vote, 692,202 against, 605,019 for, he won.

Stockholders who care enough can often take matters into their own hands rather than bow to the inevitable. In the railroad industry, where hardly a day goes by without someone making a merger proposal, dissident holders of the Western Pacific voted two-to-one to block management's plan to take control of the Atchison, Topeka & Santa Fe.

Stockholders who do rise up in protest usually can expect to have some effect on the management of their company. Under pressure from insurgent groups of investors, management may hustle to exploit every opportunity to increase dividends immediately, or, if possible, develop a plan for insuring greater profits and dividends in the future.

The incumbent management, in fact, may even wish to avoid a troublesome proxy fight by compromising with the insurgents. Not too long ago, for example, the management and dissident stockholders of U. S. Smelting, Refining & Mining Company reached an accord on who the company's directors and key executives should be, in order to head off a major battle. In effect, the agreement virtually gave full control of the lead, zinc, and petroleum producer to the insurgents who gained control of the board. Not everyone wins that easily, to be sure.

But few, in or out of management these days, relish or necessarily wish to indulge in the public scrap that a proxy fight can be. For one thing, such fights are costly, running anywhere from $25,000 all the way up—as in the case of Robert Young's battle for the New York Central—to well over $1 million. Each side needs a veritable army of expensive retainers to carry out a proxy contest, paralleling the specialists required in a good, rousing national political campaign.

There are the lawyers and accountants who must be paid to examine corporation books and records, to fight in court the allegations of the opposite side, and to file the proper solicitation material with the SEC. There are the high-powered public relations consultants who specialize in proxy wars and are hired to supplement both management's and the dissidents' regular publicity men.

There are the fees for security analysts capable of examining a corporation's earnings, standing in the industry, and other statistical data. And no campaigner worth his proxies would be without some heavy advertising talent from Madison Avenue to turn out the copy and layouts to make his case in media everywhere.

It is also just about imperative to put professional proxy solicitors on the payroll. The professional proxy solicitor is, in fact, one of the most important, though one of the least publicized, members of the business community. He is what the precinct workers who get out the vote are to the political candidates who are up for election.

Proxy contestants—particularly the insurgents—soon find out they just do not have the manpower or the experience of experts such as Georgeson & Company, the Kissel-Blake Organization, or Dudley F. King & Company, which is needed to track down the existing votes tucked away under the names of brokers, nominees or other fiduciaries. For example, Georgeson, which regularly does one-half of all professional proxy solicitations of any kind, already has one hundred people in the field. At annual meeting time, Georgeson will supplement this full-time force with fifty to seventy-five retired bank vice-presidents, security analysts, and other financial men.

Georgeson serves some 200 corporations such as Reynolds Metals Company, Olin Mathieson Chemical Corporation, and United Air Lines, at an average cost of $2500 to $7500 for a routine meeting. The price depends on the number of stockholders to be polled. In proxy fights costs may mount higher. In the Montgomery Ward contest Georgeson received a fee plus expenses estimated at $50,-000.

What the client—management or insurgent—pays for is a time-tested system of collecting votes carefully evolved over the years. Georgeson, for instance, has solicitors in thirty-eight cities. Each solicitor gets a card on each stockholder who lives in his area and is to be polled. It tells him who the stockholder is, where he lives, how many shares he owns, and whether or not the stockholder has voted in the election or meeting in question. This stockholder card in the field is kept current with a duplicate card on the stockholder in Georgeson's headquarters, which in turn is kept current with a duplicate card in the hands of the transfer agent who counts the votes as they come in. Thus, even before he calls a stockholder, the professional solicitor knows whether or not a stockholder has voted. He may ask him if he has voted only as an opening wedge for his sales talk on behalf of his client.

The solicitor, however, must keep his "sell" softly confined to the arguments on the proxy statement itself. The Securities and Exchange Commission is finicky about this. The SEC must approve all the proxy material the solicitor's client sends out. It also scrutinizes the memoranda that a vote-getting firm like Georgeson sends to its men in the field.

Even so, there is no limit, except common courtesy, on the number of contacts that can be made with stockholders. A good field solicitor can get in anywhere from twenty to forty phone calls a day. If a stockholder is big enough, he may rate a personal visit to his home or office.

But even if the solicitor doesn't get the vote, the client, if it is management, does get something for its money. All gripes and other comments a stockholder makes during a call goes on the solicitor's card, thus giving management an over-all gauge of stockholder sentiment about its policies. This puts the professional proxy solicitor in a unique position to spot a brewing contest and nip it in the bud. The professional proxy solicitor also comes in handy when a management suddenly finds itself confronted with that successor to the proxy fight—the tender offer. This happened when Curtiss-Wright made a tender offer to the stockholders of the Garrett Corporation, the Los Angeles aerospace concern. Georgeson solicitors, who had handled Garrett's annual meetings for fourteen years, went on to collect the votes necessary to bring about Garrett's saving move—a merger with Signal Oil. Not incidently, one of the early steps a wide-awake management takes when faced with a distasteful tender bid is to find another company it can live with which might be interested in acquiring the firm or merging with it.

The proxy professional has also become increasingly useful as more and more managements seek the passage of major proposals that, under law, usually require a full two-thirds vote for stockholder approval, i.e., mergers, liquidations, and authorizations of new issues of preferred stock.

In a major proxy contest, the professional solicitor can be invaluable in providing the administrative and clerical help which will also be needed to receive, tabulate, and examine the proxies as they come in. This is very important because improperly executed proxies, which could be subject to challenge, must go back for correction or new proxies must be requested. Also important are all the telephone calls and special correspondence with bankers, brokers, stockholders, and the financial press, as well as entertaining some of the biggest shareholders quite lavishly. Not to be overlooked, too, is the constant analysis of geographical areas so that the campaign can be directed to where stockholder strength lies. Finally, of course, either side will need everybody concerned for the actual count of the proxies and the vote, the tabulation of which can run into several weeks in a big contest.

Altogether there is, however, something quite ironic about the immensity and complexity of this vote-gathering apparatus. It is the relative simplicity of what is at stake, the proxy ballot itself.

Stockholders receive their proxy ballots in the mail accompanied by a proxy statement which, by law, must describe the time and place of the annual meeting, the directors proposed by management, and the proposals of management or stockholders. By law, too, the proxy statement must list the company's directors, their pay, their biographies, and their holdings, as well as the remuneration of the three highest-paid officers. Other items that must be included: election of auditors, stock splits and dividends, mergers, acquisitions, and an increase in the amount of common stock outstanding. Management is also obliged to mail to stockholders slates of directors proposed by share owners themselves.

The proxy statement is the only report that all publicly held corporations must send to their stockholders. Proxy statements are unusually well read. One major oil company, for example, found that the readership of its proxy statement totaled 61 per cent compared with 42 per cent for its annual report and 33 per cent for its quarterly reports.

Proxy ballots can come in almost any form, from an elaborate letter to a post card. But whatever it looks like, the stockholder must sign it exactly as his name appears on the proxy form he gets, otherwise, his proxy is invalid.

All this, of course, makes voting sound pretty cut and dried. But getting that vote is another matter, particularly for the insurgents. For in almost every proxy contest, management starts out with an upper hand. For one thing, bankers and brokers who have done business with the company usually remain loyal to management, even if only for selfish purposes. They often can and do influence blocks of stocks. They tread a thin line, of course, since the SEC frowns on brokerage firms who advise their customers how to vote in proxy contests. Such a warning, for example, was issued by the SEC when a leading brokerage house turned out a research report covering the battle between the Union Pacific and the Chicago & Northwestern for control of the Rock Island railroad. Even so, the law is still vague in regard to such advice.

Even more important, though, is management's prime advantage —its control of the stockholders' list. This is the one direct channel of communication to the nominal owners of a company. Management, if it chooses to do so, can delay giving a list of stockholders to the opposition, thus hampering the insurgent group's analysis and strategy as well as adding to its costs. Under the rules and regulations of the SEC, management has the choice of supplying the insurgents with a stockholders' list or of mailing the insurgents' proxy material to the stockholders directly. In most cases where the insurgents do not have the list, management not surprisingly will prefer to mail the material itself.

In major fights, this usually means the insurgents may have to wage a long court action to get an order for direct access to the list. When the Murchison group of Texas sought to upend the management of Allegheny Corporation a few years ago, for example, its members took their fight for the list right up to the New York State Court of Appeals. But by the time the court confirmed it, five and one-half months had elapsed since the Murchisons had asked management for the list. Obviously such a delay only hurts the chances for insurgents to analyze correctly the amount of votes they need to win.

Experienced managements also take the precaution of watching hawklike for the first signs of a raid: unexplained strength in a company's stock, a sharp increase in shares held in brokers' names (anything approaching 20 per cent of the outstanding shares is considered a red alert). In fact, so preoccupied has management become with the subject that it is not all uncommon for a company to post an officer—often the secretary—as a sentry.

So forewarned, there are other precautionary measures at management's disposal. American Broadcasting-Paramount Theatres, Inc., is a case in point. In early 1964, there were rumors that outsider Norton Simon, with somewhere between 100,000 and 180,000 shares of AB-PT acquired in recent months, was already angling for a seat on the board for his financial adviser and banker, Gustave L. Levy, a partner in Goldman, Sachs.

President Leonard H. Goldenson wasted little time. Almost immediately he set out to convince the present board to scrap its system of cumulative voting. Cumulative voting gives minority stockholders a better chance of getting representation on a board since they can multiply the number of their shares by the number of directorships being voted on and cast the total for one man. Not surprisingly, the American Broadcasting board unanimously decided to call a special stockholders meeting to abolish cumulative voting, and Norton Simon's supposed ardor for AB-PT was apparently cooled off.

Forewarned, too, management also can blunt the insurgents' most important tactical weapon, surprise. One reason suggested for Louis Wolfson's failure to gain control of Montgomery Ward was that he attacked too soon and too publicly. Although he caught management unawares at first, Wolfson gave them too much time to regroup and fight.

Each situation is different, of course, but experience, according to many a scarred proxy fighter, dictates that a major contest must be started at least three months before the stockholders' meeting. If a stockholders' list is needed, at least three more months should be added; and even more time will be required if it is necessary to purchase stock for the fight.

Experience dictates, too, that insurgents are best led by a stockholders' committee, not by just one or two individuals. This only rounds out the representation that insurgents can present to the entire body of a company's stockholders. It is not always easy, of course, to persuade well-qualified people to serve on a stockholders' committee. The rules and regulations of the SEC require full disclosure of their interest, background, and experience. Management also will subject them to grueling examination.

As a result, the insurgent side must take great care not to lay itself open to well-publicized innuendoes and smears. A good example of this was the big fight for Decca Records in 1954 between its president, Milton R. Rackmil, and George L. Lloyd, a director and one of the company's founders.

Lloyd had quite an argument when he kicked off the fight. Decca's sales had been slipping for three years and the market values of the stock had been sliding too. Meanwhile, Rackmil's salary had risen from $39,750 in 1948 to $122,500 six years later. The odds, viewed from the outside, favored Lloyd. Unhappily, the late financier Serge Rubinstein took an interest in the battle. His reputation was such that any name linked with his became soiled. Rackmil claimed that Rubinstein supported Lloyd. Lloyd called the claim a management smear. But two members of Lloyd's slate of directors turned out to be associated with a company said to be controlled by Rubinstein, and a third had once acted as his attorney in a deportation hearing. In the end Lloyd lost. His big mistake had been to overlook the chinks in his own armor.

Management is in somewhat the same boat—but with an important difference. Once it learns that a contest is in the making, it generally will re-examine its slate of directors to strengthen and defend its hold on the company. It must move faster to make changes in candidates, however, since it is responding to the earlier moves of the opposition, yet like the opposition it must fill in the SEC fully with information on its candidates. Late substitution of candidates may, in fact, prove impossible for a management that is not on its toes.

Once both sides have completed the complex jockeying and have fulfilled the SEC requirements that accompany the opening phases of a contest, the fun begins in earnest. For it is then that the issues and grievances go directly to the stockholders in the field, and few holds, short of the law, are barred.

The fight for proxies at the grass roots, in fact, is just as bitter today as it was in the great corporate fights in earlier years. In A. P. Giannini's stupendous recapture of the Bank of America in 1932, management used its branch managers to call on large stockholders in their areas. Thirty-two years later the management of a small firm in another industry, Arden Farms, a Los Angeles dairy, turned the same technique to its own advantage. By using Arden's own milkmen to solicit proxies, management fended off, by a vote of three to one, the attempt of former President J. Frank Holt to return to power after he was ousted the month before. Holt challenged the use of company milkmen in court. But his case was thrown out.

As a proxy campaign goes on, the more bizarre it becomes. For example, opposing sides were said to have made twenty-one separate contacts with the owner of a large block of New York Central stock. She signed a different proxy every time someone approached her. And her stock was finally voted in support of management when a professional proxy solicitor happened to be the last to visit her.

In the Montgomery Ward contest, an unknown Wolfson solicitor got in touch with Mrs. Rogers Follansbee (daughter of the incumbent chairman of the board, Sewell Avery). But Avery forces got their revenge. They invaded the headquarters of Merritt-Chapman & Scott (a Wolfson-dominated company) seeking proxies for their man. In the same contest one owner of one hundred shares failed to answer his telephone or even answer his mail. But the professionals tracked him down in a remote New Jersey village where he was trying to avoid it all by camping in a trailer. He was willing to give his proxy but was too old to sign it. "That didn't stop me," said the solicitor quite proudly later on. "I guided his hand while he signed the proxy before a notary public."

Nothing, not even the spare statements of a proxy ballot, has kept some stockholders from venting their full sentiments. Several stockholders in one fight, for instance, scrawled a simple message for the company president across their proxies: "Go to Hell!" Even so, the object of their scorn carried the day. But he was lucky, say the professionals. He and his colleagues in management started out with a large enough block of stock to assure their continued control. Some, to this day, never do. And they are ripe for plucking.

They might best heed the advice offered early in the game by one old hand in the proxy wars who believes there are at least seven simple, though often overlooked, questions management may ask itself to test its vulnerability to a proxy attack:

1. Has the stockholder list been analyzed recently with the help of professionals?

2. Have the daily transfer sheets been studied to detect a new concentration of stock?

3. Is management friendly with large stockholders?

4. Have earnings been favorable in the past year?

5. Have dividends been maintained?

6. Do you have a program of action to follow if a proxy fight is threatened?

7. Is 70 per cent or more of your stock held by individuals?

According to the battle-scarred expert, if the answers to three or more of these questions are "No," management is not only vulnerable but is inviting serious trouble unless it has a substantial block of company stock itself. And those managements which fail to take heed may learn that the old crutch "We have confidence that the stockholders will support us when they know the facts" is a statement that has come to rank high among Famous Last Words of American business.

13

CHARITY BEGINS AT HOME:

THE STOCKHOLDER AS CUSTOMER,

PARTNER, AND PROPAGANDIST

The Silvray Lighting Company, of Bound Brook, New Jersey, makes lighting fixtures, and silvers light bulbs for other manufacturers. One day not long ago, Silvray's president, James M. Gilbert, sent the firm's 2000-odd share owners a questionnaire asking them for sales leads. More than 500 stockholders replied, 137 volunteered to recommend the use of Silvray Products to school boards and other prospects, while still others interviewed local store managers in an effort to find out why they didn't stock Silvray products.

American stockholders have a lot more money to spend than their fellow citizens, and whenever they buy something made by a company they've invested in it's money in their pocket. Yet far too few investors go out of their way to buy their companies' products, and fewer still recommend them to others. The very idea of stockholders going out and beating the bushes in an effort to drum up sales leads for their companies' wares—as Silvray's owners did successfully—is so unusual that it rated a news story in *Business Week*.

This is so even though corporations are constantly reminding their owners that charity begins at home. "Just try to imagine," said the chairman of General Foods in a special letter to stockholders, "the boost to sales if every one of you used General Foods products across the board in preference to competitive brands. With our families we total 300,000 people. Consider the still added sales boost if we took it upon ourselves to promote the regular use of our products among our friends. Why, they total in the millions."

"Try them—buy them—recommend them," said Chairman Henry Ford II in a letter to stockholders that accompanied a thirty-two-page, four-color booklet describing the company's new models. "When you do," Mr. Ford added, "you not only make a wise choice in product value, but you also contribute importantly to the continued success of your Company."

"Shareholders who become policy holders," said Daniel S. Winston, president of the General Corporation of Ohio, in the company's first annual report to its owners, "not only gain all the advantages of General Life coverage, service, and cost factors but contribute to the Company's growth and earnings potential."

St. Regis Paper offered stockholders its Refuse Sack System for getting rid of garbage, Chrysler included a booklet describing its new models plus a "Special Invitation" to share owners to test-drive the car of their choice. Avis Rent-A-Car encouraged share owners to hire their company's autos by enclosing a button emblazoned with the words "We try harder" because Avis is only the No. 2 company in the auto renting business. General Foods sent each of its stockholders a three-cup sample of Sanka coffee stapled to their quarterly report, and Lily-Tulip Cup offered a thirty-two-page recipe book of dishes which use cottage cheese as a key ingredient; 50 per cent of the company's stockholders asked for the book, much to the satisfaction of the company's dairy customers who use its containers to package cottage cheese.

These sales appeals, of course, can be intensified by offering stockholders some kind of special deal, which usually comes down to a discount on the company's products. American Motors, for example, offered to trim $100 off the price of new cars purchased by stockholders. Sheraton Corporation sends share owners "room dividends" which entitle them to 50 per cent discounts at Sheraton hotels over July 4 and Labor Day. National Dairy offered a special price on "Fourteen tasty Kraft favorites packed in a handsome reusable leatherette two-layer chest." Remington Corporation, a small manufacturer of air-conditioners in Auburn, New York, offered investors a 45 per cent discount on their products. (The *New York*

Times acidly described the discount as a "consolation prize," as the company's directors had recently passed the dividend.)

Is management's effort to get stockholders to buy and boost their companies' products worth the trouble? The answer is decidedly yes, even though the facts to support this conclusion are limited and complex.

The best piece of evidence is contained in a 308-page doctoral dissertation called "Stockholders as Customers for Their Corporations' Products," which an economist named Kenneth Paul Uhl submitted to the State University of Iowa.

Uhl talked with companies such as Bristol-Myers, Minute Maid, Texaco, and American Tobacco, which actively solicit investor support of their products. These companies believe stockholders do favor their wares, but admit they have no concrete evidence to back up their contention. The more convincing part of Mr. Uhl's belief that stockholders have a bias in favor of their companies' products is founded on three pioneering investigations of the subject done by Ford, General Motors, and General Electric.

The Ford study, based on a non-random sample of 1000 stockholders taken in 1956—the year the company went public—showed that investors did prefer Ford Motor cars. This was notably the case with the low-priced Ford, which was owned by 25 per cent of the company's stockholders in contrast to the 14 per cent who owned Chevrolets. This was the case even though 24 per cent of all cars registered in 1956 were Chevrolets, as against 20 per cent for Fords. An interesting sidelight to this study was that Ford stockholders who also owned shares of General Motors stock preferred G.M. cars to Ford models.

The General Motors study of stockholder purchasing bias was made in 1948, when questionnaires were mailed to a sample of 39,418 share owners along with the annual report. The study indicated that 62.4 per cent of the stockholder respondents owned General Motors cars even though only 42.7 per cent of all cars registered in 1948 were G.M. brands. The survey also showed that 37.5 per cent of G.M.'s stockholders owned the company's Frigidaire refrigerator, despite the fact that only an estimated 20 per cent of all refrigerators in use throughout the country in 1948 were Frigidaires.

The General Electric study, which was based on personal interviews with a random sample of 2000 G.E. stockholders in 1958, showed decided share owner purchasing bias for seven of the company's major consumer products.

G.E. stockholders exhibited a 2.5-to-1 bias in favor of the company's automatic clothes washers, food freezers, and refrigerators. This means that stockholders had two and one-half times as many of these products in their homes as the public at large. Stockholders also indicated a 2.4-to-1 preference for G.E. television sets and vacuum cleaners, a 2.1-to-1 bias for G.E. electric clothes dryers, and a 1.7-to-1 predilection for G.E. toasters.

The General Electric survey also proved that stockholders who owned their shares when they purchased an appliance were far more likely to buy a G.E. brand than investors who did not have a position in the company's stock at the time.

Thirty-two per cent of the stockholders who purchased an automatic clothes washer when they had money invested in G.E. stock, for example, bought a G.E. model. This compares with only 10 per cent of the stockholders who selected G.E. clothes washers before they owned shares of the company's stock.

In concluding his discussion of the G.E. survey, Mr. Uhl noted that "The marketing significance of this particular study was expressed by a General Electric spokesman, who said in effect: We would distribute our stock free to all takers if the marketing implications were the only considerations and if these stockholders would react as favorably to General Electric appliances in their purchasing decisions as do our present stockholders."

Stockholders unquestionably represent an important, if still largely unrecognized, market for their companies' products.

They can also represent a vital force in their companies' battles with state and federal legislative bodies.

One of the very few companies that not only appreciate the political power of its stockholders but capitalize on it as well is the Wisconsin Power and Light Company, of Madison, Wisconsin.

Wisconsin Power and Light, which serves some 275,000 electric, gas, and water customers, first glimpsed the potential political strength of its stockholders back in the depths of the Depression. In those days, the company's business was so bad that it was forced to stop paying dividends on its common stock, all of which was owned by a holding company called Middle West Utilities. It was also obliged to slash the dividend on its preferred stock—at one time by as much as 75 per cent—and as a result its preferred stockholders saw the value of their investment plummet from the $100 a share they originally paid for their stock down to a low of $15.

To make matters worse, the municipal and public ownership of utilities was actively being promoted by the state administration. There was a Wisconsin Development Authority Bill before the state legislature to create a kind of TVA in the Wisconsin River Basin, and scores of communities—many of them served by Wisconsin Power and Light—were voting to take over their electric distribution systems with the aid of PWA grants from the state government.

It was against this bleak background that the company's president Grover C. Neff decided to bring its problems to the preferred stockholders. He invited them to special meetings, told them why they were not receiving a full dividend, what they as stockholders could do to improve the company's income by encouraging the greater use of electricity, and how they could help save the utility from having its distribution systems taken over by municipal governments. It is interesting to note that during those troubled years, principally in the 1930s, Wisconsin Power and Light had twenty-two communities considering the purchase of its distribution systems— yet lost nary a one to public ownership.

Thousands of Wisconsin Power and Light preferred stockholders attended these meetings, which were held in every district served by the company. The meetings were conducted by management representatives who explained the utility's plight, told stockholders how they could help, and then suggested that share owners form a permanent committee to act as liaison between themselves and management.

These committees have been in continuous operation since 1935. Meetings are held once or twice a year, at which a management man describes the company's recent progress, outlines its construction plans, and reports on any financing plans which may be coming up. Committee members are urged to ask questions, and management sees to it that they receive straight-from-the-shoulder answers. After the meeting, the commitee's officers send letters out to all stockholders in the area telling them what went on.

Since 1958, the company has augmented these meetings with general stockholder information meetings. They are held in the company's operating districts, as well as in Madison, Wisconsin, where the company's head office is located, and in Milwaukee, where a large number of stockholders live. The stockholder committees send out the invitations to all share owners within the area, and an average of 300 turn up at each meeting. These meetings, which are attended by the company's five top officers, have an annual theme such as "Investors Help Build America's Future" or "Power in the Electronic Age." Management addresses these meetings in an off-the-cuff fashion, there is a question and answer period, and refreshments are served so that the company's officers can get a chance to chat with stockholders personally.

Wisconsin Power and Light's long and determined wooing of its stockholders has resulted in a sharp rise in the number of the company's shares owned by people living within the state. In 1948, when the company sold its common stock to the public, only 21 per cent of its shares were owned by Wisconsin residents. Today the figure is 70 per cent.

Wisconsin Power and Light has some 28,000 stockholders living in the state. These investors, together with their families and friends, represent a significant pro-company political force on the state and federal level. They can also get things done on the local level, as illustrated by the following two stories.

Up until 1950, W.P. & L. had a hot water building heating service in a community of 5000 people. This became a very uneconomical operation, and the company wanted to abandon it. At the hearing before the Public Service Commission, many customers appeared against abandoning the service. Then a group of businessmen came forward who were also Wisconsin Power and Light stockholders. They testified that continuing the heating service was against the best interests of both the company's owners and its customers. This testimony had a considerable effect, and a favorable ruling on abandonment was secured.

Early in the company's history an antiutility merchandise bill was introduced into the state legislature. Passage of the bill would have meant that W.P. & L. could no longer sell electrical appliances and other merchandise associated with its business. Naturally, the company opposed the legislation. The hearing started in late afternoon, and it appeared that the number of people in favor of the bill far outnumbered those opposing it. W.P. & L. got on the telephone and talked to a dozen or so shareholders who came down of their own accord to the hearing in early evening. They testified that it was their company which would be discriminated against if the antimerchandise bill went into effect, and that they represented a lot of voters in their area who were shareholders of Wisconsin Power and Light. The bill was defeated.

Wisconsin Power & Light is by no means the only company to enlist its stockholders in political struggles. Armour & Company, for example, sends its owners reprints of newspaper stories and editorials giving the pros and cons of government actions affecting the company. Gulf Oil sends copies of congressmen's voting records to its stockholders. And International Telephone & Telegraph share owners were thanked by president Harold S. Geneen for the telegrams they fired off to their congressmen protesting the seizure of some $7.3 million of ITT properties in Brazil. It was these telegrams, together with management's own efforts, Mr. Geneen said, that was to a large extent responsible for the Hickenlooper Amendment, which now requires the suspension of American aid to countries appropriating privately owned United States property without adequate compensation.

Stockholders will also march into political combat on their own, without management prodding, if they feel their cause is just. The most recent illustration of this is the "Committee of 100,000" which was formed to represent A.T. & T.'s more than 3 million stockholders at the Federal Communications Commission hearings investigating the telephone company's rates and profits. The announcement of the FCC's investigation is credited with touching off a substantial slide in the price of A.T. & T. stock, which in turn led to the formation of the committee under the sponsorship of the United Shareowners of America, Inc.

The "Committee of 100,000" is headed by United Shareowners' President Benjamin Javits, former General Electric President Charles E. Wilson, Franklin National Bank Chairman Arthur T. Roth, and

Arnold Bernhard, founder of *The Value Line Investment Survey*. A.T. & T. stockholders are urged to support the committee (a minimum membership costs $5.00) because, as one of its ads in the *New York Times* said, "You have a stake in the investigation. As one of the owners of the Telephone Company you should be represented in these hearings; your views considered by the FCC. The Commission needs to hear what you have to say. It should understand what effect any decision it makes would have on the 2.8 million individual shareholders of A.T. & T. Your management can't do it for you; it is concerned with defending its actions. The FCC can't do it; it is the examining body. As an individual you can't do it; proper representation requires large expenditures for economic research, legal fees, distribution of information. You *can* have great influence. You *can* make a significant contribution to the economic welfare of your company . . ."

While stockholders can make a difference in the political arena and in the marketplace, they can also be helpful to their corporations in ways even less generally appreciated by management. Take the case of the little Animal Trap Company of America, founded in 1848.

The directors of this company recently asked its approximately 400 stockholders and 250 employees to suggest a new name for Animal Trap which would be shorter and more descriptive of its diversified line of products. The prize for the winning entry was a complete fishing outfit (tackle box, two rods, two reels, and a complete set of lures), and, to get everyone warmed up, the directors themselves suggested three sample names—Sports Mfg., Trappe, Inc., and Sports Unlimited. Close to 300 replies ranging from Tackle & Trap, to Trappe a Go Go, poured into the company's headquarters in Lititz, Pennsylvania. The Animal Trap Company of America is now known as the Woodstream Corporation, and the winner of the fishing kit is stockholder the Rev. Dr. Henry Luffberry, of St. Paul's Lutheran Church, in Washington, D.C.

What is really fascinating about stockholders today is that they are not only one of the largest untapped resources in America, but also one of the fastest growing.

When the New York Stock Exchange took its first Census of Share-owners in 1952, an estimated 6.5 million Americans owned shares in our nation's publicly held companies. Thirteen years later, that figure had grown to 20.1 million (one out of every six adult Americans), and N.Y.S.E. president G. Keith Funston predicts that the number may hit 25 million in 1970, and may rise to 35 million in 1980. "Although share ownership had expanded faster than even the most optimistic observers predicted a decade ago," says Mr. Funston, "it is also apparent that only a start has been made."

The number of share owners in American business now exceeds the combined population of New York, Los Angeles, Chicago and Philadelphia—the four largest cities in the U.S.

There are now more stockholders in America than there are workers in the organized labor movement. And while the stockholder population is expanding rapidly, union membership is on the decline.

Many corporations such as A.T.&T., Standard Oil (New Jersey), Du Pont, IBM, and General Motors now have far more stockholders than employees, and this trend is decidedly on the rise.

While the sheer size and growth rate of the investing public is impressive, its composition is hardly less so. Witness these statistics taken from the Exchange's 1965 Census of Shareowners.

Income: The median annual household income of the nation's share owners was $9500 in 1965 (compared to a national average of $6600) and had grown from $6200 in 1959. The largest rise in share ownership was among investors with household incomes of from $10,000 to $15,000 a year. Among individuals with household incomes in excess of $25,000, six out of every ten now own stock.

It's also interesting to note that American stockholders are oriented in the direction of thrift. According to the N.Y.S.E's 1965 census, 88 per cent of American stockholders also have savings accounts, 88 per cent have life insurance, 79 per cent own their own homes, 53 per cent own U. S. Savings Bonds, and 12 per cent have invested in corporate, municipal, or other U. S. Government bonds.

Education: More than 80 per cent of all adult stockholders— better than four out of five—are high-school graduates. This, as in the case of income, is substantially higher than the national average. What's more, over half of these stockholders have some college training, while nearly one-third are college graduates. Ninety-five per cent of the people who have become stockholders since 1959, incidentally, have a high school education or better.

Age: The average American stockholder is middle-aged (the median age of the share-owning population in 1965 was forty-nine). People aged thirty-five to fifty-four are becoming share owners in the greatest numbers. But the largest absolute and percentage increase in share ownership reported in the 1965 survey was among young people under twenty-one years of age, which nearly tripled from 450,000 to 1,280,000 since 1962.

The statistical picture painted by the New York Stock Exchange shows the typical American stockholder to be a mature individual with a significantly higher-than-average education and income. We also know from the examples given earlier that stockholders are willing to act in their company's behalf if encouraged to do so. This fact is supported by an Opinion Research Corporation survey titled "Mobilizing Stockholder Support."

This study showed that 95 per cent of the share owners interviewed were willing to buy their companies' products, 90 per cent were willing to recommend them to others, and 83 per cent were willing to test new products before they were put on the market. The survey also revealed that 77 per cent of the stockholders questioned would write to their congressmen about legislation affecting their companies, 71 per cent would vote for political candidates friendly toward business, and that 44 per cent were actually willing to take an active part in the political campaigns of these candidates.

The willingness of America's 20 million stockholders to act in their companies' behalf either economically or politically represents one of the greatest untapped reservoirs of power in our country's history. If it could be harnessed as effectively as the union movement has organized the power of the laboring man, it could alter the shape of our capitalistic society forever.

But who will organize investors? Is it possible that there are capitalist George Meanys, David Dubinskys, and Walter Reuthers waiting in the wings to lead the crusade that will give stockholders as commanding a voice in business and government as the AFL-CIO? Are there men and women with fire in their bellies who yearn to organize a countervailing force to challenge the men who manage our corporations?

Maybe such individuals don't exist. Perhaps there's no reason for them to exist; after all, the federal government is doing a pretty good job of looking after stockholders' fundamental interests.

But if ever such militants appear, they will probably bear some resemblance—vague or otherwise—to the handful of people de-scribed in the next chapter. These flamboyant individuals have been called many things in their day—most of them profoundly uncomplimentary. But whatever else they may be, they are certainly not careless capitalists.

CRACKPOTS OR CRUSADERS?

DEFENDING THE RIGHTS OF

MINORITY STOCKHOLDERS

Shortly after his appointment as chairman of what is now the Sperry Rand Corporation, the late General Douglas MacArthur presided over his first annual meeting. Stockholder Lewis Dusenbery Gilbert, unawed by a man who was already an American legend, inquired as to why the chairman owned no shares of stock in the company he headed. General MacArthur stiffly told Mr. Gilbert the answer was none of his or anybody else's business. Gilbert quickly made clear that he considered the general's holdings in the company were very much the stockholders' business, and the confrontation made headlines. By the next meeting, General MacArthur had unbent sufficiently to purchase several hundred shares.

"The role of the minority shareholder is not for the timid," says Gilbert, the articulate, pugnacious leader of the evangelical band of shareholders who are sometimes called "professionals" because they make almost a full-time job of advancing stockholder causes. Regarding themselves as crusaders in behalf of corporate democracy, they refuse to be cowed by a battery of big-name officers and directors gazing severely at them from a raised dais at an annual meeting. With irrepressible persistence, they ask questions, criticize management decisions, and introduce proposals to change any company practices they regard as unfair to minority stockholders. When not holding forth at meetings, they bombard management with letters of inquiry or suggestions, while rallying other small stockholders to the cause.

The members of this group have no ties other than common cause. In fact, some aren't on speaking terms. Evelyn Y. Davis, a cigar-smoking *femme fatale* with a Viennese accent, identified herself at a Twentieth Century-Fox annual meeting as, "Cleopatra, Queen of the stockholders." President Darryl F. Zanuck chivalrously replied, "I subscribe to that." Red-haired actress-song writer Gloria Parker, another annual-meeting regular, would disagree with that billing. At the same session, the two ladies scuffled over possession of a microphone and Mrs. Davis angrily accused Miss Parker of socking her in the eye. At an IBM meeting, Chairman Thomas J. Watson, Jr., had to assign two bodyguards to protect the vociferous Mrs. Davis from possible harm at the hands of a glowering male stockholder incensed over her efforts to monopolize the meeting.

But Lewis Gilbert is by all odds the Number One spokesman for the small stockholder—for the "independents," as they like to call themselves. When Gilbert started going to annual meetings in the 1930s and asking questions on subjects not covered in the annual report, he was viewed by corporation officials and the press as "comic relief," "a self-appointed Sir Galahad," "a ham actor," "an irritating gadfly," and other things less polite. In the course of his career he has engaged in shouting matches with John J. McCloy, former American High Commissioner in Germany, who became head of Chase National Bank, survived caustic remarks by a host of other chief executive officers and was once told, "I wish you were dead," by an irate chairman who was losing a verbal battle.

Yet three decades of dogged effort have had an effect. Today a good many corporation officials credit Gilbert with bringing about beneficial changes, and almost all of them admit that he represents a legitimate point of view. He lectures at colleges and clubs, testifies before congressional committees, is consulted, surreptitiously or openly, by many firms planning some change that affects stockholder relations, and has even followed comedian Dick Shawn as the star performer at a resort hotel where he was billed as the "Leo Durocher of the investment world." Gilbert has even been asked to serve on boards of directors—offers he turned down for fear of jeopardizing his independent position. An officer of General

Mills said that Gilbert had "done more for the little stockholder than anyone who ever lived."

Gilbert and his brother, John, who aids him in his work, inherited small amounts of stock in about fifty companies. In 1932 Gilbert attended the annual meeting of a gas company in which he owned ten shares. It was a sleepy affair. When Gilbert tried to get the chairman's attention to ask a question, he was ignored; in his own words, he was "treated like a tramp." He went away resolved to devote the rest of his life to seeing that small shareholders, as legitimate owners of businesses, got more considerate attention when they asserted their rights.

His method was to attend meetings of as many companies as he could, year after year, asking for information that he thought stockholders should have, and making proposals tending to give stockholders more control over affairs that affected them. To widen his scope, he acquired shares of other companies. Now he is entitled to attend so many meetings that his brother and several close friends have to help out in order to cover them all. Their group is referred to by wary corporate public relations men as "Gilbert and Company."

Gilbert, a youthful-looking bachelor in his fifties, lives with a handful of servants in a rambling, overstuffed co-operative apartment on fashionable Park Avenue in New York City, where one cluttered room is set aside as an office. There, with the assistance of some college students who work for him in their off hours and occasionally represent him at annual meetings, he maintains voluminous files of annual reports, postmeeting reports, proxy statements, and newspaper clippings. A small cot against one book-laden wall is used for occasional catnaps when not serving as an extension of the battered desk nearby.

Gilbert had not been long in action before he began to inspire other stockholders who had questions or complaints they had never dared to voice in public before. Some got in touch with him for tactical advice. Others simply followed procedures set up by the SEC to allow shareholders to put their ideas forward.

Under the authority granted by the Securities Exchange Act of 1934, the Securities and Exchange Commission requires companies listed on the national exchanges to mail a proxy statement containing certain information to each shareholder before voting takes place at the annual meeting. Rule X-14A-8 of these regulations permits a shareholder, even if he owns only one share of stock, to put up a proposal of his own and, along with a one-hundred-word statement of explanation, have it included in management's own proxy material mailed out to all stockholders.

Lew Gilbert once forced the giant Bethlehem Steel Corporation to adjourn an annual meeting before any business was transacted because the company had failed to include two of his resolutions in its proxy statement. Bethlehem's management was obliged to pack its bags, travel from Wilmington, Delaware (site of the meeting), to New York, reprint and mail out 74,000 new proxy statements and ballots, and hold another meeting two weeks later.

Shortly after World War II, the ranks of the vigorous minority shareholders were strengthened by a determined band of women under the leadership of Mrs. Wilma Soss, the sixty-ish president of the Federation of Women Shareholders in American Business, who was uproariously profiled in a five-page story "Queen of the Corporate Gadflies" in *Life* magazine. Campaigning for most of the same reforms as the Gilberts, they have added a strong feminist slant —for instance, they would like to see a woman on every board of directors.

At one contentious three-hour annual meeting of Metro-Goldwyn-Mayer stockholders, Mrs. Soss nominated the former Mrs. Sybil Burton, divorced wife of actor Richard Burton, to the MGM board. The nomination was in the way of a protest, she proclaimed, against the lack of a female director. Mrs. Soss, speaking in support of her nominee, said Mrs. Burton was an "excellent" business woman who was better acquainted with the movie business than most MGM directors. "She is better qualified," she snapped, "than a general, a Secretary of the Navy or someone running a steamship line." Among the MGM directors re-elected at the meeting were retired General Omar N. Bradley; John L. Sullivan, former Navy Secretary, and George L. Killion, president of American President Lines and chairman of MGM.

In the Midwest and Far West are still other leaders who follow a definite route of annual meetings and mastermind the offering of proposals, praise, and criticism very much the same way Gilbert runs his mammoth operation. They are not bashful about probing into officers' salaries, the profitability of one division compared to another, merger prospects, conflicts within management.

The activity of the professionals has emboldened other shareholders, not necessarily interested in the same causes but holding strong opinions, to speak up on such subjects as union disputes, racial discrimination, peace, and politics. At a Chase Manhattan Bank meeting a lady criticized the bank's collection of abstract paintings.

When the vocal critics arouse the ire of pro-management stockholders in the audience, a free-for-all sometimes threatens, which the chairman needs iron lungs and a heavy gavel to control. The very stockholders Gilbert believes he is helping often offer him a punch on the nose. At one stormy session Gilbert and an opponent wrestled for the microphone. Lady stockholders arguing with each other create an especially delicate problem for the meeting's chairman. Henry Alexander of Morgan Guaranty found his diplomacy strained when both Mrs. Soss and Mrs. Davis clamored loudly for his attention. His decision, "I will recognize age," only drew an indignant look from Mrs. Soss, to whom he was pointing, while the younger Mrs. Davis shouted, "What about beauty?"

Such undignified contention does not bother the "independents" a bit. "Every stockholder has a right to be heard," Gilbert maintains. "Whether or not it is something management wants to hear. The management worshippers who are tired of listening to the views of shareholders are for the most part current or retired employee-shareholders, or doing business or hoping to do business with the company. They are often the ones who think that having a free lunch is the object of the annual meeting. Needless to say, we independents are responsible only to those who send us their proxies. Others do not have to agree with us. We do intend, however, to be heard." Gilbert takes special pride in having had a hand in "recreating the annual meeting from a state of innocuous disquietude into the lively forum it was originally intended to be."

Some thought it was getting too lively. Sidney Weinberg, a partner in Goldman, Sachs & Company and a director of many corporations, suggested a while ago that annual meetings were being turned into circuses. He blasted the "few publicity seeking characters who attended stockholder meetings primarily to ask impertinent, irrelevant, sometimes abusive questions. . . . I understand that people are training themselves to follow in their footsteps," he lamented.

Gilbert has long battled to get companies to hold annual meetings in easily accessible places. "There is no reason why nation-wide companies like Pepsi-Cola and Coca-Cola, or Southern Pacific Railway, which has its headquarters on the West Coast, should meet in Wilmington, Delaware," he says. Over the years Gilbert has tried to convince managements of the desirability of moving meetings to places where shareholders in large numbers can attend. Today many companies from A.T.&T. to F. W. Woolworth are doing this and Lew Gilbert is delighted. These companies, he says, "are getting the idea." There are still a few states where antiquated laws require companies to hold annual meetings within the state boundaries. In all other cases, Gilbert insists, "you have to conclude that if they won't meet in a convenient place, they don't really want to encourage shareholder interest."

Gilbert and Mrs. Soss chalked up a victory of sorts when U. S. Steel in 1964 sponsored a resolution in its proxy statement which would enable it to hold annual meetings in cities other than Hoboken, New Jersey, site of its stockholder conclaves for many years. The resolution, which passed handily, listed as possible locations for future annual meetings New York City, San Francisco, Pittsburgh, Birmingham, Chicago, and Cleveland, site of its 1966 meeting.

Gilbert has some well-developed ideas on how annual meetings should be run. Annual reports and proxies should be mailed out in advance; most companies now do this, particularly since 1961, when the New York Stock Exchange made proxy solicitation mandatory for its listed companies. "At the meeting," he says, "the question and answer period is the important time. Stockholders resent having it curtailed for lunch or a company movie. When they get up to speak, stockholders should be asked to identify themselves, though the chairman will sometimes try to embarrass one of us by asking how many shares we own. That isn't the point. A person with one share is as much entitled to speak as a person with a thousand shares."

Gilbert gives away several thousand copies of his *Annual Report of Stockholders Activities at Corporation Meetings,* a half-inch-thick publication Gilbert started in 1939, when he began to get hundreds of letters asking him what went on. Now, he sends a copy of his report in response. He writes it himself and spends about $5000 a year of his own money publishing the document. The balance of its $10,000 annual cost is picked up by its readers.

In the Gilbert report, no punches are pulled. "Our first example of how not to conduct the annual meeting is furnished by General Electric," said his 1962 report, criticizing the arrangements that provided only one microphone for 3518 shareholders present. At the 1963 meeting, G.E. provided five microphones and won Gilbert's thanks. Certain chairmen may be singled out for praise if they handle meetings impartially and show a willingness to answer questions. All who meet Gilbert's standards are listed in the annual report. "Nothing better displays the calibre of corporate leadership than the way the annual meeting is run," Gilbert says.

"A question at an annual meeting can sometimes bring out information the stockholder could never get otherwise," Gilbert maintains. "I often ask about advertising expenditures—very important for certain types of product. This used to be called a secret for 'competitive reasons,' even though the information was always known on Madison Avenue. Now I usually get an answer, and I learn why advertising went up or down.

"In some cases the annual meeting is the only way to get important information. That's the case with the state-chartered banks. Many big New York banks are state banks and not under SEC or Federal banking rules, so they are not required to solicit proxies or disclose in proxy material things like the directors' stock ownership or options. The SEC has asked Congress to make every commercial bank with 500 or more shareholders subject to the same rules as are now applied to industrial corporations. Until banks are forced to make full disclosure to stockholders, I will have to go to the meetings and ask about those things from the floor."

A great victory was claimed by the small-stockholder representatives in 1963, when New York City's oldest bank, the Bank of New York, founded in 1784 by a group headed by Alexander Hamilton, acceded to the request to hold an annual meeting. Under its long-standing charter, the Bank of New York was not required to hold annual meetings at all. There were no directors to elect—vacancies on the bank's board of trustees, the governing body, were filled by persons appointed by other trustees. There had been a few brief, formal meetings to deal with specific changes requiring stockholder approval, but none to discuss the bank's affairs generally. A few of the stockholders had been demanding a real confrontation. Margaret Gilbert, wife of Lewis's brother John, had been particularly insistent, and the power of a woman finally won over 180 years of policy. When the bank's president, Samuel H. Wooley, finally invited shareholders to "gather informally" he gave full credit to the Gilberts for his decision. He even anticipated their questions by revealing the salary and stock holdings of the top officers and directors, facts that the Gilberts had dragged from other bank presidents only by constant nagging and questioning.

An executive who conducts a fair and informative meeting may still be subject to attack by a minority shareholder for his high salary, high pension, or policy on stock options. Gilbert feels executive salaries should have a top limit; ones that exceed $200,000 per year, including fringe benefits, are generally too high, especially in companies that are not paying a cash dividend. At General Motors, for instance, where in some years Chairman Frederic G. Donner received aggregate remuneration of more than $750,000, Gilbert and the Federation of Women Shareholders jointly proposed a ceiling of $200,000 including bonus, with no bonus to be in excess of 100 per cent of salary. Such resolutions are seldom passed, but can get as much as 25 to 30 per cent of the vote when companies are doing poorly. Because such stockholder criticism focuses public attention on high salaries in an embarrassing way, some firms have felt they should act even after defeating a Gilbert or Soss proposal. In 1963 Sperry Rand announced that officers who were also directors as a group were taking a salary cut that totaled about $130,000 for the year, and that the President, Harry F. Vickers, was taking an additional voluntary cut. After Sperry notified the Gilberts of their intentions the Gilberts withdrew a proposal on executive pay they had intended to offer in the proxy statement.

Officers' pensions should have a top limit of $25,000 excluding any amounts derived from employee contributions, Gilbert believes. When a company shows a disposition to accept the principle of some reasonable limit, however, he is willing to compromise. American Tobacco, P. Lorillard, National Dairy, General Foods, Congoleum-Nairn, and National Biscuit instituted ceilings on pensions after considering the opinion of the minority shareholders, Gilbert maintains.

In recent years restricted stock options granted to corporate officers have come under heavy attack. Many option plans already exist, however, and three out of five companies listed on the New York Stock Exchange have them. "First, the option plans should always be submitted to stockholders for approval," says Gilbert, "since they represent a dilution of stockholder equity." Some option plans, says Gilbert, "are just a way for insiders to enrich themselves at the expense of other stockholders and the government. If the optioned stock has a fixed price and the market goes down, management wants to have the price reset lower. If the market goes up, officers can take up the options and then unload the stock for profits taxed at the capital gains rate."

Gilbert sees encouraging signs that the stockholder campaign on options is getting support from other stockholders, tax authorities, and financial writers. "It was particularly gratifying that the 1963 tax law embodied some of the provisions we had advocated for years. To receive capital gains treatment stock acquired through the exercise of options must be held a minimum of three years. Such holding periods had already been adopted at our urging by General Foods, P. Lorillard and others. We also believe that options should be granted in annual installments and the rights should expire if not exercised. Franklin National Bank included such a non-cumulative installment clause in a plan it proposed for stockholder ratification; so did Glen Alden and Foremost Dairies. Burlington Industries defeated in 1956, 1957 and 1962 our resolution asking that all future option plans involving more than 1000 shares be submitted to stockholders. But in 1963 the company did ask approval, saying that because of some of the proposals made in the past, the directors had decided as a matter of policy to submit outstanding options for stockholder approval even though not required to do so."

Because of its far-reaching implications, cumulative voting for directors is regarded by the professional stockholders as the single most important plank in their platform. In twenty-three states, stockholders are allowed to cast all their votes—the number of shares they own multiplied by the number of director candidates—for one person, instead of dividing the votes among the several candidates standing for election. If minority stockholders can put up a candidate of their own and cast all their votes for him, they have some hope of success. They argue that cumulative voting would ensure the election of a "watchdog" particularly sensitive to matters affecting the small stockholders. He could also insist that they get the information to which they are entitled. Somewhat like proportional representation, the device has a good body of support outside of shareholder ranks. For instance, in California the Commissioner of Corporations takes the view that, even though companies are incorporated elsewhere, he will consider the absence of cumulative voting a point against them when they apply for a permit to issue or exchange securities within the state borders.

In several states, however, including New York, cumulative voting is merely permitted by state law, rather than required; the corporations themselves have to decide that they want it. Gilbert and the independents frequently use the proxy to introduce resolutions to adopt cumulative voting. "It does not enable a minority to block a majority; it enables minorities to be heard," Gilbert contends. "As it is now, owners of 49 per cent of the stock might have no voice in management. Naturally, when managements wish to perpetuate themselves they oppose cumulative voting. They say a minority representative might work at cross purposes with the rest of the board. It is hard to see how this might come about—certainly many directors now represent special interests—brokerages, banks, funds, large shareholders—but are assumed to act in the interests of the corporation as a whole when they get together. Cumulative voting is a way to make American capitalism more democratic."

Morton Adler, another active minority stockholder, has been stumping for cumulative voting: "We are seeing on every hand the growing financial power of investment companies, fiduciaries, foundations and insurance companies," Adler says. "With huge sums to invest they take big blocks of stock in leading companies. When it comes to voting on proposals that affect the way the company is run, they generally dodge the issue and cast their vote for management. The minority shareholders could get together and get a watchdog, without altering the balance of power substantially."

Like most proposals of the independents, cumulative voting wins its greatest support among stockholders when things are not going well for the company. At Sperry Rand, for instance, after a period of declining profits and no cash dividends, a proposal for cumulative voting received an impressive 11.2 per cent of the votes cast. While twenty-five to fifty companies a year adopt cumulative voting, a number of those already having it decide to eliminate it, so that any gain is hard to measure.

In some companies, directors all stand for re-election every year, while at others directors hold office for two or three years under an arrangement whereby only a handful come up for election each year. This is called a "stagger system." Though supposed to guarantee continuity of management, it can be used, the independents contend, to keep certain interests represented on the board long after they might otherwise have been eliminated. For instance Jay Gould, who assisted in the passage of the first law permitting a stagger system in New York State, promptly put himself in a five-year slot on the Erie Railway directorate so he could not be ousted even if he lost control of the company. On the stagger system issue the independents have had some success, and many companies have ended it. Annual election of all directors is by now the more common practice.

One of Gilbert's first corporate skirmishes came when he pursued the idea that there should be a mandatory retirement age for directors. He suggested that Charles M. Schwab, chairman of Bethlehem Steel, be retired because he was seventy-five. Schwab was hurt, other Bethlehem officials were enraged, and a fellow stockholder threatened a right to the jaw. Gilbert is still making such proposals, however, and except in companies with strong one-family control, the notion that younger men should take over the reins has come to be pretty widely accepted.

A few "outside" directors on the board are also regarded as desirable. Such men, Gilbert thinks, are more likely to bring independent thinking and are not shy about criticizing management because they are not beholden to the president or chairman for their jobs.

Morton Adler once nominated Nikita Khrushchev as a director of Virginia-Carolina Chemical Corporation, telling the president and chairman, Justin Potter, that the company "needs men as strong as you are who can stand up and object and make it stick." The premier received 1500 votes, not enough for election.

"We think that every director of a public corporation should own some stock in the company," Gilbert says. "It shows his faith in the company, that he is willing to take the same risks as other shareholders. Some state laws and the national banking laws require ownership of stock as a condition for running for the office of director.

"The Missouri-Kansas-Texas Railway used to be among the worst offenders—one proxy statement noted no less than ten directors without a share of stock. Today, all directors are stockholders, and management has endorsed a resolution—sponsored by an independent stockholder—that equity holdings be required of all directors and nominees. Even when officers have put up an argument on the floor of the annual meeting or opposed a proxy resolution, we often find that by the next year all directors have quietly acquired some stock. More and more companies have come around to our way of thinking and amended their by-laws to require it."

While conceding that annual reports have improved greatly in appearance and content over the years, the spokesmen for minority shareholders still find that some companies are not candid enough, or do not make their financial statements clear. "We constantly urge owners to read and study the pages of the annual report on which appear the notes to the financial statements," the Gilberts say. "They often relate important information which has to do with the core of the company's profit picture."

For the difficulties inherent in understanding financial statements Morton Adler places part of the blame on the practices of auditing firms. "It is common practice to change the method of reporting financial figures from year to year," says Adler. "Whenever you see the statement that some practice has been changed, you know there is a reason—either to improve or reduce reported earnings, shifting some item or credit from one period to another. This makes it impossible to compare one year to another with any accuracy, or tell how one company in an industry is really doing compared to some other company. The SEC and the Exchanges should require that when the method of reporting is changed, the figures for at least three years back be recalculated so that comparisons are possible.

"The implication of the change for earnings should be spelled out," says Mr. Adler. "Remember that when price-earnings ratios are running twenty to one, a change of $1 in earnings means $20 in the price of the stock. Think of the significance where stock options are involved. Earnings can be hidden while options are being taken up, and disclosed in years when management wants to sell its stock at a profit. The ordinary shareholder can be completely unaware that he has missed the dividends on higher earnings that he was entitled to.

"A shareholder is apt to think, in fact encouraged to think, that the phrase 'according to generally accepted practices' in the auditor's statement means something," Mr. Adler says. "Sometimes the SEC recommendation differs from that of the Accounting Principles Board. The stockholder is never told these things unless he asks, and sometimes can't even get the answer then.

"Over the years there has been a change in the role of the auditor. Originally he was brought in by the owner, when companies were one-man or family affairs. As share ownership became widely dispersed and owners delegated the running of the business to managers, the auditor became responsible to these officers, hired and directed by them. Actually, the auditor should be responsible first to the people who pay him, the shareholders who own the business."

The campaign for corporate democracy as conducted by Wilma Soss and the Federation of Women Shareholders is a good deal more colorful than that of other minority shareholders, outdoing in sheer daring even the Gilberts, who have an excellent sense of public relations. Mrs. Soss, who is short, blond, and lives in a fantastically cluttered apartment on New York's fashionable East Side, began her career as a Broadway press agent, moved on into publicity for department stores and finally corporate public relations. B. C. Forbes considered her "one of the country's ace public relations consultants" in 1945 when he hired her to write an article on women shareholders for *Forbes* magazine. "My interviews convinced me that women who held securities had no consciousness of the power of their position," Mrs. Soss says. "They did not know what their companies were doing, seldom attended annual meetings and rarely spoke up except to compliment the management on some minor point. They might complain if they couldn't get the company's product at the corner store, but that was as far as the criticism went.

"I decided to attend a meeting of U. S. Steel where I owned a few shares of stock. It was an educational experience. If they had treated me better there would have been no Federation of Women Shareholders. I simply suggested they ought to have a woman on the board of directors. They refused to take me seriously. So I announced that I was going to organize women shareholders to fight for such things. When I got home I was rather appalled at what I had done, and so was my husband, especially after my statement received some publicity. I was on the spot. I decided to go ahead and organize women shareholders, thinking it would take two or three months and then I could let the group run itself while I merely handled the publicity for it or something like that. It didn't work out that way. I couldn't let go, so many things kept happening. Much of the Federation's work is educational," Mrs. Soss says. "We try to educate women about managing their financial affairs, including their rights as shareholders. Our women aren't speculators but long-term investors—we are not an investors' club."

Like the Gilberts, Mrs. Soss gets around to many of the major annual meetings which she often enlivens by appearing in costume to dramatize her ideas. She appeared in widow's weeds, complete with veil, to mourn the passing of the dividend by the New York Central. At CBS's 1960 meeting she took mop and pail "to clean up the mess" of the TV quiz scandal that had just exploded. Anticipating a stormy session with Robert Young at the New York Central's 1956 meeting, she brought along a lady wrestler "for protection."

Mrs. Soss can be a terror at an annual meeting. She once got the late Irving S. Olds so furious at a U. S. Steel meeting that the distinguished old gentleman brought his gavel down on his watch,

which he had placed on the lectern in front of him, smashing it to
bits.

At the annual meeting of Standard Oil (New Jersey) in 1966,
when stockholders loudly applauded the defeat of a resolution
sponsored by Mrs. Soss for secret balloting in the election of
directors, she turned to the audience and snapped "How dare you
applaud for the defeat of secret balloting in the U.S.?" A focus of
Mrs. Soss's campaigns has been the idea of a secret ballot in the
election of directors, which she regards as particularly important if
there is much stock held by employees. Proxies, of course, are signed
and management can easily check how any one stockholder voted.
"Employees should not have to reveal to the management how they
vote. Even some company officers are afraid to vote their stock for
things they really believe in that go against the official position. It
may be that the overall outcome of the voting wouldn't be changed.
So I might get a ten per cent vote for my proposal instead of three
per cent. Why should management care? But it would be a great
thing for corporate democracy."

The influence of people like the Gilberts and the Federation of
Women Shareholders, they believe, cannot be fairly judged by the
vote they marshal in support of their reform propositions. Under
the original SEC rules, an independent proposal in the proxy had to
receive 3 per cent of the votes cast in order to be proposed again
the next year. Because so many poorly supported proposals were
appearing time after time, the SEC in 1954 amended its rule to
require votes of 3 per cent the first year, 6 per cent the second and
10 per cent the third. If a stockholder proposal fails to get this
proportion of the vote, it cannot be reproposed for four years. As
a result, there are years when certain favorite ideas cannot be
brought up by the minority. They have learned to stagger the resolutions so that something they regard as needed will, however,
come up each year.

"The chief reason why we fail to pass our resolutions year
after year," Gilbert explains, "is because fiduciary holders of large
blocks of stock almost invariably vote with the management. By
gathering the votes of several thousand individual owners, however,
we try to show the management that a good many people are with
us, even though their combined holdings are only 5 per cent or 6 per

cent of the stock outstanding. And often the companies come to feel this numerical vote is worth paying attention to.

"Some years ago in a large company an independent proposal to place ceilings on pensions was receiving yearly more than the ten per cent of the vote cast, and thus was eligible under the SEC proxy rules to be repeatedly re-introduced. Because of mechanical voting of proxies by trust funds and mutuals and because of un-marked proxies, a ten per cent vote against management is really far greater than might appear. The president of the company eventually called me on the phone, asking if the issue of a pension ceiling could be compromised. 'As president of a publicly owned corporation I have no right to reject in toto what 10 per cent of the voters told me they wanted,' he said. We came to an agreement."

On the issue that Gilbert has fought for most successfully, getting a postmeeting report sent out at company expense for the benefit of those unable to be present, he has never won a majority of the votes when the issue was voted on. "The companies oppose it as too expensive, or unnecessary. But the next year they may surprise us by coming out with an excellent post-meeting report. They can see people want it. When Du Pont asked on a post card how many stockholders wanted the post-meeting report, they got 12,800 requests. The Pennsylvania Railroad opposed us when we used the proxy to ask for a more detailed post-meeting report. Our proposition lost by about eight million shares. But 3,670 people had voted with us. The next year, the Pennsy report was full and complete. It is gratifying to see how shareholder criticism of omissions or perfunctory accounts often leads to a greatly improved post-meeting report the next year.

"Sometimes we get results just by calling attention in public to things that are embarrassing. If I ask how often the directors meet, and everyone learns that they meet only two or three times during the year, the next year you may be sure they'll want to increase it to nine or ten times."

Another organization of investors is the United Shareowners of America headed by Benjamin A. Javits, New York attorney and brother of Senator Jacob K. Javits, of New York. In many respects Mr. Javits' ideas coincide with the Gilberts', but Javits' group also concerns itself with such national issues as inflation, foreign aid, tax legislation, and the policies of the government.

To further the interest of investors, and also savings depositors, small businessmen, property owners, and others that United Shareowners broadly construes as "share owners of America," the organization has particularly focused its attention on tax legislation. It has called for lower individual income taxes and corporate taxes, with the substitution of excise taxes and sales taxes. It has also campaigned for less government spending and less intrusion of the government, including the SEC, into the business picture.

"There are too many impedimenta now in the SEC rules and regulations," Mr. Javits maintains. "The 1933 and 1934 Securities Exchange Acts and their administrations have been reasonably good, but unbalanced. No one can say whether the country might have been better off without them, provided that an organization like the United Shareowners of America, and the Stock Exchange, and the National Association of Security Dealers did the job jointly, rather than leaving it to a government agency."

While no officer or director of a publicly owned corporation can be an officer of United Shareowners, they can join as individuals and Javits points to such prominent members as Frank Magee, former board chairman of Alcoa, Joseph Martino, president of National Lead, Paul Manheim, a partner in Lehman Brothers, plus a sprinkling of economists and professors on the National Policy Advisory Committee of United Shareowners. Once a year an awards committee selects 300 corporations for a Corporate Management Award in recognition of their activities in keeping their stockholders fully informed and "doing an exemplary job for their investors, their country, their employees and their customers."

The reformers insist that their efforts have played a major role in giving stockholders the respected voice they now have in the affairs of the companies they owned.

John Gilbert, Lewis Gilbert's brother, takes some amount of pride in reviewing what he feels he may have contributed to the excellent relationship that exists today between the owners and managers of the General Motors Corporation.

"When I first went to a General Motors meeting, in the thirties," Mr. Gilbert says, "I was the only stockholder there," he says. "This was at Wilmington. The assistant general counsel and the secretary of the corporation were the only other people there. They had the Du Pont proxies. On the way back on the train they said I had spoiled their golf game by being there and taking up so much time with questions, but they weren't unfriendly to me. Over the years I improved the whole General Motors stockholder program. Everything was bit by bit. I got Mr. Sloan to come to a stockholders meeting—and finally to conduct one. Nearly all the things we suggested they eventually adopted—a ceiling on pensions, buses to take owners to the meetings, and a superb post-meeting report."

Many corporate officers, on the other hand, sincerely believe that the greater stockholder interest and the adoption of some of the minority's ideas would have come about anyhow.

The trend of the times has been in that direction.

An increasing self-consciousness has pervaded American democracy, in which any highhanded practices on the part of the corporations have come to be condemned.

The very high salaries of some officers and their option and pension benefits have come under closer scrutiny by those who want to show that a "people's capitalism" eliminates great disparities of wealth. The press, which has a natural stake in more information, has come to give a good deal of support to stockholder pleas for full disclosure.

Recent management scandals involving conflicts of interest, price fixing, and the hiring of private detectives to harass corporate critics have convinced an increasing number of stockholders that they must take a far more active interest in the prudent conduct of their company's affairs.

In short, history has been on the side of the professional stockholders in recent years. But regardless of where the credit should lie, the fact is that many of the things the professionals have fought for are winning acceptance by the men who manage many of America's finest corporations.

15

THE CAREFUL CAPITALISTS

In a softly carpeted and marvelously quiet expanse of offices fifty-five floors above New York's fashionable Fifth Avenue sit twelve men hired to manage what is probably the greatest family fortune the world has ever known—the Rockefeller billions.

People who have money regard it very highly—that's why they have it in the first place—and the esteem in which the Rockefellers hold their riches can be seen in the caliber of the men they've retained to look after them.

The Rockefellers' senior investment adviser is J. Richardson Dilworth (BA, LLB, Yale), a fifty-one-year-old patrician who was a partner in the Wall Street investment banking firm of Kuhn, Loeb & Company, and whose wide-ranging outside interests include serving as a trustee of the Metropolitan Museum of Art, trustee of the Yale Corporation, and member of the Council on Foreign Relations. Reporting to Mr. Dilworth are eleven investment advisers such as fifty-seven-year-old Harper Woodward (AB, LLB, Harvard) an aeronautical authority whose office is crowded with scale model airplanes of every description; and Joseph A. Lee, Jr. (Yale, Harvard, MBA) formerly a vice-president and deputy director of investment research at Bankers Trust Company, and before that manager of the institutional department at Reynolds & Co.

These twelve men, who are directors of more than fifty corporations of interest to the Rockefeller family, including Chrysler, Eastern Airlines, Cutler-Hammer Inc., and the Chase Manhattan Bank, consult with members of the family on financial ventures of every conceivable hue. One example: resort hotels. Laurance S. Rockefeller alone has invested millions in Puerto Rico's Dorado Beach Hotel twenty miles west of San Juan, Caneel Bay Plantation in the Virgin Islands, and the lavish Mauna Kea Beach Hotel on the island of Hawaii.

But the fundamental job of these money managers is to supervise the Rockefeller family's massive portfolio of stocks and bonds embracing everything from obscure firms such as Mithras, Inc., of Cambridge, Massachusetts, to household names like the Standard Oil Company of New Jersey, principal offshoot of the Standard Oil Company, which was founded in Cleveland, Ohio, on January 10, 1870, by a small group of men headed by a thirty-year-old merchant named John D. Rockefeller, and from which the family's considerable blessings have flowed.

The elevation of an investment expert to handle money matters for the Rockefellers is a newsworthy event in the world of finance. When Joseph A. Lee, Jr., joined the group in 1966, for example, the *New York Times* carried his photograph and a biographical sketch about him under the headline "Investment Aide Named for Rockefeller Family."

Lee is an earnest young man who has devoted his adult life to the business of investing other people's money. Joe Lee calls himself "a manager of money whose basic function is to create investment portfolios designed to optimize investment objectives whatever they may be." To do this job for the Rockefellers, he says, means collecting factual information on some three hundred companies from a wealth of sources including:

1. The companies' own reports to stockholders.

2. Stockholders meetings. Mr. Lee, who pays particular attention to banks, printing and publishing companies, and office equipment firms, attended International Business Machines' annual meeting in Endicott, New York, for example, because it was held right after the company had announced its new System/360 family of computers. "I know some of IBM's officers," he said, "and I wanted to chat with them about the new computer line at the lunch served after the meeting. There were some other stockholders sitting with us," he volunteers, "but the only questions they asked management had to do with why there wasn't more butter on the table."

3. Analytical materials prepared by Standard & Poor and others.

4. American newspapers and magazines including the *New York Times,* which Mr. Lee reads over breakfast "for fun," *The Wall*

Street Journal, which he devours on the train in to New York from his home in Greenwich, Connecticut, *Business Week, Fortune,* the *Analysts Journal,* and trade publications such as the *Oil and Gas Journal,* as well as foreign publications like the *Statist* and the *Economist,* which he feels provide an "objective point of view about the United States."

5. Wall Street security analysts. Mr. Lee feels that the analysts provide very good information, he always has analysts from three "reliable" Wall Street sources feeding him data at any one time, and he expects a little special service, i.e., "when one of them makes a field trip to visit a company we're interested in we expect to be told about it."

6. Consultants who Mr. Lee says "tend to be very costly, sometimes charging several hundred dollars an hour" for their services.

7. Personal contacts. "I might call a fellow at the Mellon Bank," says Mr. Lee, "to ask what he thinks of Alcoa."

Information, as you can see, is very important to Mr. Lee and his employers, and they spend a great deal of time and money making certain they have just about the best there is.

Business, in Mr. Lee's opinion, is essentially a quantitative matter that can be measured by yardsticks such as the price of a company's stock from one day to the next, the size of its dividend, and most important of all—its earnings per share. If you have good information on what a stock's future earnings will be, he says, you can do a pretty good job of predicting its future price. If a company's earnings start to vary from Mr. Lee's projections, he starts looking for more information about what's going on within the company. It may be a new product with major long-term implications, or a strike at one of its plants, or something else. But if the information suggests that a fundamental shift in the company's earnings outlook is underway, Mr. Lee will move to either buy or sell the company's stock, and he'll do it quickly. "We are not particularly sentimental about any company," he says.

If Mr. Lee's quantitative outlook toward investing makes him sound, in part, like a computer in a gray flannel suit—you may have a point. He thinks the computer may be "the principal investment weapon of the future" for by examining hundreds of stocks simultaneously it will enable an investor to maximize his return based on whatever risk he's willing to take, or minimize his risk for any desired return. But information, no matter how reliable, and computers, no matter how awesome, are not all that it takes to make a successful investor, and nobody knows this better than Joe Lee. It also takes people with wide-ranging minds who are interested in everything that's going on, and have the ability to relate what all this means to business and the stock market. "People in this business," says Joe Lee, "tend to be more interesting at age seventy than anybody else I know of."

While Mr. Dilworth and his colleagues are responsible for guarding the Rockefellers' wealth, they are also available to provide each member of the family with a personal review—not infrequently held over tea and cookies—of how his or her piece of the family's fortune is being invested. They may even be asked to give the children of the family their first lessons in finance. Some of the boys and girls will actually spend several weeks in residence being taught as much as they wish to know about the care and feeding of the money that is or will one day be theirs to enjoy.

That's a glimpse of how the Rockefellers, Mellons, Phippses, Whitneys, W. A. M. Burdens and other exceedingly fortunate families care for their capital. Occasionally, they even work together for their common good as Laurance Rockefeller and the Paul Mellon family interest did in forming Cryonetics Corporation of Burlington, Massachusetts.

But supposing you can't figure out a way to stretch the family budget to cover the weekly pay checks of a dozen high-priced investment advisers. What do you do then? The answer is that professional investment advice is available in all shapes and sizes, and at any price you care to pay from thousands of dollars per year to absolutely nothing per year.

Let's begin with the wealthy man who owns securities worth many millions, and work our way down to the man who owns a few shares of stock worth five or six hundred dollars.

The person who's rich, yet not rich enough to afford a personal investment advisory staff, will most likely turn to a firm of professional money managers, or to the investment counseling department of a bank or trust company.

One of the oldest and most prestigious investment counseling firms in the nation is Scudder, Stevens & Clark, whose New York offices occupy three floors at 320 Park Avenue directly opposite St. Bartholomew's Episcopal Church. The firm's senior partner is Hardwick Stires, son of an Episcopal bishop, who was born in Chicago eighteen years before the firm was founded right after World War I.

Anyone with $400,000 or more can become a client of Scudder, Stevens & Clark and receive a continual flow of confidential recommendations on whether to hold or sell the securities he already owns, as well as interesting opportunities for investing whatever liquid funds he may have available. These investment recommendations and opportunities are the brain work of the firm's 100-man research department, which devotes its energies to the analysis of general economic forces, including political and social trends, the study of individual industries and companies, and finally a continuing analysis of bonds and preferred stocks. Scudder, Stevens & Clark's research effort is headed by Thomas W. Phelps, a gentleman with one of the most probing and perceptive minds in the securities business. A little while ago, Tom Phelps summed up his basic recommendations for "Investing in the 'New' World of the Nineteen Sixties" in an article in the *Financial Analysts Journal*. "I have three suggestions," said Mr. Phelps to his fellow investment professionals, "all of which you have heard before:

"1. Continue to favor equities over bonds simply on the basis that the opportunity-risk ratio in well selected stocks still is superior to that in bonds, though much less so than it used to be.

"2. Be sure you are insured against confidence crises, both by owning the kind of stocks you would like to have if the stock market were to close down for the next five years and by holding enough high grade bonds to put you in a buying frame of mind if bargain day comes on the stock market.

"3. Bet on mankind's ability to achieve."

Scudder, Stevens & Clark charges a minimum fee of $2000 a year, which can rise to many times that sum depending on the value of the fund being supervised. A client with $10 million, for example, would be charged an annual fee of $27,500. The firm makes a habit of shooting straight from the shoulder when it comes to advising its clients on everything from the long-term changes taking place within the U.S. economy, to what kind of stocks to hold, to the best way to judge whether the firm is earning its retainer. If you were a client sitting across from a Scudder investment counselor, he might talk to you in the following fashion:

On long-term economic trends: "Today the production of goods and services in our economy is over six times as great as in 1928. About half of this growth is attributable to price inflation. The other half can be explained by the rise in population and in productivity. Looking back, we regard as probably the most significant development affecting investment in the middle of this century as the determination to use the full power of government as an instrument of the national economy. It now appears that this has become established national policy. In the years ahead, we believe that this national policy and the decisions which flow from it will probably have more effect upon the uncharted course of investment and upon the financial well-being of investors than any other single factor except total war."

On what kind of stocks to avoid: "A perfect example was uranium in its heyday. The cry 'uranium, uranium, uranium' was heard throughout the land, and any moose pasture in Canada was considered to be a potential gold mine. We were against making any major commitments in uranium stocks because the whole business was shrouded in national security and we couldn't find out enough about it to make any kind of sensible investment decisions."

On whether Scudder, Stevens & Clark is earning its retainer: "I think Bernard Baruch would have made more money if he had employed us, because we could have given him more investment opportunities to consider. In the final analysis, of course, it's up to the client to decide if we're worth our fee. We're your servant, dear client, not your master, and because we never ask you to sign a contract with our firm you are at liberty to fire us any time you wish. There are many ways to measure whether we're earning our fee and I'll give you three easy ones: are we making your capital appreciate faster than the purchasing power of the dollar is depreciating, are we making it grow faster than the economy as a whole as measured by the gross national product, and are we making it go up in value at a faster rate than the Dow-Jones average."

There are many advantages to be gained from hiring a top-flight investment counseling firm. Perhaps the three most commonly mentioned ones are that they provide the help you need to conserve your original capital, to improve your purchasing power through the growth in the size of this capital (and the income you receive from it), and finally to relieve you of the job of banking dividend checks, exercising options, filling out income tax forms and the like.

But the biggest, and most valuable single service a professional investment counseling firm can give you is probably protection against committing stupid mistakes. Investment firms recognize the wisdom in the old adage that "A fool and his money are soon parted," and they take pride in protecting their clients from throwing their money down the drain. A recent full-page advertisement in *Harper's* magazine, for example, showed a lovely-looking young girl obviously full of innocence—particularly about financial matters—standing beneath a headline that read: "Gerald and I were discussing my money, Daddy, and he has some really neat ideas . . ." The copy went on to read: "Fortunately, Lucy's father consented to giving Gerald only her hand in marriage. Not the tidy sum Great-Aunt Agatha left her. That's safely tucked away in an investment management account at Old Colony (The First National Bank of Boston and Old Colony Trust Company).

"Under this arrangement, Old Colony assumes full responsibility for Lucy's money. Makes the day-to-day investment decisions, clips the coupons, exercises the options, keeps the records and supplies the necessary data at tax time.

"Father sleeps better nights, knowing that Lucy's nest egg is under the full-time care of a team of investment specialists whose expertise he knows from personal experience.

"And Gerald? He might as well forget the tip his barber gave him about sesame-seed futures!"

This is the way people with important money go about protecting themselves and their children against smart guys with big ideas who are always ready with a hot tip guaranteed to double their nest eggs overnight.

But suppose you don't have this kind of money? Are you doomed to go through life as little more than a barefoot boy in Wall Street, or is there some way you can purchase professional investment service at bargain basement prices? There is a way, of course, and it is called the investment trust.

Investment trusts are like investment clubs, only instead of the members picking which stocks to buy or sell they pay professionals to do this job for them. More than 3.5 million Americans have entrusted pretty close to $34 billion to investment trusts, which come in a staggering variety of shapes and sizes to fit almost anyone's purse and investment philosophy.

First of all there are closed-end and open-end trusts.

Closed-end trusts, such as the Lehman Corporation, Madison Fund, and Tri-Continental Corporation, are formed when a group of investors pool their money and buy shares in a portfolio of securities selected by the trust's professional staff. These original investors then "close" the door to anyone else who wishes to add some capital to the pot. The only way an outsider can buy shares in the trust's portfolio is when one of the founders decides to sell out. It is these shares that are traded on the exchange.

Open-end trusts, or mutual funds, as they are more popularly called, welcome all the fresh capital they can get whenever they can get it. The trust's professional staff simply takes the new money and buys whatever securities it thinks will advance the trust's investment philosophy. Shares of open-end trusts are bought and sold on the basis of their net asset value, which, of course, changes from one day to the next as the market value of the securities they own moves up and down.

If you are interested in seeing your capital grow you can buy shares in "performance" funds such as Fidelity Trend, Dreyfus, Channing Growth, or the Manhattan Fund, which will invest your capital in common stocks they think will outperform the market. If, on the other hand, you prefer to put your money in something more conservative, you can purchase shares in "balanced" funds like Investors Mutual and Wellington Fund, which will invest your capital in a mixture of common stocks, preferred stocks, and bonds.

If you care to concentrate your capital in one or in just a handful of specific industries, you can buy shares in specialized investment companies such as the Chemical Fund, Aero-space & Science Fund,

Insurance & Bank Stock Fund, Television-Electronics Fund, or the Energy Fund.

There are also funds which will invest your capital in certain areas of the United States, such as the Florida Growth Fund, or according to a special way of playing the stock market, such as the Dow Theory Investment Fund, or in securities traded only on one market such as the Over-the-Counter Securities Fund, or speculative funds, of which the new Hubshman Fund is one example, which are permitted by the SEC to sell stocks short, borrow money on the securities in its portfolio, buy puts and calls, and indulge in quite a bit of short-term trading.

The Securities and Exchange Commission, as mentioned earlier in this book, issued a report on December 2, 1966, which recommended that mutual funds reduce the management fees they charge their stockholders, cut their sales charges from 9 per cent to under 5 per cent, and end the sale of installment plan "front-end loads" in which about 50 per cent of the buyer's first year's payment goes to commissions. The SEC plans to draft these and other recommendations into legislative proposals which it hopes to submit to Congress in early 1967 after obtaining the views of the mutual fund industry, other interested segments of the financial community, and the investing public.

Mutual funds are strange animals. Even though they're all proud of their highly paid staffs of investment experts, there's hardly a month goes by when you won't see some funds buying the very same stocks other funds are unloading. You would also think that the funds with the best performance records would sell better than those which do only so-so. Well, it doesn't work that way, and the reason is the people don't buy mutual funds to make a lot of money fast. Instead, they buy them to get professional management for their savings, to diversify their savings, to keep a couple of jumps ahead of inflation, or to save for a certain objective such as retirement, or sending the children to college.

There's also a difference in the way investment companies charge their stockholders for looking after their money. Both closed-end and open-end trusts charge their share owners a management fee of about ½ to 1 per cent of the value of their holdings. This fee is normally deducted from the trust's dividend income before it is passed along to the stockholders.

Buyers of closed-end trusts pay the usual commission when they purchase their shares, and again when they sell their shares on the exchange, plus the yearly management fee. Mutual fund buyers, on the other hand, pay the annual management fee plus, in most cases, another fee of about 9 per cent that is "loaded" on to the cost of their shares when they purchase them. There is usually no fee involved when mutual fund shares are sold.

Most mutual funds are "load" funds with about three-quarters of the 9 per cent fee going to the dealers who sell them. There are such things as "no-load" funds, however, which are not aggressively pushed by salesmen and hence do not need to pay any sales commission. One of the firms that offer "no-load" funds is Scudder, Stevens & Clark, and not too long ago its senior partner journeyed out to Minneapolis—home of Investors Diversified Services, which is the biggest seller of "load" funds in the business—to talk about the pros and cons of "loads" and "no-loads." Some of Mr. Stires's comments on the subject of what's in a name are well worth repeating.

"The nicknames of 'loads' and 'no loads' to characterize investment companies with and without selling commissions," said Mr. Stires, "are, of course, a boon to the 'no loads' and a plague to the 'load' funds. You will recall that in golf every shot pleases someone. The good shots delight him who executes them. His bad shots delight his opponent. Whoever first described the commission involved in the sale of mutual funds as a 'load' should be sought out by the large, nationally distributed investment companies and, if found, he should be tortured and then destroyed. On the other hand, the 'no loads' should immortalize him gratefully with a monument erected in his honor. The 'load' is burdensome to an investor. It conjures up an image of an investor struggling along under it like a burdened pack animal. The absence of a 'load' permits the fortunate one to speed past the less fortunate. The key, of course, is the brevity of the word 'load.'

"In this connection," Mr. Stires concluded, "I might offer you a story connected with the late Arthur Kudner, who founded the advertising agency that bears his name, the Kudner Agency. At one point in the 1930's, when Wall Street was being accused of responsibility for almost every evil that befell this country—fomenting wars, creating depressions, and the like—Arthur Kudner was asked how, as a public relations man, he would accomplish removing Wall Street from the headlines of a newspaper. He suggested a foolproof remedy, and when asked to describe it, he said, 'Simply change its name from Wall Street to Alexander Hamilton Boulevard and you will never again see it in the headlines.'"

Whether they're "load" or "no-load," "performance" or "balanced," broad-spectrum or highly specialized, the job of any investment company is to preserve your capital and make it grow in keeping with the company's investment objectives. It does this through the securities it selects for its portfolio, and in the long run the stocks and bonds it decides to buy or sell will determine its future success.

How a fund goes about buying or selling securities, therefore, is a crucial matter. To appreciate just how crucial, consider what the Massachusetts Investors Trust—the oldest and second largest mutual fund in the country after Investors Mutual—went through when it bought and then twenty years later sold shares in a company whose name is a household word but which MIT prefers to refer to as "Company X."

"For many years," says an officer of the fund, "Company X had been an important manufacturer and supplier of products for the residential sector of the building materials field. The company has been characterized by a strong industry position as well as an unusually solid balance sheet. Examination of Company X was originally carried out by one of MIT's Industry Specialists who devote full time to studying all aspects of a specific industry, and to visiting companies within the industry in order to make a first hand judgement of each company's prospects. Field trip reports written by these Specialists, together with recommended investment action, are submitted to five Trustees who have previously worked as Industry Specialists themselves. The final decision to buy or sell a stock is made by a majority vote of the Trustees. If the decision is to buy, it then becomes the job of the Industry Specialist to keep in close touch with the company, and to review continually the possibility of further investment action.

"MIT first purchased shares in Company X 20 years ago. A careful study of the company, based on visits with its management, and inspection trips to its facilities, as well as a thorough study of the construction industry generally, led to additional purchases of the stock in subsequent years. Management seemed competent; the company's financial position was very strong, and a good growth in sales appeared in prospect for the company's major product line.

"A sizable holding in the stock of this company was fully justified when, in the post-war years, the pent-up demand for housing brought about by World War II led to one of the greatest building booms in the history of the country. Following the peak of this boom in 1950, additional purchases of stock in Company X were made as the company further improved its already strong industry position by developing new products, and expanding its manufacturing capacity.

"In 1959, the company's earnings reached a record level. Its balance sheet was also so strong that cash alone far exceeded current liabilities, and it had increased its dividend each year since 1953. Early 1960 might well have seemed a good time to purchase stock in Company X's stock thereby starting the complete elimination of the stock from the fund's portfolio.

"If, in mid-1960, one could have foreseen that the next six years would witness one of the longest periods of economic expansion in the history of the country, as well as a substantial increase in the general level of the stock market, the sale of stock in Company X might indeed have appeared questionable. In this case, the key to MIT's sale came from a thorough knowledge of the industry in which Company X operated and a careful analysis of future trends within the industry.

"In the late 1950's a number of large companies began making plans to enter the field long dominated by Company X. Plans for substantial expansion in the industry made likely the possibility of price competition in an industry which had hitherto seen little of it. At the same time, a careful study of housing in the United States led to the conclusion that an overbuilt situation was beginning to appear. The possibility of problems in the residential housing field in 1960, together with the likelihood of increased competition for the principal product produced by Company X, made the outlook for improved earnings questionable. It also became increasingly apparent that in spite of the cash resources available, management showed little inclination to put funds to work in areas which might have partially compensated for the potential problems in the company's main line of business.

"What actually happened in the years following 1960? Housing starts declined to a ten year low late in the year. Although a recovery took place in 1961 and 1962, this recovery masked the unhealthy state of the residential construction industry, particularly in the Far West. From 1963 to mid-1966, housing starts declined steadily. On top of this poor industry environment, substantial new competition did enter the field long dominated by Company X, and severe price competition resulted. Consequently, in spite of the strong upward trend of the economy throughout this period, the earnings of Company X failed in each year from 1960 through 1965, to reach the level of earnings reported in 1959. In fact, earnings in 1965 fell to the lowest level in eleven years. The decline in earnings reported by Company X in 1965 in the face of peak earnings for most industrial companies, was the direct result of the problems foreseen by MIT as early as 1960.

"What happened to the price of Company X's stock during this period? From mid-1960 until mid-1966, the stock market as measured by S & P's Index of 425 Industrials *increased* more than 50 percent. During the same period, the price of the stock of Company X *declined* almost 50 percent.

"MIT is now considering a new set of questions," says the officer of the fund. "When does the decline in the price of Company X's stock sufficiently discount the problems in the industry? When are we likely to see an uptrend in housing starts which have been declining since 1963? When can we expect to see the earnings of Company X start increasing? In short, when does the stock again become a candidate for purchase by MIT?"

So there we have one in-depth illustration of the kind of analytical research that is yours when you buy shares in a mutual fund.

But suppose you don't want to, or feel you can't afford to spend a penny for investment guidance. What do you do then? One good answer· you join an investment club. For close to seventy years, more and more Americans have been funneling their savings into the stock market via the investment club route, which is sophisticated, inexpensive, a lot of fun—and above all quite profitable.

The oldest known club was formed by a group of Texans back in 1898, according to the National Association of Investment Clubs, headquartered in Detroit. Today, says the NAIC, there are some 40,000 clubs in the United States alone with more than 600,000 members and assets exceeding $765 million. A good many of these clubs have engaging names such as the Highland Flings, Baby Blue Chips, Super-Dupers, Near Mrs., Green Berets, and the Paupers. But the model for today's thriving groups bears the somewhat sedate name of the Mutual Investment Club of Detroit, which was started in 1940 by six young fellows who had attended high school together. The founders invited six more investors to join them, got a stock broker to advise them, and started pooling their money to the tune of $10 and later $20 a month each. When the club's first year ended on February 28, 1941, it had invested $800 in stock worth $812. Ten years later, this investment had risen to $10,190 and the liquidating value of the club's stocks had grown to $27,471. A decade after that, in 1961, the investment had grown to $45,470, but the value of the club's portfolio was now at $171,655. And as of the end of 1965 the members had invested $61,685 in stocks worth about four times that much or $246,738. It's interesting to note that, once the value of the club's portfolio reached the $15,000 mark, it doubled in value on an average of once every five years, taking into consideration the regular monthly investments, retained dividend income and realized capital gains. A 100 per cent appreciation in the value of an investment club's portfolio every five years is the goal the National Association of Investment Clubs holds up before its nearly 9000 member organizations, made up of housewives, clergymen, doctors, auto mechanics, engineers, mailmen, and others who do not profess to be Wall Street wizards yet regularly do well in the stock market because they have learned how to invest their capital with care.

The National Association of Investment Clubs deserves a lot of credit for this record, which it has helped to build through a fine program of investor education. "This emphasis on education," says George A. Nicholson, Jr., chairman of the NAIC's Advisory Board, "is one essential difference between the early days of the investment club movement and the modern day clubs." NAIC members can buy a wide variety of investment aids from their association including the *Investment Club Manual* ("The Handbook for Learn-by-Doing Investing.") This manual goes into considerable detail on the techniques of investing wisely, and some of its most basic rules should prove valuable to all stockholders whether they belong to an investment club or not:

Invest Regularly. Money should be invested regularly without thought as to whether the stock market itself is high or low. Forecasting short-term movements in the stock market is very difficult. It is practically impossible to find anyone who has built a fortune in this way over a lifetime. But historically, stock prices have moved upward over a long period of time and millions have found that the regular purchase of stocks has been profitable.

Reinvest All Earnings. Reinvesting your stock market earnings enables you to apply the principle of compounding to your savings. Try to maintain a 4 per cent to 6 per cent yield from dividend income even though this will be difficult at some times and impossible at others. Dividend income is important because it provides funds for the purchase of securities in a low market, and because compound income builds up your net worth.

Invest in "Growth" Companies. Investing in growth companies is a thrilling experience. You might compare such securities with a maple tree that produces sugar every year (income) and ultimately grows into valuable timber (principal). Buying securities of companies which are growing faster than their competitors is important because such growth, if it is on a sound basis, can usually be depended upon to produce higher stock prices.

Diversification. Buying stocks in a variety of industries should produce a sufficient number of good performers to ensure profitable results.

Buy Both Large and Small Companies. In selecting stocks for your portfolio choose about 25 per cent from major companies in major industries, which tend to have a more predictable rate of growth and more resistance to price declines during weak periods in the stock market. Choose the remaining 75 per cent of your portfolio from among companies in the range from very small to the reasonably large. Among major companies seek ones which have prospects of growing from 5 per cent to 7 per cent a year. Among the smaller companies you may be able to find growth at 12 per cent a year and upward, and in the companies in between you should search for growth at the rate of 7 per cent to 12 per cent. Your total portfolio can achieve a distribution of small and large companies and yet have an over-all average growth rate of from 8 per cent to 10 per cent.

Buy Management. The management of the company is almost always the most essential factor in its growth. Giving major emphasis to the industry's outlook (such as recreation, which is bound to grow) or the products a company makes (the compact car or supersonic washing machine) is where clubs often go wrong because it is really only the best managed companies that make money in the long run. Investment clubs, accordingly, make three tests which indicate the past success of the management in producing growth and augur well for continuance:

1. Rate of Growth: Other things being equal, an investment is likely to increase in value at about the same rate that sales grow. Stocks selected should be in companies whose sales have increased and give promise of continuing to increase.

2. Profit Margins Before Taxes: Profit margins are how much the company makes on its sales before taxes. This determines by comparison with other companies whether the company is earning normal profits. Excellent investment opportunities are presented if a company's profit margin is subnormal, and your study indicates that better management is likely to improve profit margins significantly in the future.

3. Earnings On Invested Capital: A mark of good management is high earnings on invested capital. The company that consistently earns 10 per cent to 25 per cent after taxes on its invested capital (the sum of preferred stock, common stock, and surplus) should prove to be a good investment. Low earnings on invested capital warn that management is not presently meeting its problems.

Buy Stocks Which Are Reasonably Priced. Growth and good quality in a security can mean nothing if you pay an excessive price for it. Try to determine how high and how low the stock may sell in the next five years, and relate its current price both to this range and to the objective of doubling your money. Three studies can be made which will prove helpful in testing to see if you are paying a reasonable price, i.e., do some investigating of the price before you invest:

1. Earnings Per Share: Earnings per share should have a record of growing at approximately the same rate as sales. It is desirable to find growing companies (especially the smaller ones) which can be bought at a price no more than the sum of the estimated earnings per share for the next five years. This is equivalent to investing money at about 20 per cent a year, but such opportunities are not too frequent and this standard is almost never applicable to high quality, large growth companies. Nevertheless, the calculation of total five-year future earnings to current price is an "eye opener."

2. Dividends: Generally speaking, a good growth company pays out 50 per cent or less of earnings. The remainder is kept in the business to help build it.

3. Price Range: Study the price range of the stock over the past five years. A review of the "lows" will give an indication of where the stock might be bought at some time during the year, while the "highs" will show where the stock might be sold, should the club want to sell in the future. This is a very rough test, but often warns against paying too high a price for a stock. Where rapid growth is evident, the historical price range is less significant, especially in respect to the "high." If a nongrowth company is purchased, the price range test is very necessary and significant.

This is but a sample of the kind of investment education the National Association of Investment Clubs makes available to its members. So if you're interested in becoming a more careful capitalist, don't have the money to pay high-priced advisers, and enjoy the fellowship of other investors, it might be a good idea to get together with a few friends and start up your own investment club. The NAIC will be happy to show you everything you should do from the moment you decide to get going.

But maybe you're the kind of person who prefers to make your investment decisions on your own, who doesn't care to spend a dollar on investment study aids of any description, yet recognizes the importance of sound advice and counsel when it comes to sinking your savings into securities. Well, some of the most astute investment counselors in the business, backed up by extraordinarily well-informed staffs of security analysts are waiting to serve you absolutely free of charge at the office of your nearest stock broker who is a member of the New York Stock Exchange, American Stock Exchange, and the other major exchanges throughout the nation. All you have to do is walk in and introduce yourself, and one of the firm's registered representatives (sometimes called customer's men, or account executives) will talk to you, advise you, give you free reports on securities that interest you, ask his firm's security analysts to give you their up-to-the-minute opinion of these same stocks—all at no charge to you. You don't have to pay anything, buy anything, or even make any promises to do business with the broker or his company in the future.

"Member firms of the New York Stock Exchange give more free personal service than any other industry in the United States," says Richard D. Weinberg, a customer's man at the 505 Park Avenue office of H. Hentz & Company, which has been in business since 1856. Mr. Weinberg, who was born in London in 1909 and came to this country twenty years later, has been a dedicated investment adviser to hundreds of Americans, including a good many who have never given him a dime's worth of business. In many respects, Mr. Weinberg is typical of the thousands of men and women waiting to serve you at brokerage houses in every city of any size in America.

"People come in to see me once, twice, three times and never give me an order," says Mr. Weinberg. "But that's all right, I give them all the time in the world, and if they ever decide to buy something there's a good chance I'll get the order. A lot of people think about buying stocks, but I figure a person should have a little money in the bank, proper insurance, all that sort of thing before he does any investing. There's nothing certain in this life, you know, the stock market fluctuates, and there's always the possibility of loss. And if a person decides to enter the market I think he should have a minimum of $1000 to invest. One reason is that it costs six points to get in and six points to get out ($6 broker's commission when you buy an odd lot of less than 100 shares, and another $6 commission when you sell), which means your original investment has to increase by $12 before you can start making any kind of capital gain.

"Some individuals come in here and ask for my opinion about certain stocks," says Mr. Weinberg, "which I am happy to check out with Standard & Poor's or whatever other analytical services we carry, or I may talk to our research department down at 72 Wall Street. Then I'll mull all this data over in my mind and give the person my opinion about the stock, which, I might say, sometimes differs from our security analysts point of view. But most of the time people ask me what I think they should buy. So, I'll pick out some kind of security which in my judgement is favorably priced and tell the customer I think he should buy it, put it away, keep an eye on it, have a little patience, and relax in the knowledge that he'll be all right.

"Today, as you know," explains Dick Weinberg, as he settles back and relights his cigar, "the market is off roughly 20 per cent from its all-time high of about 1000 on the Dow-Jones. I think a lot of good stocks are attractively priced right now, and one I'm recommending to my customers is Kimberly-Clark. Five years ago this stock sold at 91, or 23 times earnings. Today, it's selling at approximately 45, or about 13 times earnings, even though it's earning more money than it did when it was at 91 and should even earn more in 1967. That's a good buy at these low levels, and I usually give my customer a copy of Standard & Poor's latest report on the stock which gives details on the company's Prospects, Recent Developments, Dividend Data, Income Statistics and Per Share Data, Pertinent Balance Sheet Statistics, Fundamental Position, Finances, and Capitalization, as well as a Recommendation as to whether the stock should be bought, sold or held. With all this data, plus the information I've given him, my customer is in a good position to make up his own mind.

"I've got somewhere around 500 customers who I deal with more or less regularly throughout the year. Most of my new customers are recommended to me by my old customers, but if someone walks in off the street I'll be happy to serve him. I remember one gentleman who came to see me some years ago and asked if I'd handle a little order for him of 10 shares of American Telephone & Telegraph then selling for $140 a share. I said I'd be delighted, and since that time I've done over $250,000 worth of business with this man.

"If a new person wants to do business with me, I'll ask him to fill in a card with his name, address, social security number, place of employment, bank reference, and so on so I'll know who I'm dealing with. If the man wants to buy say $1000 worth of stock on his first visit, I'll probably ask him for a $250 deposit and then a day later mail him a routine confirmation asking him to send in the balance within four days. After that, I'll be glad to do business with him over the telephone which is the way I work with almost all of my regular customers.

"I keep a record of every customer, what they bought, at what price, etc., and whenever anything important happens to one of their stocks, like a change in the dividend, or the gain or loss of a major contract, I call them up and tell them the news. It's just part of the free service I told you about. Another free service most brokers offer is to keep their customers securities for them. We'll put them in our safe deposit box, insure them against loss, and mail the customer all his dividends, proxies, reports and the like at no charge. We'll even keep his shares in our firm's name if he wishes so that all he has to do when he wants to sell is give us a call on the telephone and a week or so later we'll send him a check. This means the customer doesn't have to get the shares out of his own deposit box, sign them, and mail them in to us—it's a great convenience.

"The most frustrating thing about being an account executive," says Mr. Weinberg, "is that it's a million times easier to get people to buy stocks than it is to convince them they should sell stocks. I remember one of my customers who bought 300 shares of TWA at an average price of $64 a share. When the stock got up to $100, I phoned him and recommended that he take his profit which would have amounted to about $10,000. He didn't do it, and as a result he now has a loss instead of a nice profit." Or, put another way, "Bulls make money. Bears make money. But pigs go broke."

A wealth of free investment information worth many millions of dollars awaits the careful capitalist willing to take the trouble to ask for it. An idea of the extent of this data can be had by looking at the amount of free information made available by one brokerage firm, albeit it the largest one in the world—Merrill Lynch, Pierce, Fenner & Smith, Inc., which maintains 168 offices in the U.S. and abroad, belongs to 41 stock exchanges from New York to Paris, has

2800 customers men, and plays a part in 12 per cent of all the round-lot (100 shares or more) and 20 per cent of the odd-lot transactions on the New York Stock Exchange.

Merrill Lynch employs more than two hundred analysts budgeted at about $9 million a year who keep track of 4400 companies. The firm also has a staff of eighty which does nothing but analyze the securities portfolios of customers and prospective customers free of charge. Also free are some 3.5 to 4 million booklets and pamphlets such as "How to Invest in Stocks and Bonds," along with nearly 6 million copies of its biweekly business magazine *Investor's Reader* and many millions of short market bulletins and stock analyses which Merrill Lynch distributes each year. Every three months, about fifty research specialists and analysts and a team of editors turn out the fifty-six-page "Security and Industry Survey" which contains studies of thirty-eight industry classifications, as well as a discussion of the domestic securities market, foreign stocks, and the business outlook. In addition, the firm operates a News Wire of financial and business news which connects all Merrill Lynch offices and runs from 8 A.M. to 5 P.M. every business day.

In the course of this book we have seen how such diverse institutions as the Securities and Exchange Commission, the stock exchanges, enlightened corporations, the financial press, the nation's brokerage houses, and similar groups are all at work to help the American public invest its money wisely. If you are a careless capitalist in spite of all this, you have no one to blame but yourself.

BIBLIOGRAPHY

CHAPTER 1: "The Careless Capitalists"

Bazelon, David T., *The Paper Economy*. New York: Random House, 1963.

Berle, Adolf A., Jr., and Means, Gardiner C., *The Modern Corporation and Private Property*. New York: Commerce Clearing House, 1932.

Drucker, Peter F., *The Future of Industrial Man*. New York: The New American Library, 1965.

Owen, Geoffrey, *Industry in the U.S.A.* Baltimore: Penguin Books, 1966.

CHAPTER 2: "Promoting the New World"

Cowles, Virginia, *The Great Swindle: The Story of the South Sea Bubble*. New York: Harper & Bros., 1960.

Davis, Joseph Stancliffe, *Essays in the Earlier History of American Corporations*. Cambridge: Harvard University Press, 1917.

Gras, N. S. B., and Larsen, Henrietta, *Casebook in American Business History*. New York: F. S. Crofts, 1939.

Hacker, Louis Morton, *Alexander Hamilton in the American Tradition*. New York: McGraw-Hill Book Co., 1957.

James, Marquis, *Biography of a Business, 1792–1942*. New York: Bobbs-Merrill, 1942.

Kingsbury, Susan M., "A Comparison of the Virginia Company with the other English Trading Companies of the Sixteenth and Seventeenth Centuries." American Historical Association, *Annual Report,* 1906, Vol. 1.

Mailloux, Kenneth, *The Boston Manufacturing Company of Waltham, Mass., 1813–1848*. Boston: Boston University Graduate School dissertation, 1957.

Poor, H. V., *History of the Railroads and Canals of the United States*. New York: John Schultz & Co., 1860.

Scott, William Robert, *The Constitution and Finance of English, Scottish and Irish Joint-Stock Companies to 1720*. 3 vols. Cambridge: The University Press, 1910–12.

"Speculation in the Colonies," Massachusetts Historical Society, *Proceedings,* Vol. 65.

"Virginia Company Abstracts," Virginia Historical Society, *Collections,* New Series, Vols. 7 and 8.

Warshow, Robert Irving, *The Story of Wall Street*. New York: Greenberg, Inc., 1929.

CHAPTER 3: "Riding the Rails to Capitalism"

Adams, Charles Francis, Jr., and Adams, Henry, *Chapters of Erie, and Other Essays*. New York: Henry Holt & Co., 1886.

American Railroad Journal, various issues 1854–59.

Chandler, Alfred D., *Henry Varnum Poor, Business Editor, Analyst and Reformer*. Cambridge: Harvard University Press, 1956.

Clews, Henry, *Twenty-Eight Years in Wall Street*. New York: Irving Publishing Co., 1888.

Cochran, Thomas, and Miller, William, *The Age of Enterprise*. New York: Macmillan Company, 1942.

Communication of the President and Report of the Engineer of the Indianapolis and Bellefontaine Railroad Co. December 4, 1849. Indianapolis: Chapmans and Spann, Printers, 1849.

Fowler, William W., *Ten Years in Wall Street*. Hartford, Conn.: Worthington, Dustin & Co., 1870.

Gras, N. S. B., and Larson, Henrietta, *Casebook in American Business History*. New York: F. S. Crofts, 1939.

Grodinsky, Julius, *Jay Gould: His Business Career, 1867–1892*. Philadelphia: University of Pennsylvania Press, 1957.

Hartz, Louis, *Economic Policy and Democratic Thought: Pennsylvania, 1776–1860*. Cambridge: Harvard University Press, 1948.

Hicks, Frederick (ed.), *High Finance in the Sixties*. New Haven: Yale University Press, 1929.

Hungerford, Edward. *Men of Erie*. New York: Random House, 1946.

Kirkland, Edward Chase, *Men, Cities and Transportation: A Study in New England History*. Cambridge: Harvard University Press, 1948. 2 vols.

Mayer, B. H., *Railroad Legislation in the United States*. New York: Macmillan Company, 1903.

Moody, John, *The Art of Wall Street Investing*. New York: Moody Publishing Corp., 1906.

Mott, Edward Harold, *Between the Ocean and the Lakes: The Story of Erie*. New York: John S. Collins, 1901.

Poor, H. V., *History of the Railroads and Canals of the United States*. New York: John Schultz & Co., 1860.

Swanberg, W. A., *Jim Fisk: The Career of an Improbable Rascal*. New York: Charles Scribner's Sons, 1959.

Van Oss, Solomon Frederick, *American Railroads as Investments: A Handbook for Investors in American Railway Securities.* New York: G. P. Putnam's Sons, 1893.

CHAPTER 4: "Shearing the Lambs for Fun and Profit"

Clews, Henry, *Twenty-Eight Years in Wall Street.* New York: Irving Publishing Co., 1888.

Dewey, Davis R., *Financial History of the United States.* New York: Houghton Mifflin Co., 1903.

Eames, Francis L., *The New York Stock Exchange.* New York: Thomas G. Hall, 1894.

Emery, Henry Crosby, *Speculation on the Stock and Produce Exchanges of the United States.* Columbia University Studies in History, Economics, and Public Law, Vol. 7, No. 2, 1896.

Hedges, Joseph Edward, *Commercial Banking and the Stock Market before 1863.* Johns Hopkins University Studies in Historical and Political Science. Series LVI, No. 1. Baltimore: Johns Hopkins University Press, 1938.

Hill, John, Jr., *Gold Bricks of Speculation.* Chicago: Lincoln Book Concern, 1904.

Kirkland, Edward C., *Industry Comes of Age: Business, Labor and Public Policy, 1860–1897.* Vol. 6, The Economic History of the United States. New York: Holt, Rinehart & Winston, 1961.

Meeker, James Edward, *The Work of the Stock Exchange.* New York: Ronald Press, c. 1922.

Moody, John, *The Art of Wall Street Investing.* New York: Moody Publishing Corp., 1906.

Noyes, Alexander Dana, *Forty Years of American Finance: A Short Financial History of the Government and People of the United States Since the Civil War, 1865–1907.* New York: G. P. Putnam's Sons, 1909.

Smith, Matthew Hale, *Twenty Years Among the Bulls and Bears of New York.* Hartford: J. B. Burr and Hyde, 1871.

Warshow, Robert Irving, *The Story of Wall Street.* New York: Greenberg, Inc., 1929.

CHAPTER 5: "The Rich Get Richer"

Berle, Adolf, A. Jr., and Means, Gardiner C., *The Modern Corporation and Private Property.* New York: Commerce Clearing House, 1932.

Brandeis, Louis D., *Other People's Money.* New York: F. A. Stokes, 1914.

Clews, Henry, "Publicity and Reform in Business," *Annals of the American Academy of Political and Social Science,* July 1906.

Cochran, Thomas, and Miller, William, *The Age of Enterprise*. New York: Macmillan Company, 1942.

Danielson, N. R., *American Telephone and Telegraph Company*. New York: Vanguard Press, 1939.

Dodd, David D., *Stock Watering*. New York: Columbia University Press, 1930.

Faulkner, Harold U., *The Decline of Laissez-Faire (1897–1917)*. New York: Rinehart & Co., 1959.

Hendrick, Burton J., *The Age of Big Business*. Chronicles of America Series, Vol. 39. New Haven: Yale University Press, 1904.

Moody, John, *The Truth About the Trusts: A Description and Analysis of the American Trust Movement*. New York: Moody Publishing Corp., 1904.

Ripley, William Z., *Main Street and Wall Street*. Boston: Little, Brown & Co., 1927.

Sears, John H., *The New Place of the Stockholder*. New York: Harper & Bros., 1929.

Sells, Elijah W., "Publicity of Financial Affairs of Corporations," address before a convention of the Associated Advertising Clubs of America, Boston, August 2, 1911.

Soule, George, *Prosperity Decade* (1917–29). New York: Rinehart & Co., 1947.

Werner, M. R., and Starr, John, *Teapot Dome*. New York: Viking Press, 1959.

Williams, Charles Marvin, *Cumulative Voting for Directors*. Boston: Division of Research, Graduate School of Business Administration, Harvard University, 1951.

CHAPTER 6: "Taming the Wolves of Wall Street"

Allen, Frederick Lewis, *Only Yesterday*. New York: Harper & Bros., 1931.

Aranow, E. R., and Einhorn, Herbert, *Proxy Contests for Corporate Control*. New York: Columbia University Press, 1957.

Atkins, Willard, *et. al.*, *Regulation of the Securities Markets*. Washington: Brookings Institution, 1946.

Bonbright, James C., and Means, Gardiner, *The Holding Company*. New York: McGraw-Hill Book Co., 1932.

Berle, Adolf, and Means, Gardiner, *The Modern Corporation and Private Property*. New York: Commerce Clearing House, 1932.

Brookings, Robert S., *Industrial Ownership: Its Economic and Social Significance*. New York: Macmillan Company, 1925.

Cherrington, Homer V., *The Investor and the Securities Act*. Washington: American Council on Public Affairs, 1942.

"Contemporary Problems in Security Regulation," *Virginia Law Review*, Vol. 45, No. 6, October 1959.

Cook, Donald C., and Feldman, Myer, "Insider Trading under the Securities Exchange Act," *Harvard Law Review,* Vol. 66, January 1953.

Douglas, William O., *Democracy and Finance.* New Haven: Yale University Press, 1940.

Emerson, Frank D., and Latcham, Franklin C., *Shareholder Democracy.* Cleveland: Press of Western Reserve University, 1954.

Galbraith, John Kenneth, *The Great Crash.* Boston: Houghton Mifflin Co., 1955.

Kessler, Friedrich, "The American Securities Act and Its Foreign Counterparts," *Yale Law Journal,* May 1935.

Livingston, Joseph A., *The American Stockholder.* Philadelphia: J. B. Lippincott, 1957.

Loss, Louis, and Cowett, Edward M., *Blue Sky Law.* Boston: Little, Brown & Co., 1958.

Murray, Roger F., "Urgent Questions about the Stock Market," *Harvard Business Review,* September–October 1964.

"New Trading Rules," *Financial World,* October 7, 1964.

Pecora, Ferdinand, *Wall Street under Oath.* New York: Simon & Schuster, 1939.

Reed, Robert R., and Washburn, L. H., *Blue Sky Laws.* New York: Clark Boardman Co., 1921.

Rubin, Robert S., and Feldman, Myer, "Statuatory Inhibitions upon Unfair Use of Corporate Information by Insiders." Philadelphia: *University of Pennsylvania Law Review,* Vol. 95, 1947.

Williams, Charles M., *Cumulative Voting for Directors.*

CHAPTER 7: "Beware of Barbers, Beauticians, and Waiters"

Baruch, Bernard M., *Baruch, My Own Story.* New York: Henry Holt, 1957.

CHAPTER 8: "The High Cost of Ignorance"

Funston, Keith G., Address Before the *Financial World* Annual Awards Banquet, New York, October 26, 1965.

Girdler, Reynolds, "18,000,000 Books Nobody Reads," *Saturday Review,* April 13, 1963.

Merrill Lynch, Pierce, Fenner & Smith, Inc., "How to Read a Financial Report," New York: 1962.

Smith, Richard A., *Corporations in Crisis.* Garden City, New York: Doubleday, 1963.

CHAPTER 9: "The Professionals"

"A Company Guide to Effective Stockholder Relations," New York: American Management Association, 1953.

Beveridge, Oscar M., *Financial Public Relations*. New York: McGraw-Hill Book Co., 1963.

Blood, Jerome W., *Investor Relations*. New York: American Management Association, 1963.

Childs, John, *Coordination & Communications Problems of the Financial Executive*. New York: American Management Association, 1954.

Graham, Benjamin, Dodd, David L., and Cottle, Sidney, *Security Analysis*, Fourth Edition. New York: McGraw-Hill Book Co., 1962.

Hettinger, Herman S., *Financial Public Relations for the Business Corporation*. New York: Harper & Bros., 1954.

Shultz, Birl E., *The Securities Market and How It Works*. New York: Harper & Bros., 1946.

CHAPTER 10: "My Pilot Light Leaks"

"Annual Meetings Cut Frills," *Business Week,* April 20, 1963.

Dixon, Edgar H., "Footnotes to a Visit with European Stockholders," *"Investment Dealers' Digest,* June 6, 1960.

"President's Panel," *Dun's Review,* July 1963.

Speech Quotation, *The New Yorker,* July 6, 1963.

Wise, T. A., *The Insiders*. New York: Doubleday, 1962.

CHAPTER 11: "Our Man in the Board Room"

Broehl, Wayne G., Jr., "Independence in Control," *The Controller,* June 1955.

———, "Letter to a Director," *Management Review,* September 1960.

Brown, Courtney C., and Smith, E. Everett (eds.), *The Director Looks at His Job*. The record of a symposium sponsored jointly by the Graduate School of Business, Columbia University, and the McKinsey Foundation for Management Research. New York: Columbia University Press, 1957.

Chamberlain, John, "Why It's Harder and Harder to Get a Good Board," *Fortune,* November 1962.

"Company Presidents Size Up the Board," *Dun's Review,* November 1958.

Copeland, Melvin T., and Towl, Andrew R., *The Board of Directors and Business Management*. Cambridge: Harvard University Press, 1947.

Fever, Mortimer, *Handbook for Corporate Directors*. New York: Prentice-Hall, 1966.

Ford, Henry, II, "Business Ethics in 1961," Speech before the Minneapolis Junior Chamber of Commerce, April 20, 1961.

"Inside the Board Room," *Time*, February 28, 1964.

Jackson, Percival E., *What Every Corporation Director Should Know*. New York: William-Frederick Press, 1949.

Kennedy, Robert E., Jr., and West, Rhea H., "The Board of Directors; Its Composition and Significance," *Advanced Management*, November 1959.

Martindell, Jackson, *The Scientific Appraisal of Management*. Harper & Bros., 1950.

Moore, Wilbert E., *The Conduct of the Corporation*. New York: Random House, 1962.

National Industrial Conference Board, *Corporate Directorship Practices. Studies in Business Policy*, No. 103, 1962.

"Retire Yourself into Active Consultancy," *Business Management*, December 1964.

Securities and Exchange Commission, *Report of Special Study of Securities Markets*. Part 1. Eighty-eighth Congress, 1st Session, House Document No. 95, Part 1., April 3, 1963.

Smith, R. A., "How a Great Corporation Got out of Control," *Fortune*, January and February 1962.

———, "Incredible Electrical Conspiracy," *Fortune*, April and May 1961.

Vance, Stanley C., *Boards of Directors: Structure and Performance*. Eugene, Ore.: School of Business Administration, University of Oregon, 1964.

Weinberg, Sidney, "A Corporation Director Looks at His Job." *Harvard Business Review*, September 1949.

CHAPTER 12: "The Power of Your Proxy"

Aranow, Edward Ross, and Einhorn, Herbert A., *Proxy Contests for Corporate Control*. New York: Columbia University Press, 1957.

Broehl, Wayne G., Jr., "The Proxy Battle." Hanover, N.H.: Amos Tuck School of Business Administration, 1955.

Karr, David, *Fight for Control*. New York: Ballantine Books, 1956.

Whetten, Leland Carling, *Recent Proxy Contests: A Study in Management Stockholder Relations*, 1959, *The Influence of Recent Proxy Contests on Social and Economic Trends, The Rise of Professional Proxy Solicitors*. 1961, Atlanta: Georgia State College of Business Administration.

CHAPTER 13: "Charity Begins at Home"

Shareownership U.S.A., 1965 Census of Shareowners, New York Stock Exchange.

"Stockholders Provide Sales Leads," *Business Week,* May 2, 1959.

Uhl, Kenneth Paul, "Stockholders as Customers for Their Corporations' Products," doctoral dissertation. Ann Arbor: University Microfilms, 1960.

CHAPTER 14: "Crackpots or Crusaders"

Bainbridge, John, "The Talking Stockholder," *The New Yorker,* December 11, 18, 1948.

Gilbert, Lewis D., "Management's Responsibility to the Corporate Shareholder," *Atlanta Economic Review,* June 1961.

———, *Dividends and Democracy.* Larchmont: American Research Council, 1956.

———, and Gilbert, John J., *Annual Report of Stockholders Activities at Corporation Meetings.* 1958 through 1964. New York: Lewis D. Gilbert, 1165 Park Avenue, 1959–65.

Securities and Exchange Commission, *Annual Report,* 1963, 1964. Eighty-eighth Congress, 2nd Session, House Document No. 269; and eighty-ninth Congress, 1st Session, House Document No. 19. 1964, 1965.

"The Man Who's Been to 2,000 Meetings," *Fortune,* April 1961.

United Shareowners of America, Inc., 45 Rockefeller Plaza, New York City, miscellaneous releases and publications.

CHAPTER 15: "The Careful Capitalists"

Engel, Louis, *How to Buy Stocks.* New York: Bantam Books, 1957.

H. Hentz & Co. 1856/1956, New York: privately printed by the Beck Engraving Co., 1956.

"Investing in the 'New' World of the Nineteen Sixties," *Financial Analysts Journal,* May–June 1966.

"Stockbroker James Thomson," *Time,* August 19, 1966.

Wise, T. A., *The Insiders.* Garden City, New York: Doubleday, 1962.

INDEX

J3